A SPECIAL RELATIONSHIP: OUR TEACHERS AND HOW WE LEARNED

A Special Relationship

Our Teachers and How We Learned

Edited by
John C. Board
With a foreword by
Mary Hatwood Futrell

Pushcart Press

ISBN: 0–916366–68–5

LC90-63923

This book was produced in
The United States of America
by RAY FREIMAN & COMPANY
Stamford, Connecticut 06903

ACKNOWLEDGEMENTS

From MY LORD, WHAT A MORNING by Marian Anderson. Copyright © 1956, renewed, 1984 by Marian Anderson. Reprinted by permission of the publisher, Viking Penguin, a division of Penguin Books USA Inc.

From the book, SATCHMO My Life in New Orleans by Louis Armstrong. © 1982, 1954. Used by permission of the publisher, Prentice-Hall, Inc., Englewood Cliffs, NJ.

Excerpt(s) from IN MEMORY YET GREEN by Isaac Asimov, copyright © 1979 by Isaac Asimov. Used by permission of Doubleday, a division of Bantam, Doubleday, Dell Publishing Group, Inc.

Reprinted from THE PAST HAS ANOTHER PATTERN, Memoirs, by George W. Ball, by permission of W. W. Norton & Company, Inc. Copyright © 1982 by George W. Ball.

From BERNARD M. BARUCH, MY OWN STORY by Bernard M. Baruch. Copyright © 1957 by Bernard M. Baruch, © 1985 by Bernard M. Baruch, Jr. and Renee B. Samstag.

From *What Are People for?* by Wendell Berry. Copyright © 1990 by Wendell Berry. Reprinted by permission of the publisher, North Point Press, Berkeley, California.

Excerpt(s) from A CASUAL PAST by Francis Biddle, copyright © 1961 by Francis Biddle. Used by permission of Doubleday, a division of Bantam, Doubleday, Dell Publishing Group, Inc.

From MY LIFE: The Memoirs of Claude Bowers by Claude Bowers, edited by Patricia Bowers. Copyright © 1962 by Patricia Bowers. Reprinted by permission of Simon & Schuster, Inc.

Excerpt from AMERICAN MEMOIR by Henry Seidel Canby. Copyright 1934, 1936, and 1947 by Henry Seidel Canby. Copyright renewed © 1975 by Edward T. Canby. Reprinted by permission of Houghton Mifflin Company.

From Carter, Jimmy. *Why Not the Best?* (Nashville: Broadman Press 1975) 29–30. All rights reserved. Used by permission.

Excerpt(s) from WAITING FOR THE MORNING TRAIN by Bruce Catton, copyright © 1972 by Bruce Catton. Used by permission of Doubleday, a division of Bantam, Doubleday, Dell Publishing Group, Inc.

From *Unbought and Unbossed* by Shirley Chisholm. Copyright © 1970 by Shirley Chisholm. Reprinted by permission of Shirley Chisholm.

Excerpt from *My Quarter Century of American Politics* by Champ Clark. Copyright © 1920 by Champ Clark. Renewed © 1947 by Bennett Champ Clark and Genevieve Clark Thompson. Reprinted by permission of Harper & Row, Publishers, Inc.

Excerpts from TRUST YOUR HEART: AN AUTOBIOGRAPHY by Judy Collins. Copyright © 1987 by Judy Collins. Reprinted by permission of Houghton Mifflin Company.

From *The Autobiography of Calvin Coolidge* by Calvin Coolidge. Excerpts, pp. 45–47, 60–62 and 63–70, reprinted by permission of John Coolidge.

Excerpts from *Copland, 1900 Through 1942* by Aaron Copland and Vivian Perlis. Copyright © 1984 by Aaron Copland and Vivian Perlis. Reprinted by permission of St. Martin's Press, Inc., New York and The Robert Lantz-Joy Harris Literary Agency as agents for the authors.

From *An Autobiographical Sketch (1815–1842)* by Richard Henry Dana, Jr. Edited by Robert F. Metzdorf. Copyright © 1953 by Robert F. Metzdorf. Published by The Shoe String Press, 1953.

From ANGELA DAVIS, AN AUTOBIOGRAPHY by Angela Davis. © 1974 by Angela Davis. Reprinted by permission of Angela Davis.

Excerpts from *This House of Sky: Landscapes of a Western Mind,* copyright © by Ivan Doig, reprinted by permission of Harcourt Brace Jovanovich, Inc., and Ivan Doig.

From GO EAST, YOUNG MAN: THE EARLY YEARS by William O. Douglas. Reprinted by permission of Random House, Inc., the Estate of William O. Douglas and The Robert Lantz-Joy Harris Literary Agency as agents for the author.

From *Dawn: A History of Myself* by Theodore Dreiser. Excerpts, pp. 274–280, 294–295 and 368–370, reprinted by permission of The Dreiser Trust.

From *An Indian Boyhood* by Charles A. Eastman. Published by McClure, Phillips & Company, 1920.

From ABRAHAM FLEXNER: An Autobiography by Abraham Flexner. Copyright © 1960 by Jean Flexner Lewison and Eleanor Flexner. Renewed © 1988 by Allen Nevins. Reprinted by permission of Simon & Schuster, Inc.

Excerpt from *THE LIVING OF THESE DAYS: An Autobiography* by Harry Emerson Fosdick. Copyright 1956 by Harper & Brothers; copyright © renewed 1984 by Dorothy Fosdick and Elinor F. Downs. Reprinted by permission of Harper & Row, Publishers, Inc.

Excerpt from CHRONICLES OF A GENERATION by Raymond B. Fosdick. Copyright © 1958 by Raymond B. Fosdick, Renewed © 1986 by Elizabeth Miner Fosdick. Reprinted by permission of Harper & Row, Publishers, Inc.

Reprinted from THE RIGHT TIME An Autobiography by Harry Golden. Copyright © 1969 by Harry Golden. (G. P. Putnam's Sons.)

From BOSTON BOY by Nat Hentoff. Copyright © 1986 by Commonsense Productions, Inc. Reprinted by permission of International Creative Management, Inc. and Alfred A. Knopf, Inc.

From *Cheerful Yesterdays* by Thomas Wentworth Higginson. Excerpt, pp. 49–54. (Arno Press and The New York Times, 1968).

From RECOLLECTIONS OF A LIFE by Alger Hiss. Copyright © 1988 by Alger Hiss. Reprinted by arrangement with Seaver Books/Henry Holt and Company, Inc., and by kind permission of Unwin Hyman Ltd.

From DUST TRACKS ON A ROAD by Zora Neale Hurston. Copyright 1942 by Zora Neale Hurston. Renewed 1970 by John C. Hurston. Reprinted by permission of Harper & Row, Publishers, Inc.

From the book, JOURNEY TO WASHINGTON by Daniel K. Inouye with Lawrence Elliott. © 1967. Used by permission of the publisher, Prentice-Hall, Inc., Englewood Cliffs, NJ.

From *Wayfaring Stranger* by Burl Ives. Published by McGraw-Hill Book Company, Inc., 1948. Copyright © 1948 by Burl Ives.

From ALONG THIS WAY: THE AUTOBIOGRAPHY OF JAMES WELDON JOHNSON by James Weldon Johnson. Copyright © 1933 by James Weldon Johnson, renewed © 1961 by Grace Nail Johnson. Reprinted by permission of the publisher, Viking Penguin, a division of Penguin Books USA Inc.

From *But Look, the Morn: The Story Of A Childhood* by MacKinley Kantor. Copyright © 1947 by MacKinley Kantor. Copyright © renewed 1974 by MacKinley Kantor. Reprinted by permission of Layne Shroder and Tim Kantor.

Excerpts from *The Story of My Life* by Helen Keller. © 1902, 1903, 1905 by Helen Keller.

From DADDY KING: AN AUTOBIOGRAPHY by The Rev. Dr. Martin Luther King, Sr. with Clayton Riley. Copyright © 1980 by The Rev. Dr. Martin Luther King, Sr. Reprinted by permission of William Morrow & Co. and Joan Daves.

Reprinted with permission of Macmillan Publishing Company from ROBERT M. LAFOLLETTE by Belle Case and Fola LaFollette. Copyright 1953 by Fola LaFollette; copyright renewed © 1981 by Fola LaFollette.

From *Early Memories* by Henry Cabot Lodge (Charles Scribner's Sons, N.Y., 1913).

From GRASSROOTS by George McGovern. Copyright © 1977 by George McGovern. Reprinted by permission of Random House, Inc.

From BORN TO REBEL: AN AUTOBIOGRAPHY by Benjamin E. Mays. Copyright 1971 by Benjamin E. Mays. Reprinted by permission of the University of Georgia Press.

From BLACKBERRY WINTER by Margaret Mead. Copyright © 1972 by Margaret Mead. Reprinted by permission of William Morrow & Co.

From *The Trouble Bush* by Earl Schenck Miers. Excerpts, pp. 33–35, 109–110, 118–120 and 214, reprinted by permission of Mrs. Earl Schenck Miers.

Excerpts from THE STORY OF MY BOYHOOD AND YOUTH by John Muir. Copyright 1912 and 1913 by The Atlantic Monthly Company. Copyright 1913 by John Muir. Copyright 1916 by Houghton Mifflin Company. Copyright renewed 1940 and 1941 by Wanda Muir Hanna.

From RN: THE MEMOIRS OF RICHARD NIXON by Richard Nixon. Reprinted by permission of Warner Books, New York.

From *Reflections Without Mirrors: An Autobiography of the Mind* by Louis Nizer. Published by Doubleday & Company, Inc. Copyright © 1978 by Louis Nizer. Reprinted by permission of Louis Nizer.

From *Fighting Liberal: The Autobiography of George W. Norris* by George W. Norris. Copyright © 1945 by Macmillan Company. Reprinted with permission by Marian N. Nelson and the cooperation of the George W. Norris Committee, High Plains Historical Society, 423 Norris Avenue, McCook, Nebraska 69001.

From BEHOLD THIS DREAMER! by Fulton Oursler. Copyright © 1964 by Fulton Oursler, Jr. By permission of Little, Brown and Company.

Excerpted with the permission of the publisher, Bernard Geis Associates, from VICTORY OVER MYSELF by Floyd Patterson © 1962 by Floyd Patterson.

From THE TRUE JOY OF POSITIVE LIVING by Norman Vincent Peale. Copyright © 1984 by Norman Vincent Peale. Reprinted by permission of Willaim Morrow & Co., and Dr. Norman Vincent Peale.

From *And Gladly Teach: Reminiscences* by Bliss Perry. Copyright © 1935 by Bliss Perry. Published by Houghton Mifflin Company, 1935.

From THE CAMERA NEVER BLINKS: THE ADVENTURES OF A TV JOURNALIST by Dan Rather with Mickey Herskowitz. Copyright © 1977 by Dan Rather and Mickey Herskowitz. Reprinted by permission of William Morrow & Co., and Bill Adler Books, Inc.

Reprinted by permission of the Estate of Norman Rockwell from *Normal Rockwell, My Adventures as an Illustrator* (New York: Harry N. Abrams Inc., 1988. Second Edition.) Copyright © 1988 Estate of Norman Rockwell.

Excerpt from THIS IS MY STORY by Anna Eleanor Roosevelt. Copyright by 1937 by Eleanor Roosevelt; copyright © renewed 1965 by Franklin Roosevelt, Jr., and John Roosevelt. Reprinted by permission of Harper & Row, Publishers, Inc.

Corner, G., ed., *Autobiography of Benjamin Rush.* Copyright 1948 American Philosophical Society © 1975 renewed by Princeton University Press. Excerpt, pp. 28–32, 33–34, 35–37 reprinted with permission of Princeton.

Excerpt from A JOURNEY FOR OUR TIMES (in England as DISTURBER OF THE PEACE: MEMOIRS OF A FOREIGN CORRESPONDENT) by Harrison E. Salisbury. Copyright © 1983 by Harrison E. Salisbury. Reprinted by kind permission of Harper & Row, Publishers, Inc., Curtis Brown Ltd., and Unwin Hyman Ltd.

From *Ever the Winds of Chance* by Carl Sandburg. Copyright © 1983 by Maurice C. Greenbaum and Frank M. Parker, Trustees of the Sandburg Family Trust. Excerpt, pp. 26–32, reprinted by permission of the University of Illinois Press.

Reprinted from I KNEW A PHOENIX, Sketches for an Autobiography, by permission of W. W. Norton & Company, Inc. and Russell & Volkening as agents for the author. Copyright © 1959, 1956, 1954 by May Sarton. Copyright renewed 1987, 1984, 1982 by May Sarton.

Excerpt from THE STORY OF A PIONEER by Anna Howard Shaw. Copyright 1915 by Anna Howard Shaw. Copyright 1915 by Anna Howard Shaw; copyright renewed 1943 by Lucy E. Anthony. Reprinted by permission of Harper & Row, Publishers, Inc.

From PARTICULARS OF MY LIFE by B. F. Skinner. Copyright © 1976 by B. F. Skinner. Reprinted by permission of Alfred A. Knopf, Inc.

Excerpt from ELIZABETH CADY STANTON by Theodore Stanton and Harriot Stanton Blatch. Copyright 1922, copyright renewed 1950. Reprinted by permission of Harper & Row, Publishers, Inc.

Excerpt from *The Autobiography of Lincoln Steffens* by Lincoln Steffens, copyright 1931 by Harcourt Brace Jovanovich, Inc. and renewed 1959 by Peter Steffens, reprinted by permission of the publisher.

Excerpted from TO TEACH, TO LOVE by Jesse Stuart. Copyright © 1970 by Jesse Stuart. Published by The Jesse Stuart Foundation and reprinted with their permission. The Jesse Stuart Foundation, P.O. Box 391, Ashland, KY 41114.

From *The Autobiography of an Idea* by Louis Sullivan. Copyright © 1924 by The American Institute of Architects. Reproduced by permission from The American Institute of Architects, under license number 90020.

From *All In The Day's Work: An Autobiography* by Ida Tarbell. Copyright © 1939 by Ida Tarbell. Published by The Macmillan Company, 1939.

Excerpt(s) from THE LIGHT OF OTHER DAYS by Rexford G. Tugwell, copyright © 1962 by Rexford G. Tugwell. Used by permission of Doubleday, a division of Bantam, Doubleday, Dell Publishing Group, Inc.

From *The Autobiography of Mark Van Doren* by Mark Van Doren. Copyright © 1958 by Mark Van Doren. Reprinted with permission by Mrs. Mark Van Doren.

Excerpt from *Lew Wallace, An Autobiography, Volume 1* by Lew Wallace. Printed by Harper & Brothers Publishers, 1906.

Reprinted by permission of the publishers from ONE WRITER'S BEGINNINGS by Eudora Welty, Harvard University Press, Copyright © 1983, 1984 by Eudora Welty. All rights reserved. Reprinted, also, by permission of Russell & Volkening as agents for the author.

Excerpt from IN SEARCH OF HISTORY: A PERSONAL ADVENTURE by Theodore H. White. Copyright © 1978 by Theodore H. White. Reprinted by permission of Harper & Row, Publishers, Inc., and The Julian Bach Literary Agency, Inc.

From STANDING FAST: THE AUTOBIOGRAPHY OF ROY WILKINS by Roy Wilkins with Tom Mathews. Copyright © 1982 by Aminda Wilkins. Reprinted by permission of the publisher, Viking Penguin, a division of Penguin Books USA Inc.

"A teacher, finally, has nothing to go on but faith,
a student nothing to offer in return but testimony."

Wendell Berry in *What Are People For?*

In gratitude this book is dedicated to the following forces in my life: God; the memory of my father, Victor; my mother, Pearl; my wife, Mait, and our sons, John-David and Andrew; the taxpayers of Illinois, Indiana, Montana, Wyoming and Oregon who made my schooling possible; the teachers who taught me; the teachers with whom I taught; the teachers I have served and serve; and the more than 4,000 men and women who are my former students.

CONTENTS

FOREWORD

Readers of this anthology will no doubt describe it most often as a tribute to America's teachers. And there is truth in that description. But it's not the whole truth. For what this volume celebrates is not merely the miracle of teaching and learning, but the miracle we call democracy.

What John Board has created is a testimonial to those individuals who devote their lives to the principle that before a child can know the blessings of liberty, that child must first know the blessing of learning. Each of the special relationships chronicled in this volume begets the same result: freedom from ignorance. And those who are freed from the chains of ignorance will not for long endure the chains of tyranny. In this precise sense, teaching is the lifeblood of democracy. And the special relationship between teacher and student is its heart.

That heart has never pulsed more strongly. Recent developments—in Eastern Europe and the Soviet Union—give substance to this claim. And we now see, in developments still in their infancy, the faint glimmer of hope that we shall one day know a world where the size of our hearts counts for more than the size of our arsenals, and where the power of the tyrant will prove no match for the power of the tutor.

Then we shall know, beyond all doubt, that the engine of human history is the passion of the artist, not the passion of the oppressor. And then we might at long last give proper credit to those artists we call teachers.

John Board's anthology becomes, on reflection, a treatise on liberation. It is a treatise on the liberation of the human spirit from the forces of malice whose soil is ignorance. The special relationship between teacher and student is—and always will be—the antidote to every poison that disgraces reason and mocks the ideal implicit in the words "with malice toward none, with charity for all."

Those poisons remain potent. Our liberation from malice remains incomplete. The human journey toward justice has miles to go. And all of us have promises to renew, promises to keep. Among these promises, none may be more vital than the promise to cultivate and nourish, encourage and support every effort to make the special relationship between teacher and student a common occurrence rather than a rare achievement.

John Board's labor of love may take us no more than one step closer to the day we make good on that promise. For this alone, we owe him gratitude. And for this, we owe gratitude to his teacher, Miss Lucile Sizelove.

Mary Hatwood Futrell
President
World Confederation of
Organizations of the Teaching
Profession

INTRODUCTION

Although it has been more than 10 years since I first read Ivan Doig's *This House of Sky: Landscapes of a Western Mind,* it was that book that first ignited the idea for this anthology. Doig's description of his English and Latin teacher, Frances Carson Tidyman, sparked my curiosity. I wondered what other writers had said—if anything—about their teachers, and what memories—for better or worse—they had recorded. This idea burned brightly for a time, then became no more than an ember. Some years later, it was rekindled when I read Eudora Welty's *One Writer's Beginnings.* Once again, I banked the idea until the moment I came upon a single sentence, a splendidly simple sentence, from Helen Keller's *The Story of My Life:* "The most important day I remember in all my life is the one on which my teacher, Anne Mansfield Sullivan, came to me." From that time forward, I knew my search for autobiographical recollections of teachers who made a difference had begun. This time, there would be no turning back. This time, the flame would linger. And it did.

Teaching is a dynamic act, and learning a dynamic process. Each fires the other. When the untapped potential of a student meets the liberating art of a teacher, a miracle unfolds. Learning begins. A special relationship is born.

This book is about that relationship. It is about teachers who possessed the art of liberation and about students who were liberated. Such encounters defy standard description. They elude tidy definition. But they leave an indelible imprint. Henry Seidel Canby noted this truism when, at the age of 69, he wrote of his teachers at Yale, "We loved them, or hated them, or even despised them, but never escaped their daily presence in our thoughts."

What is it about teachers that affects us so?

What is it about teachers that gives rise to such powerful reactions, such vigorous emotions?

What is it that causes us to identify teachers as such lasting, vital, irreplaceable influences in our lives?

Surely some strange power is at work. And that power may remain forever shrouded in mystery, forever resistant to precise description. But it's there. We feel its presence. We know its permanence. It is for this that we love our teachers or hate them, but are unable to forget them.

The teachers described in this volume are people of rare accomplishment. They had a decisive impact on their students, on men and women who shaped—and often re-shaped—the intellectual, cultural and political character of our nation.

It is difficult to categorize these teachers. No single personality profile will suffice. It is, in most cases, just as difficult to categorize their students. Greatness eludes definition. We remember Benjamin Rush as a signer of the Declaration of Independence, but Rush was also a physician, soldier, and teacher. We recognize Shirley Chisholm as a black woman who graced Congress with her presence and stung our nation's conscience with her oratory, but she, too, was a teacher. We think of B. F. Skinner as a maverick who revolutionized the psychology profession, but Skinner was above all else a teacher. And however we may remember Mark Van Doren, Benjamin E. Mays, William O. Douglas, Rexford G. Tugwell, Abraham Flexner, or George McGovern, we do them injustice if we fail to remember that they were teachers. These teachers—like *their* teachers—are, as Louis Nizer observed of people of great accomplishment, as "different in personality as the infinite variations of color and form in nature's creation."

The mystery remains.

Who were these teachers of memorable Americans who defined—and who continue to define—our national character? Of those cited in this anthology, 51 percent were public grade and high school teachers. Five percent were private school teachers. Approximately 13 percent were private tutors or instructors of special subjects. The remaining 31 percent were professors in public (5%) and private (26%) institutions of higher education.

What characteristics, if any, do these teachers share? That question returns us, once more, to the mystery at the heart of the artistry of teaching. Pedagogical skills are as varied as the colors and shapes in a kaleidoscope. At the same time, within this kaleidoscopic variety, patterns emerge. Beneath the differences, there's sameness. These teachers, almost without exception, displayed masterful command of their subject matter. All were caring. All were possessed of an uncanny ability to unleash youthful potential. All were demanding, all relentless in their determination to ignite in every student the will to excel. And all were, to borrow Louis Nizer's words, "alike in their boundless energy."

Does this profile unlock the mystery of teaching greatness? It does not. For it omits what I believe is the uncommon characteristic great teachers hold in common—passion! Passion for learning, passion for knowledge, passion for excellence, passion for life. Theirs is a passion given, not without suffering, in the service of teaching and learning. Theirs is a passion devoted to the ideal that education is sacred, and the denial of education profane. Theirs is a passion that says—"The day you seek is the day I become the teacher . . . and you, the student."

The passion recollected in this anthology offers a portrait of the powerful and sometimes ineffable dynamic that defines the special relationship between teacher and student. Viewing it is like watching a potter working clay, shaping it into an object, and glazing it so that its special properties are emphasized when it is kilned. But this same portrait, taken in its entirety, becomes a portrait in miniature of a 250-year American journey, a journey toward inclusiveness, a journey toward expanded opportunity, a still-unfinished journey that will be finished only when the words "and justice for all" describe present reality rather than a distant ideal.

What emerges from the accounts in this volume is the gradual evolution of the understanding that education is not a privilege reserved for the few, but a right belonging to all. The evolution of this understanding parallels the evolution of our system of free public schools.

This system—the system that would in time give substance to the promises implicit in the Declaration of Independence and the United States Constitution—began, of course, on the eastern shores of our country, in Massachusetts, then spread westward. What began as an exclusive educational system created, almost solely, to educate white boys, gradually became inclusive. It expanded to include children of both sexes and all races and creeds regardless of national origin, economic status, or physical and mental condition.

This is a phenomenal national accomplishment. It is one which Harry Golden was part of during the first decade of this century. In speaking of his public school teachers in New York City, Golden wrote, "They turned an immigrant population into a citizen population and did it within a single generation. It took Rome 200 years to accomplish the same goal, and the Romans were not fully successful in transforming all the races into *cives Romani*."

The last chapter of the history of the United States has not been written. Americans are not disposed to writing conclusions. Their forte is the prologue. They are best at laying foundations, at creating beginnings. By their nature, they are prone to look forward, not backward. They are innovators, creators, builders. In this sense, they are like the teachers portrayed in this book—teachers whose power sparked and ignited the latent creativity within their students. These teachers were crucibles for change. They changed their students. Their students changed America. Because of these teachers, and because of these teachers' students, we are today a better people. And America is today a more just nation.

Teaching and learning continue in America. They continue wherever there is a teacher and a student and where their special relationship is permitted, fostered, encouraged. We need not search far to see this creative process in action. This once-rare miracle now occurs every day within every community in every state in our nation. We need only to recognize this miracle for what it is. When we do, we shall realize, as Harry Golden observed, that America's teachers have been—and America's teachers continue to be—the major legion in taking to heart our national motto, *E Pluribus Unum,* and translating it into fact.

John C. Board

A SPECIAL RELATIONSHIP: OUR TEACHERS AND HOW WE LEARNED

STUDENT: BENJAMIN RUSH

(ca. 1745–1813)

Physician, signer of the Declaration of Independence, member of the Continental Congress, Surgeon General of the Continental Army, founder of the first American antislavery society, a founder of Dickinson College, and Treasurer of the U. S. Mint.

TEACHERS: SAMUEL FINLEY SAMUEL DAVIES

My only surviving brother, Jacob Rush, and myself were sent to a country school in Nottingham, now in Cecil county in the State of Maryland, a few years after our father died. This School was taught by the Revd. Dr. Saml. Finley, afterwards President of the College of New Jersey, and who had married one of the sisters of my mother. It was then the most respectable and flourishing of any in the middle provinces of America. The character of Dr. Finley as a minister of the gospel and Scholar is well known to thousands in this country, but he is less known as a teacher of an academy, and a master of a family. Few men have ever possessed or displayed greater talents in both those capacities. His government over his boys was strict but never severe nor arbitrary. It was always by known laws which were plain, and often promulgated. The object of a law, whether it related to great or little matters, was never taken into consideration in the trial of the offender. I remember he once issued an order forbidding his boys to throw stones at his fruit trees in order to obtain fruit from them. Soon afterwards he observed a boy flinging stones up an apple tree. He came up to him, and struck him with his hand on the side of his head. The boy remonstrated against his punishment, and said the tree had no fruit on it, and that he was only amusing himself by trying to hit a decayed apple of the last year's growth which hung upon one of the highest branches of the tree. "This is no excuse for your offence (said the Doctor). By throwing at that decayed apple you injure the tree. You have moreover broken a law, which though apparently trifling, will lead you to break laws of more importance." In the infliction of punishments in his School, he always premised them by a discourse upon the nature, hainousness, or tendency of the offence. Sometimes he made all the Scholars in the School give their opinions upon the nature of an offence, before he gave his own, and now and then he obliged them to pronounce sentence of punishment, before he inflicted it. The instrument with which he corrected was a small switch which he broke from a tree. The part he struck was the palm of the hand, and that never more than three times. The solemn forms connected with this punishment were more terrible and distressing than the punishment itself. I once saw him spend half an hour in exposing the folly and wickedness of an offence with his rod in hand. The culprit stood all this while trembling and weeping before him. After he had ended his admonitions, he lifted his rod as high as he could and then permitted it to fall gently upon his hand. The boy was surprised by this conduct. "There, go about your business (said the Doctor). I mean shame, and not pain [to] be your punishment in the present instance."

He took uncommon pains to promote good manners among his Scholars. The slightest act of incivility was reproved. This he did at his table and in so elegant and delicate a manner as not to expose the person who was rebuked. He selected a number of artificial characters with which he connected all the usual follies and improprieties of boys. To these he gave the names of Thomas Broadbrim, Ned Short, Bill Slovenly, and the like. These characters he contrasted by the history of Johnny Courtley, who was an example of all that was proper and amiable in the conduct of a young man. His manner of describing these characters was so agreeable as to fix even the most volatile and desultory of his boys to their chairs. Sometimes his descriptions were interspersed with anecdotes that excited a burst of laughter. If in his walks and in his study he occasionally overheard an improper expression, or saw an improper act in any of his boys, he never failed to take notice of it at the ensuing meal, but in such a manner as not to excite a suspicion that a personal application of what was said, was intended. One evening I recollect he dwelled chiefly upon the character of Ned Short. Among other things, he informed us that he was of a quick temper, and very prone to give rude answers to the most innocent questions. "For instance (said he), if one of his companions asked him if he knew where his book was, he would answer 'Ask about.'" Here he paused. A blush appeared in the countenance of one of his boys, who had on that day given that answer to a question of a similar nature. The Doctor did not appear to be conscious that the rebuke had produced its intended effect. But his table was not made subservient only to this mode of instruction. He made it a constant practice to admit his boys to eat with all the strangers who visited him. The benefits derived from the news, anecdotes, and general conversations which young people are thus permitted to hear are much greater than is generally supposed. "Conversation (said a wise man) is education," and one of the first geniuses in Britain has declared that he learned more from the conversation of one man whom he named, than from all the books he ever read in his life. I could repeat an hundred things I heard at the table of my master to which I then was constrained to lend a reluctant and impatient ear, but which have since become the seeds of useful knowledge. I owe my present ideas of the misery connected with great wealth, to a dream which the Revd. Mr. Richd. Treat related at his table when I was about 12 years old.

He inculcated at all times a regard to the common forms of good breeding. For this purpose, he frequently exercised his pupils in delivering and receiving letters, and in asking and receiving favors. He extended his attention to forms, to the composition, folding, and direction of letters. These had their rules, and were applied by him to different ranks and subjects according as they were upon business, or mere letters of friendship.

His method of teaching the Latin and Greek languages was simple. He taught several of the Arts and Sciences usually taught in Colleges. In these he was unfortunately tied down to the principles and forms that were common in the Schools of that day. He had studied the English language, and taught the reading, writing, and speaking of it with great care and success.

In the government and instruction of his family he exhibited an example of apostolical prudence, piety and zeal. He read and explained the whole or part of a chapter in the Old or New Testament every morning and evening before prayers in his family. Many of the remarks that he made upon passages in the Bible, which then passed hastily through my mind, have occurred to me many years afterwards, and I hope not without some effect. He obliged all the boys who lodged in his house to commit the Shorter Catechism of the Church of Scotland to memory, and to repeat it every Sunday evening. Upon each of the answers, he made pertinent and instructing or pious remarks. He likewise obliged all the members of his family to repeat what they remembered of the sermons they had heard at church. I cannot commend this practice too highly. It created habits of attention and recollection. I was much struck in observing how much we improved in the knowledge we brought home of the sermon by exercise. Two of his Scholars I recollect frequently gave, between them, every idea mentioned in a sermon.

The Instructions of the Sunday evening were usually closed by delivering in a plain way some of the most striking and intelligible evidences of the truth of the Christian Religion. Many of his arguments upon these occasions, tho' cloathed in simple language, were the same which are to be met with in the most logical writers upon that subject, and to the impressions they made upon my understanding, I ascribe my not having at any time of my life ever entertained a doubt of the divine origin of the Bible. I wish this mode of fortifying the reason of young people in the principles of Christianity were more general. The impressions which are made upon their fears, or their faith, by sermons and creeds soon wear away, but arguments fixed in the understanding are indelible. They operate upon the judgement, and this process of the mind we know to yield as necessarily to the impression of truth as vision in a sound eye succeeds the impression from the rays of light.

One more branch of education remains to be mentioned which was taught in the Doctor's family, and that is practical agriculture. All his boarders shared in the labors of Harvest and hay making. I bear on one of my fingers to this day the mark of a severe cut I received in learning to reap. These exercises were both pleasant and useful. They begat health, and helped to implant more deeply in our minds the native passion for rural life. Perhaps it may be ascribed in part to their influence, that not a single instance of death, and not more than two or three instances of sickness occurred in the Doctor's family during the time I lived in it, which was five years. The family seldom consisted of less than thirty persons.

The comfort and reputation of a boarding School depends so much upon the conduct of the wife of its master, that the account I have given would be very defective without mentioning that my aunt (with a small deduction on account of irritability of her temper, occasioned by bad health) was eminently qualified for her station. She was industrious, intelligent, frugal, and in every other respect a good housewife. She possessed information upon many subjects, and some wit, which rendered her agreeable in conversation. She kept a plentiful table of country food dressed in a pleasant manner. The record of this fact will not appear trifling to those who know that the appetite is the ruling principle in young people, and that no advantages in point of education will be duly appreciated where it is not pleased, nor any acts of injustice committed by boarding Schools remembered with less forgiveness, than scanty, or ill-dressed meals. I quit the history of this delightful haunt of my youth with reluctance. There is not a fruit tree, nor a rivulet of water on it that was not dear to me. Some years after I left it, I rode several miles out of my way to visit it. I rambled with a melancholy pleasure slowly over the fields and meadows and orchard in which I had shared with my master and Schoolmates in rural labors and festivity. I sat down in the dining room of the old mansion house, and stood silent and motionless for a considerable time in the Schoolhouse, which was then used as a weaver's shop. Most of the members of that once happy family are now no more. Seven out of eight of Dr. Finley's children sleep with their father and mother in the grave.

• • •

In taking leave of the School and family of my venerable preceptor, I have only to add that he died in the city of Philadelphia in the month of July in the year 1776 in the 51st year of his age. I sat up with him every other night for several weeks, and finally performed the distressing office of closing his eyes. The annals of Christian biography do not furnish an instance of more patience in sickness, nor of a greater triumph in death. His conversation for several days before he died was elevated, pious, and eloquent in the highest degree. It was carefully recorded by one of his attendants, and afterwards published by Mr. Aitken in the United States magazine. The character and manners of this excellent man commanded respect and affection from his numerous pupils. I never met with one of them who did not admire, esteem and love him. Some of them expressed their respect for his memory in terms bordering upon idolatry. I endeavoured to show my gratitude to him by adopting and educating his youngest son, who is now a respectable physician and citizen of South Carolina. His picture forms a part of the furniture of my house.

• • •

In the spring of 1759 and in the 15th year of my age, I was removed from Dr. Finley's School to the Jersey College, where after an examination by two of the tutors I was admitted into the Junior Class. The pro tempore President of this College at that time was Revd. Jacob Green. He was succeeded in the month of August by the Revd. Samuel Davies, who had been elected some time before President of the College. This gentleman surmounted the disadvantages of scanty circumstances and a confined education by the strength and activity of a great and original genius. He was in most respects "Faber suae fortunae" that is, in the language of the world a "self made man." His reputation for classical literature, philosophy and oratory, was such as recommended him to the Trustees of the College many years before to undertake a mission to Great Britain to solicit contributions to build and endow the College. This mission was executed with success. From his intercourse when abroad with the most eminent Scholars and Divines among the dissenters, he enlarged his mind and became better qualified for the station he was now called to fill. He seemed to have been made for it. To a handsome person, he united the most elegant and commanding manners. He was truly dignified, but at the same time affable and even familiar in his intercourse with his pupils. He introduced several new subjects of instruction into the College, and gave to the old branches of education a new and popular complexion. It was my happy lot to attract a good deal of his attention. I discovered some talents for poetry, composition and public speaking, to each of which he was very partial. The facility with which I committed his lessons to memory, imposed upon him so far that he gave me credit for much more capacity than I possessed. Those who knew me at that time remember me only as an idle, playful, and I am sorry to add, sometimes mischievous boy. While I lament that my improvements here, as at Dr. Finley's school, were by no means equal to my opportunities, I hope I shall be excused in acknowledging that his mode of teaching inspired me with a love of knowledge, and that if I derived but little from his instructions, I was taught by him how to acquire it in the subsequent periods of my life. I learned from him to record in a book what he called "Liber Selectorum" such passages in the Classicks as struck me most forcibly in reading them. By recording these passages, I was led afterwards to record facts and opinions. To this I owe perhaps in part the frequent use I have made of pen and ink. I have constantly associated them with every book I have read, sometimes by making extracts from them, but more frequently by making references to them in a common place book, or by making marks or indexes in them. This method of reading I know is condemned by some people, and memorandum books have been called by them the destruction of memories, but I have not observed this to be the case in myself, nor in some others who have adopted it in a greater extent than I have done. "Studium sine calamo somnium" was the saying of one of the ancient poets. Recording facts has the usual effect of repetition. Instead of producing an oblivion of them, it imprints them more deeply in the memory.

In the month of September 1760 I was admitted to the degree of Bachelor of Arts. Before I left the College Mr. Davies asked me what profession I intended myself for. I told him I had been advised to study the law. He approved of the advice, and added that he "believed I should make a better figure at the bar, than in the walks of a hospital." This opinion fixed my determination, and my mother in consequence of it applied to a Lawyer in Philadelphia to take me into his office. Previously to my sitting down to study I was prevailed upon to accompany one of my old Schoolmates on a visit to his family in Somerset County in Maryland. On my way there and back again I stopped a few days at Dr. Finley's. Just before I took leave of him on my return home, he called me to the end of the piazza before his door, and asked me whether I had chosen a profession. I told him I had, and that I expected to begin the study of the law as soon as I returned to Philadelphia. He said the practice of the law was full of temptations and advised me by no means to think of it, but to study physic. "But before you determine on any thing (said he), set apart a day for fasting and prayer, and ask God to direct you in your choice of a profession." I am sorry to say I neglected the latter part of this excellent advice, but yielded to the former, and accordingly obtained from Mr. Davies, whom I saw soon afterwards in Philadelphia, a letter of recommendation to Dr. John Redman to become his pupil.

On what slight circumstances do our destinies in life seem to depend! All my friends objected to my choice. One of my classmates wrote me a long letter full of remonstrances against it, and reminded me of the credit I had acquired at the College as a public speaker. There were periods in my life in which I regretted the choice I had made of the profession of medicine, and once, after I was thirty years of age, I made preparations for beginning the study of law. But providence overruled my intentions by an event to be mentioned hereafter. I now rejoice that I followed Dr. Finley's advice. I have seen the hand of heaven clearly in it. This fact is recorded to shew that our feelings sometimes mislead us, as well as our reason, and that we often regret having done or omitted doing things which time discovers to have been most for our interests, or for the benefit of our fellow creatures. I might have acquired more fortune and rank in life in the profession of law, and probably have escaped much of the vexation and distress that are connected with the practice of medicine, but I am sure I have been more useful in the latter profession, and therefore acquiesce in my lot, and were I to chuse an employment again, a conviction of suffering all the persecution that has followed me for my opinions and practice would not alter my predilection for medicine.

STUDENT: RICHARD HENRY DANA, JR.

(1815–1882)
Author, editor and attorney.

TEACHER: WILLIAM H. SANDFORD

Upon returning to Cambridge [Massachusetts] I again joined the grammar school at Cambridge-Port, under two successive teachers, Mr. Tyler & Mr. Perkins, graduates of Yale College. Soon afterwards a school was opened in the old town under the charge of Mr. Ralph Waldo Emerson, since known as a writer & lecturer upon what is called the transcendental philosophy. We had a school of about 20 boys, all of us engaged in those studies which would prepare us for college; & a very pleasant instructor we had in Mr. E., although he had not system or discipline enough to ensure regular & vigorous study. I have always considered it fortunate for us that we fell into the hands of more systematic & strict teachers, though not so popular with us, nor perhaps so elevated in their habits of thought as Mr. E. The next teacher was the Rev. Jonathan Cole, & after him Rev. William H. Sandford. Mr. Sandford left college without much reputation as a scholar, & he was not given to theories & speculations upon teaching, mental processes of the young, modes of presenting motives, &c, yet he was the best teacher I ever had. He used no corporal chastisement, but had regular systems of punishment, well understood & put in force with all the certainty & inflexibility of public statutes, & pardoning power was most sparingly exercised. As an instance of this, one of his rules was that no boy should speak except in answer to a question from the master, without coming to the master's desk. This rule was partly to prevent the offering of excuses, denials, & the like. At the time a *note* for impropriety was made; a time for such excuses being set apart, after school was dismissed. Something had been thrown across the school-room from the part where my desk was. He saw it & called out to the monitor to *note* me for misconduct. I instinctively said, "I didn't throw it, Sir." "Note him again for talking," was the only reply. After school was over the boy who threw the thing confessed it to save me, & my note was taken off. I was going away, when Mr. S. called me back for my other note. I told him they ought both to go together; but no, I had to commit my ten lines of Virgil for my second note. On another occasion he had set one of the boys, as punishment, the task of committing ten lines of Latin to memory. The boy's father, who was rather indulgent to his son & thought the task too hard, wrote Mr. S. requesting him to change the punishment, if he could do so consistently with his rules. Mr. S. answered that [he] would do it with pleasure, & set the boy the same number of lines of Greek. After this he had no interference from parents. There was perfect silence, order & decorum in the school, with a good deal of hard study & sufficient emulation, & the drilling in the grammars & rudiments was constant & thorough. By these means, though but an indifferent classical scholar himself, Mr. S. fitted his boys admirably for college & they passed very creditable examinations. He left the school with the approbation of all the parents & with good wishes & kind feelings from his scholars who felt the benefits of his faithful preceptorship.

STUDENT: ELIZABETH CADY STANTON

(1815–1902)

Woman suffrage leader and author.

TEACHER: SIMON HOSACK

When I was eleven years old two events occurred which changed the current of my life. My only brother, who had just graduated from Union College, came home to die. A young man of great talent and promise, he was the pride of my father's heart. We early felt that his son filled a larger place in our father's affections and future plans than the five daughters together. Well do I remember how tenderly he watched my brother in his last illness, the sighs and tears he gave vent to as he slowly walked up and down the hall, and, when the last sad moment came, and we were all assembled to say farewell in the silent chamber of death, how broken were his utterances as he knelt and prayed for comfort and support. I still recall, too, going into the large darkened parlor to see my brother, and finding the casket, mirrors, and pictures all draped in white, and my father seated by his side, pale, immovable. As he took no notice of me, after standing a long while, I climbed upon his knee, when he mechanically put his arm about me and, with my head resting against his beating heart, we both sat in silence, he thinking of the wreck of all his hopes in the loss of a dear son, and I wondering what could be said or done to fill the void in his breast. At length he heaved a deep sigh and said: "Oh, my daughter, would that you were a boy!"

Then and there I resolved that I would not give so much time as heretofore to play, but would study and strive to be at the head of all my classes and thus delight my father's heart. All that day and far into the night I pondered the problem of boyhood. I thought that the chief thing to be done in order to equal boys was to be learned and courageous. So I decided to study Greek and learn to manage a horse. Having formed this conclusion I fell asleep. My resolutions, unlike many such made at night, did not vanish with the coming dawn. I arose early and hastened to put them into execution. They were resolutions never to be forgotten—destined to mold my character anew. As soon as I was dressed I hastened to our good pastor, Simon Hosack, who was always early at work in his garden.

"Doctor," said I, "which do you like best, boys or girls?"

"Why, girls, to be sure; I would not give you for all the boys in Christendom."

"My father," I replied, "prefers boys; he wishes I was one, and I intend to be as near like one as possible. I am going to ride on horseback and study Greek. Will you give me a Greek lesson now? I want to begin at once."

"Yes, child," said he, throwing down his hoe, "come into my library and we will begin without delay."

He entered fully into the feeling of suffering and sorrow which took possession of me when I discovered that a girl weighed less in the scale of being than a boy, and he praised my determination to prove the contrary. The old grammar which he had studied in the University of Glasgow was soon in my hands, and the Greek article was learned before breakfast.

Then came the sad pageantry of death; the weeping of friends, the dark rooms, the ghostly stillness, the exhortation to the living to prepare for death, the solemn prayer, the mournful chant, the funeral cortege, the solemn, tolling bell, the burial. How I suffered during those sad days! What strange undefined fears of the unknown took possession of me! For months afterward, at the twilight hour, I went with my father to the new-made grave. Near it stood two tall poplar trees, against one of which I leaned, while my father threw himself on the grave with outstretched arms, as if to embrace his child. At last the frosts and storms of November came and threw a chilling barrier between the living and the dead, and we went there no more.

During all this time I kept up my lessons at the parsonage, and made rapid progress. I surprised even my teacher, who thought me capable of doing anything. I learned to drive, and to leap a fence and ditch on horseback. I taxed every power, hoping some day to hear my father say, "Well, a girl is as good as a boy, after all." But he never said it. When the doctor came over to spend the evening with us I would whisper in his ear, "Tell my father how fast I get on," and he would tell him, and was lavish in his praises. But my father only paced the room, sighed, and showed that he wished I were a boy; and I, not knowing why he felt thus, would hide my tears of vexation on the doctor's shoulder.

Soon after this I began to study Latin, Greek, and mathematics with a class of boys in the village academy, many of whom were much older than I. For three years one boy kept his place at the head of the class, and I always stood next. Two prizes were offered in Greek. I strove for one, and took the second. How well I remember my joy in receiving that prize. There was no sentiment of ambition, rivalry, or triumph over my companions, nor feeling of satisfaction in receiving this honor in the presence of those assembled on the day of the exhibition. One thought alone filled my mind. "Now," said I, "my father will be satisfied with me." So, as soon as we were dismissed, I ran down the hill, rushed breathless into his office, laid the Greek Testament, which was my prize, on his table and exclaimed: "There, I got it!" He took up the book, asked me some questions about the class, the teachers, the spectators, and evidently pleased, handed it back to me. Then while I stood looking and waiting for him to say something which would show that he recognized the equality of the daughter with the son, he kissed me on the forehead and exclaimed, with a sigh, "Ah, you should have been a boy!"

My joy turned to ashes. I ran to my good doctor. He chased my bitter tears away, and soothed me with unbounded praise and visions of future success. He was then confined to the house with his last illness. He asked me that day if I would like to have, when he was gone, the old lexicon, Testament, and grammar that we had so often thumbed together. "Yes, but I would rather have you stay," I urged, "for what can I do when you are gone?" "Oh," said he tenderly, "I shall not be gone; my spirit will still be with you, watching you in all life's struggles." Noble, generous friend! He had but little on earth to bequeath to anyone, but when the last scene in his life was ended, and his will was opened, sure enough there was a clause saying: "My Greek lexicon, Testament and grammar, and four volumes of *Scott's Commentaries*, I will to Elizabeth Cady.'' I never look at these books without a feeling of thankfulness that in childhood I was blessed with such a friend and teacher.

STUDENT: THOMAS WENTWORTH HIGGINSON

(1823–1911)

Unitarian minister, abolitionist, woman suffragist, soldier, author and friend of Emily Dickinson.

TEACHERS: BENJAMIN PEIRCE EDWARD TYRREL CHANNING

Professor Benjamin Peirce, our mathematical teacher [at Harvard], was then put, by general opinion, at the head of American mathematicians,—a place which, I believe, he still retains by tradition. In his later years, and after the abandonment of the temporary elective method, he may have become discouraged or apathetic, but when I knew him he was in his prime, and he was to me of all teachers the most inspiring and delightful. He was then a very handsome man, with the most eager and ardent manner, alternating with deep absorption, and he gave beyond all others the effect of original and creative genius. We studied, by an added stroke of good luck, his "Curves and Functions," which was just passing through the press, and the successive parts of which were bound up for our use. This increased the charm; it seemed like mathematics in the process of construction. I was already old enough to appreciate the wonderful compactness and close reasoning of these volumes, and to enter with eager zest into filling the intermediate gaps afforded by the long steps often taken from one equation to another. Dr. Bowditch, the translator of Laplace's "Mecanique Celeste," used to say that whenever he came to one of Laplace's "Whence it plainly appears," he was in for an hour or two of toil in order to make this exceeding plainness visible. It was often so with Peirce's books, but this enhanced the pleasure of the chase. He himself took part in it: a thought would sometimes flash into his mind, and he would begin to work it out on the blackboard before our eyes; forgetting our very existence, he would labor away with the chalk, writing out with lightning rapidity a series of equations, smaller and smaller, chasing his scientific prey down into the utmost right-hand corner of the blackboard, and finally turning to us with a sigh when the pursuit was ended. Again was the science of mathematics being created before our very eyes; it was like being present at the first discoveries of some old Greek or Arabian geometrician. Peirce had also the delightful quality of being especially interested in all of this his first voluntary class, and indeed of greatly overrating their merits. When I left college, he gave me an indorsement which took my breath away, and had me placed, at eighteen, on the examining committee in his department. Years after, when in a fair way to pass some time in jail after an anti-slavery riot, I met him, and said that I had reserved that period of imprisonment for reviewing mathematics and reading Laplace. His fine eyes kindled, and he replied, "In that case, I sincerely hope that you may go there." He was then vehemently opposed to the abolitionists, and it seemed a double blessing to gag one of them and at the same time create a mathematician. The indictment was, unluckily, quashed, so that both his hopes were disappointed.

Next to Peirce's teaching came, without question, both in stimulus and in attractions, the English course of Professor Edward Tyrrel Channing. Professor Wendell has lately spoken of the present standard of training in English composition at Harvard as if it were quite a new thing; but with some opportunity of observing it, I have never had reason to think it any new departure as compared with that given by Professor Channing down to 1841 at least. The evidence would seem to be that between that period and 1846, when Professor Child graduated, Professor Channing had in some way lost his hold upon his pupils as his years advanced; so that when Professor Child succeeded to the chair, in 1851, it was profound distrust in the whole affair, insomuch that the very department of rhetoric and oratory came near being wiped out of existence, and was saved by the indignant protest of the late Charles Francis Adams.

Certain it is that this department was, in my time, by far the most potent influence in determining college rank, and therefore in stimulating ambition. We wrote themes every fortnight and forensics once a month; and as these were marked on a scale of 48, and ordinary recitations on a scale of 8, the importance of this influence may be seen. Never in my life have I had to meet such exacting criticism on anything written as came from Professor Channing, and never have I had any praise so encouraging as his. My marks were often second in the class, sometimes equaling—O day of glory!—those of my classmate, Francis Edward Parker, who was easily first; and to have a passage read to the class for praise, even anonymously, was beyond all other laurels, though the satisfaction might be marred occasionally by the knowledge that my elder sister had greatly helped in that particular sentence. When it is considered that Channing's method reared most of the well-known writers whom New England was then producing,—that it was he who trained Emerson, C. F. Adams, Hedge, A. P. Peabody, Felton, Hillard, Winthrop, Holmes, Sumner, Motley, Phillips, Bowen, Lovering, Torrey, Dana, Lowell, Thoreau, Hale, Thomas Hill, Child, Fitzedward Hall, Lane, and Norton,—it will be seen that the classic portion of our literature came largely into existence under him. He fulfilled the aspiration attributed to Increase Mather when he wished to become president of Harvard College: to mould not merely the teaching, but the teachers,—*non lapides dolare, sed architectos*.

STUDENT: LEW WALLACE

(1827–1905)

Attorney, army officer and author.

TEACHER: SAMUEL K. HOSHOUR

My thirteenth year was passed in Centreville, Indiana, where there was a teacher of such repute that my father decided to send me to him. An aunt dwelt there also, and it was thought she would occasionally look after me; that is, see to the buttons on my clothes, keep my hair down, and trifles of the sort. She did not fail expectation. My elder brother was assigned to me as companion, principally, I think, to assist my aunt.

Professor Samuel K. Hoshour—his name is purposely given in full—came more nearly to my ideal school-master than any to whose tender mercies it had been my lot to fall. He wielded the rod and vigorously, but with discrimination and undeniable justice, and really taught me. He even interested me in arithmetic. Getting me to his house of evenings, with infinite patience he would cipher me over the knottier problems, explaining the rules pencil in hand. Better evidence of Christian nature no man can furnish.

Professor Hoshour was the first to observe a glimmer of writing capacity in me. An indifferent teacher would have allowed the discovery to pass without account; but he set about making the most of it, and in his method there was so much wisdom that it were wrong not to give it with particularity, the more so as some modern pedagogue may in that way be helped to an understanding of what I mean by discrimination applied to pupils.

The general principle on which the professor acted is plain to me now. The lack of aptitude for mathematics in my case was too decided not to be apparent to him; instead of beating me for it, he humanely applied himself to cultivating a faculty he thought within my powers and to my taste. Or, in another form, poverty of talent in one line, as he reasoned, might be compensated for by the development of ability in another.

I remember his beginning perfectly; inasmuch as it set me to wondering that one could waste time and effort in plying a lad like me with a subject so serious and seemingly beyond my years. What had he on which to believe that I could even understand what he said to me? But when at length I saw I could understand him, and that he too saw it, how delicious the flattery! And what stimulation there was in it!

The first sitting he gave me was in one of the evening seances at his house without witnesses. By a series of questions, artfully put, he led me to expose the whole field of my reading, and I think it encouraged as well as surprised him, for he presently brought out two volumes of size.

"These," he said, "are lectures on rhetoric by John Quincy Adams. They are given to rules for composition. You must dig them out for yourself sometime, for there can be no good writing if one of them be violated."

I recall also a saying of the professor's own.

"Were you to ask me," he said, "which of the rules is the most important, which comes nearest being the essence of the whole art, here it is: In writing, everything is to be sacrificed to clearness of expression—everything."

By way of illustration, I suppose, he next produced a volume which he called *The Spectator*.

"Here," he said, "are some of the finest examples of clear English ever printed. I will select some of the best. Now listen." He read a paragraph, and declared, "You can't help understanding that."

From the table he then picked a thin pamphlet, premising, "This is a work of my own, *Lorenzo Altisonant* by name." At the end of an example he looked at me quizzically and said, "You don't understand a word of it, do you?"

"Is it English?" I asked.

The professor had a habit of tugging at the lower skin of his cheek, and as a result the skin hung to the jaw like a flabby purse of yellow leather. Giving the purse an extra pull, he chuckled inwardly, making me think of Natty Bumpo, and explained.

"This, you see, is a story in words of five syllables. I wrote it to show the absurdity of big words so striven after by young writers, and, for the matter of that, by many old ones as well."

Taking another book, he selected a passage and had me read it aloud, saying, at the conclusion, "How clear and simple that is! Now try *Altisonant* again."

I tried, but gave it up.

And he commented: "The first was from *The Vicar of Wakefield*, by one Oliver Goldsmith. You must take the book home with you. Washington Irving borrowed his style from Goldsmith. What style is we will come to after a while. Let me speak of language now. Our English is mainly composed of Saxon and Latin. *Altisonant* is very little Saxon. See how preferable the Saxon is. Our conversation is almost altogether Saxon. Let me give you an example of the very purest Saxon."

Taking a New Testament, "There," he said, "read that. It is the story of the birth of Jesus Christ."

This was entirely new to me, and I recall the impression made by the small part given to the three wise men. Little did I dream then what those few verses were to bring me—that out of them *Ben-Hur* was one day to be evoked.

I can see the professor standing in his door, lamp in hand and bareheaded, dismissing me for the night, with exactly the same civilities he would have sped an official the most important in the state. Ah, the kindly cunning of the shrewd old gentleman! He had dropped a light into my understanding and caught me.

So, step by step, the professor led me into and out of depths I had never dreamed of, and through tangles of subtlety and appreciations which proved his mind as thoroughly as they tried mine. Before the year was out he had, as it were, taken my hand in his and introduced me to Byron, Shakespeare, and old Isaiah. The year was the turning-point of my life, and out of my age and across his grave I send him, Gentle master, hail, and all sweet rest! Now I know wherein I am most obliged to you—unconsciously, perhaps, but certainly you taught me how to educate myself up to every practical need.

STUDENT: JOHN MUIR

(1838–1914)

Naturalist, conservationist, and author.

TEACHER: MR. GRISWOLD

I received my first lesson in botany from a student by the name of Griswold, who is now County Judge of the County of Waukesha, Wisconsin. In the University [of Wisconsin] he was often laughed at on account of his anxiety to instruct others, and his frequently saying with fine emphasis, "Imparting instruction is my greatest enjoyment." One memorable day in June, when I was standing on the stone steps of the north dormitory, Mr. Griswold joined me and at once began to teach. He reached up, plucked a flower from an overspreading branch of a locust tree, and, handing it to me, said, "Muir, do you know what family this tree belongs to?"

"No," I said, "I don't know anything about botany."

"Well, no matter," said he, "what is it like?"

"It's like a pea flower," I replied.

"That's right. You're right," he said, "it belongs to the Pea Family."

"But how can that be," I objected, "when the pea is a weak, clinging, straggling herb, and the locust a big, thorny hardwood tree?"

"Yes, that is true," he replied, "as to the difference in size, but it is also true that in all their essential characters they are alike, and therefore they must belong to one and the same family. Just look at the peculiar form of the locust flower; you see that the upper petal, called the banner, is broad and erect, and so is the upper petal of the pea flower; the two lower petals, called the wings, are outspread and wing-shaped; so are those of the pea; and the two petals below the wings are united on their edges, curve upward, and form what is called the keel, and so you see are the corresponding petals of the pea flower. And now look at the stamens and pistils. You see that nine of the ten stamens have their filaments united into a sheath around the pistil, but the tenth stamen has its filament free. These are very marked characters, are they not? And, strange to say, you will find them the same in the tree and in the vine. Now look at the ovules or seeds of the locust, and you will see that they are arranged in a pod or legume like those of the pea. And look at the leaves. You see the leaf of the locust is made up of several leaflets, and so also is the leaf of the pea. Now taste the locust leaf.''

I did so and found that it tasted like the leaf of the pea. Nature has used the same seasoning for both, though one is a straggling vine, the other a big tree.

''Now, surely you cannot imagine that all these similar characters are mere coincidences. Do they not rather go to show that the Creator in making the pea vine and locust tree had the same idea in mind, and that plants are not classified arbitrarily? Man has nothing to do with their classification. Nature has attended to all that, giving essential unity with boundless variety, so that the botanist has only to examine plants to learn the harmony of their relations.''

This fine lesson charmed me and sent me flying to the woods and meadows in wild enthusiasm. Like everybody else I was always fond of flowers, attracted by their external beauty and purity. Now my eyes were opened to their inner beauty, all alike revealing glorious traces of the thoughts of God, and leading on and on into the infinite cosmos. I wandered away at every opportunity, making long excursions round the lakes, gathering specimens and keeping them fresh in a bucket in my room to study at night after my regular class tasks were learned; for my eyes never closed on the plant glory I had seen.

• • •

Although I was four years at the University, I did not take the regular course of studies, but instead picked out what I thought would be most useful to me, particularly chemistry, which opened a new world, and mathematics and physics, a little Greek and Latin, botany and geology. I was far from satisfied with what I had learned, and should have stayed longer. Anyhow I wandered away on a glorious botanical and geological excursion, which has lasted nearly fifty years and is not yet completed, always happy and free, poor and rich, without thought of a diploma or of making a name, urged on and on through endless, inspiring Godful beauty.

From the top of a hill on the north side of Lake Mendota [in Wisconsin] I gained a last wistful, lingering view of the beautiful University grounds and buildings where I had spent so many hungry and happy and hopeful days. There with streaming eyes I bade my blessed Alma Mater farewell. But I was only leaving one University for another, the Wisconsin University for the University of the Wilderness.

STUDENT: ANNA HOWARD SHAW

(1847–1919)

Feminist, political activist, clergywoman, physician, woman suffrage leader.

TEACHER: LUCY FOOT

Fate, however, as if weary at last of seeing me between her paws, suddenly let me escape. Before I had been working a month at my uncongenial trade Big Rapids [Michigan] was favored by a visit from a Universalist woman minister, the Reverend Marianna Thompson, who came there to preach. Her sermon was delivered on Sunday morning, and I was, I think, almost the earliest arrival of the great congregation which filled the church. It was a wonderful moment when I saw my first woman minister enter her pulpit; and as I listened to her sermon, thrilled to the soul, all my early aspirations to become a minister myself stirred in me with cumulative force. After the services I hung for a time on the fringe of the group that surrounded her, and at last, when she was alone and about to leave, I found courage to introduce myself and pour forth the tale of my ambition. Her advice was as prompt as if she had studied my problem for years.

"My child," she said, "give up your foolish idea of learning a trade, and go to school. You can't do anything until you have an education. Get it, and get it *now*."

Her suggestion was much to my liking, and I paid her the compliment of acting on it promptly, for the next morning I entered the Big Rapids High School, which was also a preparatory school for college. There I would study, I determined, as long as my money held out, and with the optimism of youth I succeeded in confining my imagination to this side of that crisis. My home, thanks to Mary, was assured; the wardrobe I had brought from the woods covered me sufficiently; to one who had walked five and six miles a day for years, walking to school held no discomfort; and as for pleasure, I found it, like a heroine of fiction, in my studies. For the first time life was smiling at me, and with all my young heart I smiled back.

The preceptress of the high school was Lucy Foot, a college graduate and a remarkable woman. I had heard much of her sympathy and understanding; and on the evening following my first day in school I went to her and repeated the confidences I had reposed in the Reverend Marianna Thompson. My trust in her was justified. She took an immediate interest in me, and proved it at once by putting me into the speaking and debating classes, where I was given every opportunity to hold forth to helpless classmates when the spirit of eloquence moved me.

As an aid to public speaking I was taught to "elocute," and I remember in every mournful detail the occasion on which I gave my first recitation. We were having our monthly "public exhibition night," and the audience included not only my classmates, but their parents and friends as well. The selection I intended to recite was a poem entitled "No Sects in Heaven," but when I faced my audience I was so appalled by its size and by the sudden realization of my own temerity that I fainted during the delivery of the first verse. Sympathetic classmates carried me into an anteroom and revived me, after which they naturally assumed that the entertainment I furnished was over for the evening. I, however, felt that if I let that failure stand against me I could never afterward speak in public; and within ten minutes, notwithstanding the protests of my friends, I was back in the hall and beginning my recitation a second time. Possibly it hoped to see me topple off the platform again, but nothing of the sort occurred. I went through the recitation with self-possession and received some friendly applause at the end. Strangely enough, those first sensations of "stage fright" have been experienced, in a lesser degree, in connection with each of the thousands of public speeches I have made since that time. I have never again gone so far as to faint in the presence of an audience; but I have invariably walked out on the platform feeling the sinking sensation at the pit of the stomach, the weakness of the knees, that I felt in the hour of my debut. Now, however, the nervousness passes after a moment or two.

From that night Miss Foot lost no opportunity of putting me into the foreground of our school affairs. I took part in all our debates, recited yards of poetry to any audience we could attract, and even shone mildly in our amateur theatricals. It was probably owing to all this activity that I attracted the interest of the presiding elder of our district—Dr. Peck, a man of progressive ideas. There was at that time a movement on foot to license women to preach in the Methodist Church, and Dr. Peck was ambitious to be the first presiding elder to have a woman ordained for the Methodist ministry. He had urged Miss Foot to be this pioneer, but her ambitions did not turn in that direction. Though she was a very devout Methodist, she had no wish to be the shepherd of a religious flock. She loved her school-work, and asked nothing better than to remain in it. Gently but persistently she directed the attention of Dr. Peck to me, and immediately things began to happen.

Without telling me to what it might lead, Miss Foot finally arranged a meeting at her home by inviting Dr. Peck and me to dinner. Being unconscious of any significance in the occasion, I chatted light-heartedly about the large issues of life and probably settled most of them to my personal satisfaction. Dr. Peck drew me out and led me on, listened and smiled. When the evening was over and we rose to go, he turned to me with sudden seriousness:

"My quarterly meeting will be held at Ashton," he remarked, casually. "I would like you to preach the quarterly sermon."

For a moment the earth seemed to slip away from my feet. I stared at him in utter stupefaction. Then slowly I realized that, incredible as it seemed, the man was in earnest.

"Why," I stammered, "I can't preach a sermon!"

Dr. Peck smiled at me. "Have you ever tried?" he asked.

I started to assure him vehemently that I never had. Then, as if Time had thrown a picture on a screen before me, I saw myself as a little girl preaching alone in the forest, as I had so often preached to a congregation of listening trees. I qualified my answer.

"Never," I said, "to human beings."

Dr. Peck smiled again. "Well," he told me, "the door is open. Enter or not, as you wish."

He left the house, but I remained to discuss his overwhelming proposition with Miss Foot. A sudden sobering thought had come to me.

"But," I exclaimed, "I've never been converted. How can I preach to any one?"

We both had the old-time idea of conversion, which now seems so mistaken. We thought one had to struggle with sin and with the Lord until at last the heart opened, doubts were dispersed, and the light poured in. Miss Foot could only advise me to put the matter before the Lord, to wrestle and to pray; and thereafter, for hours at a time, she worked and prayed with me, alternately urging, pleading, instructing, and sending up petitions in my behalf. Our last session was a dramatic one, which took up the entire night. Long before it was over we were both worn out; but toward morning, either from exhaustion of body or exaltation of soul, I seemed to see the light, and it made me very happy. With all my heart I wanted to preach, and I believed that now at last I had my call. The following day we sent word to Dr. Peck that I would preach the sermon at Ashton as he had asked, but we urged him to say nothing of the matter for the present, and Miss Foot and I also kept the secret locked in our breasts. I knew only too well what view my family and my friends would take of such a step and of me. To them it would mean nothing short of personal disgrace and a blotted page in the Shaw record.

STUDENT: CHAMP CLARK

(1850–1921)

Teacher, attorney, Member of Congress and Speaker of the United States House of Representatives.

TEACHER: CHARLES R. WHITTERN

The best school-teacher who ever taught me was a strolling English phrenologist named Charles R. Whittern, for whose memory I have profound affection. My father induced him to teach for three months a subscription school in the neighborhood, and, finding that he was a splendid teacher, father and others induced him to teach in that vicinity for more than a year. In fact, he taught until he died. I thought then that he knew everything. I know now that he did not know very much, but what he did know he could teach better than any other man that I ever saw. As between a teacher who knows little but can incite in his pupils a love of learning and one who knows a great deal and has not the power to incite that love of learning, I prefer the former. He is by far the more valuable of the two.

STUDENT: HENRY CABOT LODGE

(1850–1924)

Attorney, editor, historian, biographer, Member of the Massachusetts House of Representatives, Member of Congress and United States Senator.

TEACHER: HENRY ADAMS

But in all my four years I never really studied anything, never had my mind roused to any exertion or to anything resembling active thought until in my senior year I stumbled into the course in mediaeval history given by Henry Adams, who had then just come to Harvard. How I came to choose that course I do not exactly know. I was fond of history, liked to read it, and had a vague curiosity as to the Middle Ages, of which I knew nothing. I think there was no more intelligent reason than this for my selection. But I builded (sic) better than I knew. I found myself caught by strong interest, I began to think about the subject, Mr. Adams roused the spirit of inquiry and controversy in me, and I was fascinated by the stormy careers of the great German emperors, by the virtues, the abilities, the dark crimes of the popes, and by the tremendous conflicts between church and empire in which emperors and popes were antagonists. In just what way Mr. Adams aroused my slumbering faculties I am at a loss to say, but there can be no doubt of the fact. Mr. Adams has told me many times that he began his course in total ignorance of his own subject, and I have no doubt that the fact that he, too, was learning helped his students. But there was more than this. He had the power not only of exciting interest, but he awakened opposition to his own views, and that is one great secret of success in teaching. In any event, I worked hard in that course because it gave me pleasure; I took the highest marks, for which I cared, as I found, singularly little, because marks were not my object, and for the first time I got a glimpse of what education might be and really learned something. I have never lost my interest in the Othos, the Henrys, and the Fredericks, or in the towering figure of Hildebrand. They have always remained vital and full of meaning to me, and a few years ago I made a pilgrimage to Salerno with Adams himself to see the burial-place of the greatest of the popes, who had brought an emperor to his feet and had died a beaten exile. Yet it was not what I learned, but the fact that I learned something, that I discovered that it was the keenest of pleasures to use one's mind, a new sensation, and one which made Mr. Adams's course in the history of the Middle Ages so memorable to me. I have often wondered since, in view of this experience, why there is so little real education to be had, and why, as a rule, what passes under that name is so dry and meaningless and sometimes so repulsive.

• • •

. . . thanks to Henry Adams, I was imbued with a realizing sense of my own abounding ignorance, which is the first rung on the ladder of learning and the best education that any college or university can give.

STUDENT: LOUIS H. SULLIVAN

(1856–1924)

Architect and author.

TEACHER: MOSES WOOLSON

[Moses Woolson] was a man above medium height, very scant beard, shocky hair, his movements were panther-like, his features, in action, were set as with authority and pugnacity, like those of a first mate taking on a fresh crew.

He was tense, and did not swagger—a man of passion. He said, in substance: "Boys, you don't know me, but you soon will. The discipline here [at English High School in Boston] will be rigid. You have come here to learn and I'll see that you do. I will not only do my share but I will make you do yours. You are here under my care; no other man shall interfere with you. I rule here—I am master here—as you will soon discover. You are here as wards in my charge; I accept that charge as sacred; I accept responsibility involved as a high, exacting duty I owe to myself and equally to you. I will give to you all that I have; you shall give to me all that you have. But mark you: The first rule of discipline shall be SILENCE. Not a desk-top shall be raised, not a book touched, no shuffling of feet, no whispering, no sloppy movements, no rustling. I do not use the rod, I believe it the instrument of barbarous minds and weak wills, but I will shake the daylight out of any boy who transgresses, after one warning. The second rule shall be STRICT ATTENTION: You are here to *learn*, to *think*, to *concentrate* on the matter in hand, to hold your minds steady. The third rule shall cover ALERTNESS. You shall be awake all the time—body and brain; you shall cultivate promptness, speed, nimbleness, dexterity of mind. The fourth rule: You shall learn to LISTEN; to *listen* in *silence* with the *whole* mind, not part of it; to listen with your *whole heart*, not part of it, for sound listening is a basis for sound thinking; sympathetic listening is a basis for sympathetic, worth-while thinking; accurate listening is a basis of accurate thinking. Finally you are to learn to OBSERVE, to REFLECT, to DISCRIMINATE. But this subject is of such high importance, so much above your present understanding, that I will not comment upon it now; it is not to be approached without due preparation. I shall not start you with a jerk, but tighten the lines bit by bit until I have you firmly in hand at the most spirited pace you can go.'' As he said this last saying, a dangerous smile went back and forth over his grim set face. As to the rest, he outlined the curriculum and his plan of procedure for the coming school year. He stressed matters of hygiene; and stated that a raised hand would always have attention. Lessons were then marked off in the various books—all were to be ''home lessons''—and the class was dismissed for the day.

Louis was amazed, thunder-struck, dumb-founded, over-joyed! He had caught and weighed every word as it fell from the lips of the master; to each thrilling word he had vibrated in open-eyed, amazed response. He knew now that through the years his thoughts, his emotions, his dreams, his feelings, his romances, his visions, had been formless and chaotic; now in this man's utterances, they were voiced in explosive condensation, in a flash they became defined, living, real. A pathway had been shown him, a wholly novel plan revealed that he grasped as a banner in his hand, as homeward bound he cried within: *At last a Man*!

Louis felt the hour of freedom was at hand. He saw, with inward glowing, that true freedom could come only through discipline of power, and he translated the master's word of discipline into its true intent: *Self Discipline of self power*. His eager life was to condense now in a focusing of powers: What had the words meant;—''silence,'' ''attention,'' ''promptness,'' ''speed,'' ''accurate,'' ''observe,'' ''reflect,'' ''discriminate,'' but powers of his own, obscurely mingled, unco-ordinated, and, thus far, vain to create? Now, in the master's plan, which he saw as a ground plan, he beheld that for which, in the darkness of broad daylight, he had yearned so desperately in vain; that for which, as it were with empty, outstretched hands, he had grasped, vaguely groping; as one seeing through a film, that for which he had hungered with an aching heart as empty as his hands. He had not known, surely, what it was he wished to find, but when the master breathed the words that Louis felt to be inspired: ''You are here as wards in my charge; I accept that charge as sacred; I accept the responsibility as a high exacting duty I owe to myself and equally to you. I will give to you all that I have, you shall give me all that you have,''—a veil was parted, as it were by magic, and behold! there stood forth not alone a man but a TEACHER of the young.

• • •

The ground work of his plan was set forth in his opening address, and is now to be revealed in its workings in detail.

The studies on which Louis set the highest value were Algebra, Geometry, English Literature, Botany, Mineralogy and French language. All these subjects were to him revelations. Algebra had startled him; for, through its portal in entered an unsuspected world of symbols. To him the symbol *x* flashed at once as a key to the unknown but ascertainable. Standing alone, he viewed this *x* in surprise as a mystic spirit in a land of enchantment, opening vistas so deep he could not see the end, and his vivid imagination saw at once that this *x*, expanded in its latent power, might prove the key to turn a lock in a door within a wall which shut out the truth he was seeking—the truth which might dissolve for him the mystery that lay behind appearances. For this *x*, he saw, was manipulated by means of things unknown.

Thus he saw far ahead; looking toward the time when he might mature. Geometry delighted him because of its nicety, its exactitude of relationships, its weird surprises—all like fairy tales, fairy tales which could be proved, and then you said: Q.E.D. He began to see what was meant by a theorem, a postulate, a problem, and that *proof* was a reasoned process based on certain facts or assertions. It was well for him, at the time, that he did not perceive the Euclidian *rigidity*, in the sense that he had noted the fluency of Algebra. As to Botany, had he not always seen trees and shrubs and vines and flowers of the field, the orchard and the garden?

Now he was learning their true story, their most secret intimacies, and the organization of their world. He loved them all the more for this. Mineralogy was new and revealing, the common stones had begun as it were, to talk to him in their own words. Concerning French he was ardent, for he had France in view. English literature opened to him the great world of words, of ordered speech, the marvelous vehicle whereby were conveyed every human thought and feeling from mind to mind, from heart to heart, from soul to soul, from imagination to imagination, from thought to thought; and to his ever widening view, it soon arose before him as a vast treasure house wherein was stored, in huge accumulation, a record of the thoughts, the deeds, the hopes, the joys, the sorrows, and the triumphs of mankind.

Moses Woolson was not a deep thinker, nor was Moses Woolson erudite or scholarly, or polished in manners, or sedate. Rather was he a blend of wild man and of poet. But of a surety he had the art of teaching at his finger tips and his plan of procedure was scientific to a degree, so far beyond the pedagogic attainments of his day that he stood unique, and was cordially hated by his craft as lambs might fear and hate a wolf. Today men would speak of such a man as a "human dynamo," a man ninety-nine per cent "efficient." His one weakness was a temper he all too often let escape him, but his high strung, nervous make-up may be averred in part extenuation, for this very make-up was the source of his accomplishment and power: He surely gave in abundance, with overflowing hands, all that he had of the best to give.

His plan of procedure was simple in idea, and therefore possible of high elaboration in the steady course of its unfolding into action and results. For convenience it may be divided into three daily phases seemingly consecutive, but really interblended; first came severe memory drill, particularly in geometry, algebra, French grammar and in exact English; this work first done at home, and tested out next day in the school room. Second, (first, next day) a period of recitation in which memory discipline and every aspect of alertness were carried at high tension. At the end of this period came the customary half-hour recess for fresh air and easing up. After recess came nature study with open book. Chief among them Gray's "School and Field Book of Botany"—Louis's playground; then came a closing lecture by the Master.

Thus it may be said, there was a period of high tension, followed by a period of reduced tension, and this in turn by a closing period of semi or complete relaxation, as the master reeled off in easy, entertaining talk, one of his delightful lectures. It was in the nature studies, and in these closing lectures, particularly those in which he dwelt upon the great out-of-doors, and upon the glories of English literature, that the deep enthusiasms of the man's nature came forth undisguised and unrestrained, rising often to the heights of impassioned eloquence, and beauteous awakening imagery. These lectures, or rather, informal talks covered a wide range of subjects, most of them lying beyond the boundaries of the school curriculum.

Thus, in a sense, Moses Woolson's school room partook of the nature of a university—quite impressively so when Professor Asa Gray of Harvard came occasionally to talk botany to the boys. He did this out of regard for Moses Woolson's love of the science. The unfailing peroration of these lectures—every one of them, was an exhortation in favor of "Women's Rights," as the movement was called at the time; for Moses Woolson was a sincere and ardent champion of womankind. On this topic he spoke in true nobility of spirit.

But the talks that gripped Louis the hardest were those on English literature. Here the master was completely at his ease. Here, indeed, he revelled, as it were, in the careful analysis and lucid exposition of every phase of his subject, copious in quotation, delightfully critical in taking apart a passage, a single line, explaining the value of each word in respect of action, rhythm, color, quality, texture, fitness, then putting these elements together in a renewed recital of the passage which now became a living moving utterance. Impartial in judgment, fertile in illustration and expedient, clear in statement, he opened to view a new world, a new land of enchantment.

One day, to Louis's amazement, he announced that the best existing history of English literature was written by a Frenchman, one Hyppolite Taine by name. This phenomenon he explained by stating that the fine French mind possessed a quality and power of detachment unknown to the English; that Monsieur Taine further possessed that spiritual aspect of sympathy, that vision, which enabled him to view, to enter freely and to comprehend a work of art regardless yet regardful of its origin in time or place; and he rounded an antithesis of French and English culture in such wise as to arouse Louis's keenest attention, for the word *culture*, had hitherto possessed no significance for him; it was merely a word! Now his thoughts, his whole being floated o'er the sea to distant France, whereupon he arose from his seat and asked Moses Woolson what culture really meant, and was told it signified the genius of a people, of a race. And what was meant by the *genius* of a people? It signified their innate qualities and powers of heart and mind; that therefore their culture was their own expression of their inmost selves, as individuals, as a people, as a race. Louis was magnificently bewildered by this high concentration. He seemed to be in a flood of light which hid everything from view; he made some sheepish rejoinder, whereupon Moses Woolson saw his own mistake.

He came down from his high perch to which he had climbed unwittingly, for it was dead against his theory and practice to talk above the heads of his boys. He thereupon diluted the prior statement with a simply worded illustration, and Louis was glad to find his own feet still on the ground. Then Louis put the two aspects of the statement side by side again, and "culture" became for him a living word—a sheer veil through which, at first, he could but dimly see; but living word and sheer living veil had come from without to abide with him. It seemed indeed as though Moses Woolson had passed on to him a wand of enchantment which he must learn to use to unveil the face of things. Thus Louis dreamed.

By the end of the school year Moses Woolson through genius as a teacher, had turned a crudely promising boy into, so to speak, a mental athlete. He had brought order out of disorder, definition out of what was vague, superb alertness out of mere boyish ardor; had nurtured and concentrated all that was best in the boy; had made him consciously courageous and independent; had focussed his powers of thought, feeling and action; had confirmed Louis's love of the great out of doors, as a source of inspiration; and had climaxed all by parting a great veil which opened to the view of this same boy, the wonderland of Poetry.

Thus with great skill he made of Louis a compacted personality, ready to act on his own initiative, in an intelligent purposeful way. Louis had the same capacity to absorb, and to value discipline, that Moses Woolson had to impart it, and Louis was not a brilliant or showy scholar. He stood well up in his class and that was enough. His purpose was not to give out, but to receive, to acquire. He was adept in the art of listening, and was therefore rather silent of mood. His object was to get every ounce of treasure out of Moses Woolson. And yet for Moses Woolson, the master and the man, he felt neither love nor affection, and it is quite likely that the master felt much the same toward him. What he felt toward the man was a vast admiration, he felt the power and the vigor of his intense and prodigal personality. It is scarcely likely that the master really knew, to the full extent, what he was doing for this boy, but Louis knew it; and there came gradually over him a cumulative reciprocity which, at the end, burst forth into a sense of obligation and of gratitude so heartfelt, so profound, that it has remained with him in constancy throughout the years. There may have been teachers and teachers, but for Louis Sullivan there was and could be only one. And now, in all too feeble utterance he pleads this token, remembrance, to the memory of that ONE long since passed on.

STUDENT: IDA M. TARBELL

(1857–1944)

Journalist and author.

TEACHERS: JEREMIAH TINGLEY GEORGE HASKINS

My pioneer childhood served me well. Moreover, I realized at the start that I had found what I had come to [Allegheny] college [in Meadville, Pennsylvania] for, direction in the only field in which I was interested—science. I found it in a way that I doubt if Cornell [University] could have given me at the moment, shy and immature as I was: the warming and contagious enthusiasm of a great natural teacher, one who had an ardent passion for those things which had stirred me and a wide knowledge which he fed by constant study and travel—Jeremiah Tingley, the head of Allegheny's department of natural science.

Professor Tingley was then a man of fifty, sparkling, alive, informal. Three years before, he had been one of the fifty chosen from many hundred applicants to spend the summer with Louis Agassiz on the island of Penikese in Buzzards Bay. Agassiz had planned with enthusiasm for the Penikese Summer School, and for those privileged to enter who could understand and appreciate it was an unforgettable experience; certainly it was for Jeremiah Tingley. He carried there Agassiz's faith in observation and classification, as well as his reverence for Nature and all her ways. For both men the material world was but the cover of the spirit. Professor Tingley would quote Agassiz sometimes: "Nature always brings us back to absolute truth whenever we wander."

This fervent faith had a profound and quieting effect on my religious tumult. I learned a new word: Pantheism. Being still in that early stage of development where there must be a definite word by which to classify oneself, I began to call myself a pantheist—and I had a creed which I repeated more often than the creed I had learned in childhood:

> Flower in the crannied wall,
> I pluck you out of the crannies,
> I hold you here, root and all, in my hand
> Little flower—but *if* I could understand
> What you are, root and all, and all in all,
> I should know what God and man is.

It reassured me; I was on the right track, for was I not going to find out with the microscope what God and man are?

Professor Tingley's method for those he found really interested in scientific study was to encourage them to look outside the book. There was where I had already found my joy; but I suspected it was the willful way, that the true way was to know first what was in the books. Here in Professor Tingley's classes you were ordered to go and see for yourself. He used to tell us a story of his first experience at Penikese. A stone was put before him, a round water-washed stone, on which he was to report. He looked at the stone, turned it over. There was nothing to report. "It is not the outside, it is the inside of things that matters," said Agassiz. And in the laboratory that became our watchword: Look inside.

Discovering my interest in the microscope, I was not only allowed, I was urged to use the magnificent binocular belonging to the college, was given the free run of the laboratory along with a few as crazy as myself. Here my most exciting adventure apart from what I found under the microscope came from actually having my hands on a "missing link." Evolution, to which I was clinging determinedly, could only be established, I realized, by discovering the links. There was one peculiar to the waters in our valley, the *Memopomo Alleghaniensis*, a creature twelve to fifteen inches long with gills and one lung, able to live in the water or mud as circumstances required. The mud puppy, as it was appropriately called, was slimy, loathsome, but I worked over it with awe. Was I not admitted into the very workshop of Nature herself—seeing how she did it?

Professor Tingley took his little group of laboratory devotees into his home circle. He and Mrs. Tingley were housed in a wing of Bentley Hall—big rooms built for classrooms. They had no children, and in the years of their study and travel they had gathered about them things of beauty and interest. The atmosphere of those rooms was something quite new and wonderful to me. It was my first look into the intimate social life possible to people interested above all in ideas, beauty, music, and glad to work hard and live simply to devote themselves to their cultivation.

And such good talks! Much of it was concerned with fresh scientific thought, the inventions and discoveries which were stirring the world. An omnivorous reader of the scientific publications of Europe and America, Professor Tingley kept us excited, not only by what had been done but what it might mean. There was the telephone. I had been in college but a few weeks when my father asked me to go with him and my brother to the Centennial Exposition of 1876. President Bugbee, who had made me his special care for a time—Mrs. Bugbee even taking me into their home until an appropriate boarding place could be found—was heartily in favor of my going. I went, and when I returned Professor Tingley's first question was, "Did you see the telephone?" I hadn't even heard of it. Two exhibits only of that exposition made a deep enough impression on me to last until today—my first Corot and the Corliss engine. Professor Tingley was greatly disappointed, and I did not understand why until a few weeks later he called the student body together to explain and illustrate the telephone by a homemade instrument. "You'll talk to your homes from these rooms one day," he told us. "New York will talk to Boston." He didn't suggest Chicago. "Dreamer," the boys said. "Dreamer," my father and his Titusville friends said a little later when an agent of the Bell Associates, the first company to attempt putting the new invention within reach of everybody, came to town selling stock. How often I heard it said later, "If I'd bought that telephone stock!"

Years later I told Alexander Graham Bell of my introduction to the telephone. "Nobody," he said, "can estimate what the teachers of science in colleges and high schools were doing in those days not only to spread knowledge of the telephone but to stir youth to tackle the possibilities in electricity."

What I best remember is not the telephone but Professor Tingley's amazing enthusiasm for the telephone. This revelation of enthusiasm, its power to warm and illuminate was one of the finest and most lasting of my college experiences. The people I had known, teachers, preachers, doctors, businessmen, all went through their day's work either with a stubborn, often sullen determination to do their whole duty, or with an undercurrent of uneasiness, if they found pleasure in duty. They seemed to me to feel that they were not really working if they were not demonstrating the Puritan teaching that labor is a curse. It had never seemed so to me, but I did not dare gloat over it. And here was a teacher who did gloat over his job in all its ramifications. Moreover, he did his best to stir you to share his joy.

But while I looked on what I was learning in the laboratory as what I had come to college for, while each term stiffened my ambition to go deeper and deeper into the search for the original atom, science was not all that interested in me. The faculty, if small, was made up largely of seasoned men with a perspective on life. There was not only deep seriousness but humor and tolerance, and since we were so small a college the student was close enough to discover them, to find out what each man as an individual had to offer him. As I learned the power of enthusiasm from Jeremiah Tingley, I learned from another man of that faculty the value of contempt. Holding the chair of Latin was one of the few able teachers I have known, George Haskins, father of that sound scholar of international repute, the late Charles Homer Haskins, at the time of his death Professor Emeritus of Medieval History at Harvard University. What deep satisfaction his career gave his father, himself a man of many disappointments!

George Haskins labored, usually in vain, to arouse us to the choiceness of Latinity, the meaning of Rome's rise and fall, the quality of her men, the relation of that life to ours. Professor Haskins' contempt for our lack of understanding, for our slack preparation, was something utterly new to me in human intercourse. The people I knew with rare exceptions spared one another's feelings. I had come to consider that a superior grace; you must be kind if you lied for it. But here was a man who turned on indifference, neglect, carelessness with bitter and caustic contempt, left his victim seared. The sufferers lived to say, some of them at least: "I deserved it. He was never unjust, never inappreciative of effort."

"Cherish your contempts," Henry James advised me once when he had drawn from me a confession of the conflict between my natural dislike of saying anything unpleasant about anybody and the necessity of being cruel, even brutal, if the work I had undertaken was to be truthful in fact and logic. "Cherish your contempts," said Mr. James, "and strength to your elbow." If it had not been for George Haskins I doubt if I should have known what he meant; nor should I ever have become the steady, rather dogged worker I am. The contempt for shiftlessness which he inspired in me aroused a determination to be a good worker. I began to train my mind to go at its task regularly, keep hours, study whether I liked a thing or not. I forced myself not to waste time, not to loaf, not to give up before I finished. If I failed at any point in this discipline I suffered a certain mental and spiritual malaise, a dissatisfaction with myself hard to live with.

STUDENT: OHIYESA, a.k.a. CHARLES A. EASTMAN

(1858–1939)

Physician and author.

TEACHER: MYSTERIOUS MEDICINE

My uncle [Mysterious Medicine], who educated me up to the age of fifteen years, was a strict disciplinarian and a good teacher. When I left the teepee in the morning, he would say: "Hakadah, look closely to everything you see"; and at evening, on my return, he used often to catechize me for an hour or so.

"On which side of the trees is the lighter-colored bark? On which side do they have most regular branches?"

It was his custom to let me name all the new birds that I had seen during the day. I would name them according to the color or the shape of the bill or their song or the appearance and locality of the nest—in fact, anything about the bird that impressed me as characteristic. I made ridiculous errors, I must admit. He then usually informed me of the correct name. Occasionally I made a hit and this he would warmly commend.

He went much deeper into this science when I was a little older, that is, about the age of eight or nine years. He would say, for instance:

"How do you know that there are fish in yonder lake?"

"Because they jump out of the water for flies at mid-day."

He would smile at my prompt but superficial reply.

"What do you think of the little pebbles grouped together under the shallow water? And what made the pretty curved marks in the sandy bottom and the little sand-banks? Where do you find the fish-eating birds? Have the inlet and the outlet of a lake anything to do with the question?"

He did not expect a correct reply at once to all the voluminous questions that he put to me on these occasions, but he meant to make me observant and a good student of nature.

"Hakadah," he would say to me, "you ought to follow the example of the shunktokecha (wolf). Even when he is surprised and runs for his life, he will pause to take one more look at you before he enters his final retreat. So you must take a second look at everything you see.

"It is better to view animals unobserved. I have been a witness to their courtships and their quarrels and have learned many of their secrets in this way. I was once the unseen spectator of a thrilling battle between a pair of grizzly bears and three buffaloes—a rash act for the bears, for it was in the moon of strawberries, when the buffaloes sharpen and polish their horns for bloody contests among themselves.

"I advise you, my boy, never to approach a grizzly's den from the front, but to steal up behind and throw your blanket or a stone in front of the hole. He does not usually rush for it, but first puts his head out and listens and then comes out very indifferently and sits on his haunches on the mound in front of the hole before he makes any attack. While he is exposing himself in this fashion, aim at his heart. Always be as cool as the animal himself." Thus he armed me against the cunning of savage beasts by teaching me how to outwit them.

"In hunting," he would resume, "you will be guided by the habits of the animal you seek. Remember that a moose stays in swampy or low land or between high mountains near a spring or lake, for thirty to sixty days at a time. Most large game moves about continually, except the doe in the spring; it is then a very easy matter to find her with the fawn. Conceal yourself in a convenient place as soon as you observe any signs of the presence of either, and then call with your birchen doe-caller.

"Whichever one hears you first will soon appear in your neighborhood. But you must be very watchful, or you may be made a fawn of by a large wild-cat. They understand the characteristic call of the doe perfectly well.

"When you have any difficulty with a bear or a wild-cat—that is, if the creature shows signs of attacking you—you must make him fully understand that you have seen him and are aware of his intentions. If you are not well equipped for a pitched battle, the only way to make him retreat is to take a long sharp-pointed pole for a spear and rush toward him. No wild beast will face this unless he is cornered and already wounded. These fierce beasts are generally afraid of the common weapon of the larger animals—the horns, and if these are very long and sharp, they dare not risk an open fight.

"There is one exception to this rule—the grey wolf will attack fiercely when very hungry. But their courage depends upon their numbers; in this they are like white men. One wolf or two will never attack a man. They will stampede a herd of buffaloes in order to get at the calves; they will rush upon a herd of antelopes, for these are helpless; but they are always careful about attacking man."

Of this nature were the instructions of my uncle, who was widely known at that time as among the greatest hunters of his tribe.

All boys were expected to endure hardship without complaint. In savage warfare, a young man must, of course, be an athlete and used to undergoing all sorts of privations. He must be able to go without food and water for two or three days without displaying any weakness, or to run for a day and a night without any rest. He must be able to traverse a pathless and wild country without losing his way either in the day or night time. He cannot refuse to do any of these things if he aspires to be a warrior.

Sometimes my uncle would waken me very early in the morning and challenge me to fast with him all day. I had to accept the challenge. We blackened our faces with charcoal, so that every boy in the village would know that I was fasting for the day. Then the little tempters would make my life a misery until the merciful sun hid behind the western hills.

I can scarcely recall the time when my stern teacher began to give sudden war-whoops over my head in the morning while I was sound asleep. He expected me to leap up with perfect presence of mind, always ready to grasp a weapon of some sort and to give a shrill whoop in reply. If I was sleepy or startled and hardly knew what I was about, he would ridicule me and say that I would never expect to sell my scalp dear. Often he would vary these tactics by shooting off his gun just outside of the lodge while I was yet asleep, at the same time giving blood-curdling yells. After a time I became used to this.

When Indians went upon the war-path, it was their custom to try the new warriors thoroughly before coming to an engagement. For instance, when they were near a hostile camp, they would select the novices to go after the water and make them do all sorts of things to prove their courage. In accordance with this idea, my uncle used to send me off after water when we camped after dark in a strange place. Perhaps the country was full of wild beasts, and, for aught I knew, there might be scouts from hostile bands of Indians lurking in that very neighborhood.

Yet I never objected, for that would show cowardice. I picked my way through the woods, dipped my pail in the water and hurried back, always careful to make as little noise as a cat. Being only a boy, my heart would leap at every crackling of a dry twig or distant hooting of an owl, until, at last, I reached our teepee. Then my uncle would perhaps say: "Ah, Hakadah, you are a thorough warrior," empty out the precious contents of the pail, and order me to go a second time.

Imagine how I felt! But I wished to be a brave man as much as a white boy desires to be a great lawyer or even President of the United States. Silently I would take the pail and endeavor to retrace my footsteps in the dark.

With all this, our manners and morals were not neglected. I was made to respect the adults and especially the aged. I was not allowed to join in their discussions, nor even to speak in their presence, unless requested to do so. Indian etiquette was very strict, and among the requirements was that of avoiding the direct address. A term of relationship or some title of courtesy was commonly used instead of the personal name by those who wished to show respect. We were taught generosity to the poor and reverence for the "Great Mystery." Religion was the basis of all Indian training.

I recall to the present day some of the kind warnings and reproofs that my good grandmother was wont to give me. "Be strong of heart—be patient!" she used to say. She told me of a young chief who was noted for his uncontrollable temper. While in one of his rages he attempted to kill a woman, for which he was slain by his own band and left unburied as a mark of disgrace—his body was simply covered with green grass. If I ever lost my temper, she would say:

"Hakadah, control yourself, or you will be like that young man I told you of, and lie under a *green blanket*!"

In the old days, no young man was allowed to use tobacco in any form until he had become an acknowledged warrior and had achieved a record. If a youth should seek a wife before he had reached the age of twenty-two or twenty-three, and been recognized as a brave man, he was sneered at and considered an ill-bred Indian. He must also be a skillful hunter. An Indian cannot be a good husband unless he brings home plenty of game.

These precepts were in the line of our training for the wild life.

STUDENT: BELLE CASE LAFOLLETTE

(1859–1931)

Teacher, attorney, editor, feminist and wife of Robert Marion LaFollette, Governor of Wisconsin, United States Senator and author.

TEACHER: DR. JOHN BASCOM

Dr. John Bascom was the great outstanding teacher of the University of Wisconsin for the thirteen years he served as president. Bob himself said Dr. Bascom's "addresses to the students on Sunday afternoons, together with his work in the classroom were among the most important influences in my early life." The university then had less than four hundred students. It was therefore possible for a man of Dr. Bascom's intellectual and moral power to impress himself on the student body in a way difficult to understand now that the university counts its students by the thousands. His manner of lecturing was formal but earnest and clear, with an occasional touch of rare humor. At times he was truly eloquent, and always impressive and moving. He "met the seniors daily throughout the year, in classes which covered the whole range of philosophy, and this meant the range of the students' serious thinking. For with him Philosophy meant not so much an inquiry into the ultimate nature of reality as a discussion of the rational side of human life. . . . Its questions were discussed from the personal and social sides."

Dr. Bascom held the strict attention of his classes without any apparent effort. His examinations were especially fair. He never asked "catch" questions, his purpose being to ascertain whether his students had grasped the principles which had been thoroughly explained and emphasized. He stressed the spiritual side of life but was ever mindful of its inseparable relationship to the everyday world. Progressive in spirit, uncompromising with what he believed to be wrong, Dr. Bascom urged us to think and reason for ourselves and to translate our convictions into action. Especially did he emphasize the obligations of citizenship. Again and again he would tell us what we owed the State and impress upon us our duty to serve the State in return. Here, as in other phases of our university course, my understanding of what President Bascom was trying to implant seems to have been rather vague and general; while to Bob it was concrete truth, the living gospel, whose application was as plain as a pikestaff. In my student days I stood somewhat in awe of Dr. Bascom. Bob loved, honored, and understood him as well then as in later life. He enjoyed and made a good record in the branches which Dr. Bascom taught.

There is more reason for the mutual friendship that existed between President Bascom and Bob throughout the years than may appear on the surface. Of strikingly different mold and method, what they had in common was the spirit of the reformer, the same faith in what they believed a righteous cause; they had a like intensity of nature, will power, and determination to achieve practical results; both had self-mastery and an inner calm that nothing could disturb. I vividly recall that at one time, when Bob was governor, President Bascom came purposely to give him the encouragement and advice he knew so well how to render. After the first affectionate greetings, the two men spoke not at all of lesser matters. For a long time they sat together in the library talking earnestly of what was at stake in the pending political struggle, President Bascom stressing the momentous importance of the ethical victory, whatever else the outcome.

More than anyone I ever met, President Bascom impressed me as being innately sincere and conscientious, always striving to guide his action by the light of reason. He led an upright, abundant, yet restrained and disciplined, religious life. He tried to inculcate a love of nature and the beautiful in the hearts of his pupils, and he taught us true respect for labor. He found joy and recreation in working with his hands, and always cultivated his own garden. In his book *Things Learned by Living*, he expressed his philosophy when he wrote that "the world seems to me to be the very garden of God, resting under the first warm spring days of his love, and our prayer becomes that we all may thrive in this vital sunshine."

Although President Bascom was awe-inspiring to some of us in the classroom, we all appreciated his social charm. His son and daughter, George and Jean Bascom, were members of our class, and for that reason we were more intimately acquainted with their ideal family life. In his home President Bascom would at times unbend and be quite playful and humorous. With his wife he was especially affectionate. They were true comrades.

Bob and I felt there never was another such strong bond of friendship among the members of a graduating class as that of 1879. Fifty years afterward, I feel that these college friendships, even though we may lose track of each other, wield an influence like that of our teachers, which enriches all the years of our lives. Bob's unusually extended personal acquaintances with the students during and after his own college days was a source of strong political support, as well as a personal joy and inspiration.

STUDENT: BLISS PERRY
(1860–1954)
Professor, critic, editor and author.

TEACHER: MARK HOPKINS

Yet I think that for the majority of our class the chief intellectual adventure of the senior year was the morning or evening hour with Mark Hopkins. He was then seventy-eight, but his powerful frame and noble features showed little or no trace of the burden of years, and there was never, up to the time of his death at eighty-five, any apparent diminution of his mental vigor. This exceptional endowment played its part in the spell which he cast upon his contemporaries. No one can furnish an adequate definition of greatness, but Mark Hopkins, like Gladstone and Bismarck, gave the beholder the instant impression of being in the presence of a great man. He had already become in his lifetime a legend, a symbol of teaching power: "Mark Hopkins on one end of a log, and a student on the other."

Four of his pupils and colleagues, Professors Bascom, A. L. Perry, Carter, and Spring, have made painstaking analyses of the Doctor's personality and methods. They all agree that he was not, in the strict academic sense, a "scholar"; the source of his power was not in his knowledge of books. But that is an old story in the history of the world: "He taught them as one having authority, and not as the scribes." Any teacher can study books, but books do not necessarily bring wisdom, nor that human insight essential to consummate teaching skill. I think that the peculiar gift of Mark Hopkins has rarely been better described than by a single phrase from my old friend Professor Dodd. I was driving with him over Mason's Hill, a year or two after my graduation, and I was telling him about attending the brilliant lectures on the history of philosophy which Stanley Hall was then giving to Williams seniors.

"After all," I said—captivated by the new horizons which Stanley Hall was opening for us— "Dr. Hopkins taught us nothing about the history of philosophy." "No," said Dodd slowly, "he taught you nothing *about* philosophy, but he taught you *to philosophize*. This is essentially what my father wrote, in pointing out that the Doctor's favorite question—"What do *you* think about it?"—was the key to his success as a teacher. After beginning by asking the pupil what the textbook stated upon this and that topic, the Doctor would almost invariably inquire: "*What do you think about it?*" "It stole the hearts of crude young men to hear such a man as he was plumping down upon them from his desk, as if it were a matter of importance, such a question as that! It suddenly increased their own self-respect."

To discover that you had a mind—narrow, common-place, or ill-trained, perhaps, but a mind of your own, was a thrilling experience. You rose when your name was called, and sometimes the Doctor's initial questions, like those of Socrates, seemed remote from the matter in hand. The fascination lay partly in the effort to guess what the Doctor was driving at. He knew, and we did not, but the game gradually revealed itself as one bland question succeeded another. He always had an objective and sometimes the class perceived it more quickly than the boy who was on his feet, trying to keep his wits and to avoid foolish answers. But often the objective was remote: we were like a party of mountain-climbers, conscious that we were well above timber-line, but ignorant of the particular peak for which the guide was headed. We were having a good climb and were made to feel that we could keep up the pace and get some grand views, even though the Doctor did not seem to care whether we reached any particular hut by nightfall. To some men in each class, no doubt, he seemed a philosopher without a system, a moralist indifferent to definitions. He was in truth a builder of character who could lay a stone wall without ever looking at a blue-print.

All of us recognized his immense latent power. "Half his strength he put not forth." Yet this apparently indolent wrestler with ideas—never dogmatic, never over-earnest, never seeming to desire converts to any creed or platform—was ceaselessly active in studying the members of each class and in directing, however subtly, the questions by which he sought to develop and test their individual capacity. "Also he knew men at once," it was said of Cosimo de' Medici, "when he looked into their eyes."

I must limit myself to a single illustration of this wise handling of one of his "crude young men." In our senior year the mutterings of the famous Andover controversy in theology began to be heard throughout New England. Was "everlasting" punishment the same thing as "eternal" punishment? What was really at issue was not the exact meaning of some Greek words, but the whole Calvinistic conception of the actuality of a fire and brimstone hell. I had been brought up in a very liberal and deeply religious household, and I knew that on this question of a material hell my father and his friend John Bascom thought very differently from Grandfather Smedley. Being now twenty and fond of debating, I was wholly on the side of the "new theology," as it was then called. Nobody knew where Dr. Hopkins really stood, although he was supposed to be a pillar of Orthodoxy. He was an old man and a wise one, and refused to be drawn into controversy.

One Saturday morning, in reviewing some passage from a textbook, he called me up and put this question: "Perry, do you think that the fear of future punishment is a proper motive for human action?" I fear the light of battle gleamed in my eyes, for I saw the whole of the New Theology at stake in the Doctor's apparently abstract and innocent inquiry. And the textbook had said "Yes"; which was only an additional reason why a self-confident youth should take the other side. So I straightened my shoulders and answered "No, sir."

The Doctor looked me over. "I will repeat the question," he said slowly. "Do you think that the fear of future punishment is a proper motive for human action?"

"No, sir, I do not." I was ready to debate against a whole Bench of Bishops; *Athanasius contra mundum*; Luther at the Diet of Worms, etc., etc.

To my disappointment, the Doctor straightway called up "Turk" Parsons, a missionary's son, who recited the textbook position with fluent precision. But by that time the Doctor seemed to have lost all interest in the question, and went on to something else. The fight was evidently off, and I sulked for the rest of the hour. When the class was dismissed, I had to pass directly in front of the Doctor's desk. He leaned over toward me, bowing his magnificent shoulders and superb head. It was as if an old lion had turned in his cage to look at you, only that all the bars were magically down.

"Bliss," he said gravely, "did I understand you to say that you thought the fear of future punishment was not a proper motive for human action?"

I was still obstinate. "Yes, sir, that is what I think."

The leonine features relaxed into a captivating smile. "Well, now, Bliss," he remarked confidentially, as if to a very intimate friend; "*a great many young men have felt about that question exactly as you do*."

All the anger and conceit went out of me. I saw myself, not as a lonely rebel, but as one of the great company of the immature. With one sentence Mark Hopkins had put me in my place, and had nevertheless managed to let me feel that he liked me. I hope I had the manners enough to thank him, for no teacher had ever rendered me a greater service.

STUDENT: GEORGE W. NORRIS

(1861–1944)

Attorney, judge, Member of Congress and United States Senator.

TEACHER: I. D. SPEIDELL
GEORGE SETZLER

I cannot remember the exact year I entered school. I looked forward to that first day. The Mount Carmel district school [in Ohio] had been moved from the earlier location only half a mile from our home to one a mile and a half away. We walked along the country road to school, carrying our lunch, and then home again.

I remember that first day.

The teacher called all of us tiny beginners to his knee, and there undertook to instruct us in the first six letters of the alphabet. I was frightened; I had never seen the letters of the alphabet. I knew I could not get the lesson, and that feeling was fully confirmed the following day when I returned to school.

I did not know the six beginning letters.

But we were fortunate in having fine instructors for the Mount Carmel district school, particularly in the last two years that I attended the common grades. The teacher then, I. D. Speidell, who lived in Clyde, was an exceptionally well educated man, with great understanding of children and sympathy for them. With the exception of the Norris family, and two or three other families of Vickerys, of English blood, each one of the latter with quite a number of children, all the pupils attending Mount Carmel were descendants of the Pennsylvania Dutch.

Today those incidents of school years which remain the most exquisite, warm recollections of American education during my boyhood would seem simple and unsatisfactory. But it was thorough, and it produced good citizenship. There had developed during the years the great rivalry of the "spelling bee"; it was the one tradition in which parents and pupils alike took a great interest. For many years the Norris girls were the leading spellers of the vicinity, and it was Mount Carmel's proud distinction to be able to "spell down" all the other schools of the region. When my sisters left, Mount Carmel lost its championship, although prior to their completion of the school term Jesse Vickery, two years my senior, had become a champion. Jesse had a sister, Flora, my age, and in the same classes.

In addition to the rivalry created by the spelling bees, the teacher in the primary arithmetic class took a great interest in teaching the multiplication table. He utilized the technique so effective in the spelling bee in order to stimulate interest in arithmetic. He would arrange the youngsters, varying in age from fifteen or sixteen, to much younger ones like Flora and myself, in a long row; and, starting at the head, he would question pupils in multiplication, allowing only a second for the answer.

When he snapped his fingers, if the pupil had been unable to answer, the question passed to the next one, and so on until finally everybody had been eliminated.

He was an excellent penman, and had prepared a prize which was to be awarded to the student who won the multiplication table contest. It was a splendid specimen of his penmanship, and in my heart I made up my mind to win it.

The news spread, and soon the entire district was talking about it; and when the hour of the contest arrived the schoolroom was packed with patrons. It took several hours to complete the elimination, but gradually the larger pupils went down one by one until no one was left except little Flora and me. We stood there for a long time while he shot questions at us, and as we gave the answers, gradually he shortened the time allowed us.

I remember when Flora missed.

The question which she had been called upon to answer was: "How much is 9 times 12?"

She answered instantly, "96."

The teacher snapped his fingers and I said, "108."

I was champion, and yet I felt ashamed.

I thought a great deal of Flora; in fact, Flora and I were little schootime sweethearts. She was my first sweetheart, and I think that the memories of boyhood attach a special sentimentality to the first schootime sweetheart. I remember the various games we played at school how always it turned out that Flora was my favorite and, apparently, I was hers. We used to play "Drop the Handkerchief." Flora always dropped it back of me, and I do not believe Flora ever ran fast enough to escape being kissed.

In fact, it seemed to me that she did not try.

That night when I reached home, I thought how cruel it had been not to let Flora win that contest. Young as I was, I knew I should have been manly enough to surrender the prize to a beautiful girl. I remember crying myself to sleep when I went to bed alone in the loft where at the moment a multiplication table contest seemed to be the biggest event in a big world. It would have been understood and applauded, I reasoned, had I permitted Flora to win. I never talked to Flora about it; she never mentioned it to me; although I knew, without a word being spoken, she was grieved sorely.

In spite of such healthy rivalries, most of these pioneer people clung to the belief that the labor of their children on the farms was infinitely more important than the study of higher mathematics or grammar. There were none more poor, and none needing labor more than my mother, but she insisted I study as extensively as the facilities permitted.

Only three—Willis and Jesse Vickery and I—completed the course in grammar.

Mr. Speidell succeeded in interesting us in algebra. Under his teaching, we completed Ray's Highest Algebra so effectively that upon entering Baldwin University, I was able to plunge into mathematics in the beginning courses of geometry.

At the Mount Carmel school there was a debating society, composed mainly of farmers, which met every Thursday night.

Such debating societies flourished widely throughout the country. They were the usual offspring of the old form of Town Hall meetings which gave such vigor to American colonial life, and which stimulated so much interest in public discussion. They were healthy and invaluable to the development of American citizenship and to American political progress. Their gradual decline has been a loss to the nation.

One of the members of the Mount Carmel debating society was a wagon-maker, George Setzler. Except for Mr. Setzler and the teacher, Mr. Speidell, all the members lived in the country. For reasons unknown the older people never took part in the discussions of the debating society.

It was a great night when Mr. Speidell told the two Vickerys and me that he was going to place our names before the society, but only on the condition that we join actively in the debates.

The leader on my side was "Bill" Wagoner, a farmer, a very fine debater, but unfortunately inclined to imbibe a little too much. That was his plight the night we were to be presented to the debating society. He came to me and said:

"Now you are near the foot of the row on my side. Under the rules, you have about ten minutes, and I want you to talk the full ten minutes. If you should forget what to say, look at me, and I will raise my right hand, and when I raise it, you take up this particular point. If I raise my left hand, it will serve to remind you of that particular point."

It was hard to remember what Bill had suggested as arguments; harder to remember his arguments than to talk without prompting. But to my great surprise, when my time came, I talked the full ten minutes without great effort.

The debating society ushered me into a new life.

The night I became a member the question under discussion was: "*Resolved*, That water is more destructive than fire."

Bill Wagoner in a moment of inspiration recalled the destruction of Vesuvius.

"Now there is Pompoy," he said in a loud voice. Everybody laughed and Bill was stopped for a moment. "Now there is Pompee," he shouted a second time. Again there was laughter. Bill did succeed in pronouncing Pompeii that night.

I remember one occasion I proposed this question: "*Resolved*, There is more pleasure living with a neat, cross woman than with a good-natured, slouchy woman." There was a great deal of laughter, but it was adopted by vote as the basis for discussion at the next meeting. I found I alone was willing to defend the slouchy woman. But the question had provoked a great deal of curiosity, and the schoolroom was crowded to capacity. Alone, I was given all the time I desired for argument and rebuttal, and when the three judges delivered their decision I was a unanimous winner.

More frequently the questions extended to history.

One was: "*Resolved*, That Grant was a greater general than Lee." Another was: "*Resolved*, That the Emancipation Proclamation of Lincoln was constitutional under the constitution at the time of the Civil War." Still a third: "*Resolved*, That under the constitution any state had the legal right to secede and withdraw from the Union."

I remember that one question in which I became greatly interested, and to which as a boy I devoted a great deal of study was: "*Resolved*, That man is a free moral agent." I was curious then concerning the independence of the individual to serve himself and fulfill his responsibilities to his fellow man. It was to bob up at the most unexpected times and under the most unlooked-for circumstances.

George Setzler was unmarried, about thirty-five years old. I had to pass his wagon shop each morning on the way to school. One day he said to me:

"I want to take you over to my room and show you my books."

It was just across the road, upstairs in a farm house. I thought his living quarters were the finest I had ever seen. There was a rug on the floor, and there were curtains at the windows. It was luxury beyond my dreams.

The furniture consisted of three ordinary wooden chairs; a little wooden table, unpainted, which he himself had made; and a bookcase consisting of three shelves about eighteen inches long, also homemade, filled completely with books.

I never had seen a library so large.

When he noted my deep interest, he told me to my delight I was welcome to any book.

All we had to read at home was the weekly newspaper, the *Cincinnati Times*, and the Holy Bible. I was hungry for books, and my pulse quickened at the thought of the nights of reading ahead of me.

Both Mr. Speidell and Mr. Setzler were skillful parliamentarians, and shortly the Vickerys and I found ourselves deeply interested in parliamentary procedure. George Setzler had a copy of Cushing's "Manual of Parliamentary Practice" which generously he loaned to us. The Vickerys and I got enough money together to get Robert's

"Rules of Order." It was not long before we participated with all of the eagerness of veterans in parliamentary squabbles and were deeply engaged in parliamentary procedure.

One of the attributes of the American system of public education, to which Jefferson looked for the perpetuation and strengthening of the ideals of democratic institutions, is the imperishable memories of teachers and their influence upon young thought. Throughout my life in Congress, I was cheered and comforted by letters from these old school associates.

George Setzler married Miss Heater, who was my teacher in the last year that I spent in the public schools of Mount Carmel. Years later I learned that she was living in Caldwell, Kansas; and so on January 17, 1931, when she had reached the age of seventy-nine years, I wrote her:

> I have a distinct and vivid recollection of the time when I was a boy and you, as Lydia Heater, were my teacher. Neither can I forget the many kindnesses shown to me by your late husband, George Setzler. It was he more than any other one person, who introduced me to join the old debating society of Mount Carmel and started me in as a debater. I have often thought and firmly believe that the experience I received in that old country schoolhouse, where we met once a week to debate various questions, was one of the main things which started me on my political career. I think of you and your husband always with a feeling of love and affection. I recall the days when I attended school and you were the teacher, with many pleasant recollections and with gratitude for your infinite patience and inspiration.

To which Mrs. Setzler replied:

> I not infrequently recall my experience at Mount Carmel. It has long been one of my pleasures to watch the careers of a number of the pupils whom I enrolled at that time. I distinctly remember that you and your two classmates, Willis and Jess Vickery, always were studious and faithful. To me, it never seemed strange that later each one of you was able to do things that made you so marked an honor, not only to your family and friends, but to your country as well. Permit me to congratulate you on always having the strength of purpose to stand by your honest convictions.

To another of the thinning circle of those early country-school days, Ambrose Jones, of Toledo, Ohio, from whose granddaughter, Irene Waranke, I had learned the whereabouts, I wrote in 1937:

> What great sport we had playing baseball, and when it was impossible to do this on account of snow on the ground, we put in time playing "dog and deer." As I look back over the years, it seems to me those were some of the happiest days of my life.

I remember distinctly the occasion when Mr. Speidell told us of a debating society in the town of Clyde, called the Boanerges, which translated means "Sons of Thunder."

It was impressive for farm boys to walk into a meeting hall which had carpet on the floor, fine lights, and nice desks.

To our embarrassment, we found that the members were well groomed. They had white shirts and fine suits; while we wore our rough, crude high-top boots, trousers tucked inside as we dressed on the farm, shirts homespun without collars. But our embarrassment soon faded away. The young lawyers and the young doctors of this debating society revealed every consideration for us.

I remember that during the summer months when the society met I worked hard in the harvest field all day; when daylight faded, walked to Clyde, three miles away, for the debates, and was back in the fields soon after daylight the next morning. It was not difficult; it was a great privilege, and a great pleasure.

I did not know then—in fact, it did not occur to me until years later—that what I learned of parliamentary procedure by this rough road in the primitive country school and the pioneer town debating society was one of the best educations of my life. It gave me an understanding of parliamentary technicalities and of human nature itself that later became of great value in congressional battles. What I learned in this frontier Ohio community on many occasions helped me on the floor of the United States Senate. Some of the bitterest, some of the most far-reaching congressional contests were determined by parliamentary tactics.

STUDENT: ABRAHAM FLEXNER
(1866–1959)

Teacher, principal, educator, medical school reformer, and author.

TEACHERS: MINTON WARREN CHARLES D'URBAN MORRIS

The decisive moment of my life came in 1884 when, at the age of seventeen, I was sent by my oldest brother, Jacob, to the Johns Hopkins University.

• • •

I went to the Hopkins in September 1884. My wardrobe consisted of the one suit of clothes, quite new, which I was wearing, shirts which my mother had made with her own hands, and a few other essentials sufficient to fill a small suitcase. I had to take entrance examinations that in scope and difficulty far exceeded my high-school education in most of the subjects. Fortunately, I was equipped with letters of introduction from Lee Sale to Minton Warren, who had recently become associate professor of Latin and afterward became professor of Latin at Harvard, and to Fabian Franklin, associate professor of mathematics, who subsequently became professor of mathematics and later a distinguished liberal journalist. These letters of introduction I had presented before I took my examinations. When I went a few days later to ask Dr. Warren whether I had passed, he said, "Your paper shows that you don't know much Latin, but Sale says that you come of a fine family, and we are going to let you in." When, something over twenty years later, Warren died suddenly at Cambridge, I wrote to my wife:

> I owe him—more than anyone else—my opportunities in Baltimore. He was patient with my ignorance; he gave me time and spared me criticism that would have hurt and discouraged me. I was a mere boy at the time—as little prepossessing as any boy you can imagine—and ready to flee if anyone had turned me down. Warren and Morris did just the reverse. I should have been satisfied to be let alone, permitted, tolerated, and even that was more than my scanty training merited. Well, they helped me. And I shall never cease to love them for that.

The examination in Greek was even more disastrous. Before going to Baltimore I had not even learned the regular verbs thoroughly and had read only a few pages of Xenophon's *Anabasis*. One look at the examination paper convinced me that it was absolutely out of my reach. The examinations were conducted by Professor Charles D'Urban Morris, who was collegiate professor of Greek. Morris, who had been a fellow of Oriel College, had come to America and opened a private school at Peekskill, New York. He had also written an elementary Greek grammar. Somewhat later in his life he edited, for a series published by Ginn and Company, the first book of Thucydides. He was one of the most lovable and high-minded men I have ever known—a polished scholar to whom Greek was a living language. I can still recall his agitation when in reading Thucydides he came to the pages describing the destruction of the Greek fleet at Syracuse. He would pace the floor as if a great calamity had just happened, murmuring under his breath, "Poor Nicias! Poor Nicias!" I also recall his saying one day, "Every man has his small economy. Myers' " (the bookkeeper downstairs) "is red ink. How that man hates to part with red ink enough to correct written exercises! Mine is string," whereupon he pulled out of the pocket of his tailcoat a huge ball of string, as varied in color as Joseph's coat.

After the examination papers had been distributed I went to the platform on which Professor Morris was seated and explained that I was unable to answer the questions. In the most kindly way imaginable, he said, "You are frightened."

"No," I replied. "I have studied very little Greek."

He took a small copy of the *Anabasis* which lay upon his desk and said, "All I have to do is to satisfy my conscience; suppose you translate this passage for me." He opened the volume at one of the later books of the *Anabasis*. I was utterly at a loss. He then turned to the familiar passages of Book I, with which I made very little progress beyond translating ἐντεῦθεν ἐξελαύνει.

Then he commented, "Well, you don't know much. How old are you?"

"Seventeen."

"Where are you from?"

"Kentucky."

After a moment's hesitation he said, "I have a class from twelve to one every day. You seem to be in earnest. Come to me promptly at one o'clock daily, and I will tell you what to study. I can't give you more than five minutes, but if you will do your work well, you can in the course of a few months learn enough Greek to join Dr. Spieker's class in Isocrates."

Conscientiously I was present at one o'clock every day. Professor Morris told me what to learn and gave me a copy of his own grammar, which I still possess, adding that for a beginner it was much better than Goodwin's. When I returned on successive days he asked me a few questions at random and made another assignment. I do not believe that he ever spent more than five minutes a day with me. I devised a system for learning declensions, conjugations, irregular verbs, etc. Having committed the verb λύω, for example, to memory, I cut a sheet of paper into small slips, writing a particular form on each, e.g., "principal parts," "aorist indicative, second person singular," "perfect infinitive," and so on. These slips I shuffled in my hat and then drew them out by chance. Unless I was able to give the correct answer immediately, back went the slip into the hat. I spent hours in thus drilling myself, for luckily I had no teacher who would waste *his* time in doing it for me. I became quite accurate and rapid in the course of the next six weeks. About Thanksgiving time Professor Morris said to me, "Go to Dr. Spieker and tell him that you are ready to enter his class." I reported to Dr. Spieker as I had been ordered to do, but at first found Isocrates far beyond my depth. There were in the class several gifted and well-trained boys, among whom I remember most vividly Robert M. Rogers, who afterward became a distinguished Hebraist, and Allen McClane, subsequently mayor of Baltimore during the great fire. The work was very hard sledding, but I gradually caught up with my fellows both in Latin and in Greek.

Professor Morris gave me a piece of advice which proved invaluable. "When you leave Baltimore for home," he said, "buy a complete Homer, the orators, and the works of the tragic poets. Get a Liddell and Scott dictionary to consult as you require. Spend four or five years reading Greek. You will never regret it." I did as I was told. All these books I still possess. I reached the point where I could read Greek with great facility, and it was for many years my chief intellectual occupation.

In my second year at Baltimore Professor Morris died of erysipelas. His students co-operated in putting his library in order. We were asked to select a memento of our beloved teacher and friend. I chose a little text of Xenophon and four small volumes of Homer without notes, which he had himself used as a student at Oriel College. There are drops of wax upon the pages, which show that he must have read them by candlelight.

STUDENT: LINCOLN STEFFENS

(1866–1936)

Journalist, editor and author.

TEACHER: EVELYN NIXON

Evelyn Nixon [a private school teacher and personal tutor in San Francisco] formed it. He was the first teacher I ever had who interested me in what I had to learn—not in myself, but in the world outside, the world of conscious culture. He was a fanatic of poetry, especially of the classic poets. When he read or recited Greek verse the Greeks came to life; romance and language sang songs to me, and I was inspired to be, like him, not a hero nor even a poet, but a Greek scholar, and thus an instrument on which beautiful words might play. Life filled with meaning, and purpose, and joy. It was too great and too various for me to personify with my boyish imitations and heroism. I wrote verses, but only to learn the technique and so feel poetry more perfectly. I wanted to read, not to write; I wanted to know, not to do and be, great things—Mr. Nixon expressed it.

"I'm nobody," he used to say. "I'm nothing but one of the unknown beings Homer and Dante, Shakespeare, Caesar, and the popes and the generals and statesmen have sung and fought and worked for. I'm the appreciator of all good words and deeds."

A new, a noble role, and Evelyn Nixon was a fine example of it: the receiver, not the giver, of beautiful inventions. He was an Englishman; he took a double first at Oxford, I heard, and came for his health to San Francisco. There was a group of such men, most of them with one story. They were athletes, as well as scholars at Oxford and Cambridge; they developed muscles and a lung capacity which they did not need and could not keep up in the sedentary occupations their scholarship put them into. Lung troubles exiled them.

"Keep out of college athletics," they advised. "Don't work up any more brawn than you can use every day afterward."

Nixon taught me Greek, Latin, and English at school, and at his house he opened up the beauty and the meaning of the other subjects I had to cram up for entrance. I worked for him; I worked more, much more, for myself. He saw this, he saw my craving for the answers to questions, and he laughed.

"I will answer no questions of yours," he shouted. "Men know no answers to the natural questions of a boy, of a child. We can only underline your questions, make you mad yourself to answer them, and add ours to whip, to lash you on to find out yourself—one or two; and tell us! That is what youth is for: to answer the questions maturity can't answer." And when I looked disappointed and balked, he would roar at me like a demon.

"Go to, boy. The world is yours. Nothing is done, nothing is known. The greatest poem isn't written, the best railroad isn't built yet, the perfect state hasn't been thought of. Everything remains to be done—right, everything."

STUDENT: JAMES WELDON JOHNSON

(1867–1902)

Poet, professor and attorney.

TEACHER: AN UNKNOWN COBBLER

The fall was ended before the [yellow] fever had run its course and the quarantine was lifted. Reluctantly I resigned myself to the necessity of missing the year at school [Atlanta University]. I talked with my father and told him I wanted to keep it from being a lost year; that I wanted to go on with as many of my studies as possible—if I could find a tutor. He said that he knew a West Indian who was reputed to be a fine scholar. We went to see this man and found him in a small, dingy, cobbler's shop that he ran, pegging away at old shoes. He was a little man, very black, partially bald, with a scraggly beard, and but for bright, intelligent eyes an insignificant presence. At the sight of the surroundings my heart misgave me, and I was embarrassed both for my father and myself. I wondered if he misunderstood so much as to think that I wanted to be coached in spelling and arithmetic and geography. I was reassured when the little cobbler began to talk. He spoke English as no professor at the University could speak it. My father made arrangements, and I began to study with him every night. By a lamp that was often smoky and in an atmosphere filled with the odor of smelly old shoes I read Caesar's *Gallic War* and Cicero's orations against Catiline. I also began the study of elementary geometry. My teacher did more than correct, when necessary, the way in which I translated or construed

Latin sentences; he had a considerable store of collateral knowledge, and gave me the benefit of it. He talked to me about Julius Caesar and Cicero, and about Roman power and Roman politics in their time. So I got more than a language out of what I read; this collateral information not only made it interesting, but gave it sense and connected it up with life. Perhaps, the most common fault among teachers is the lack of collateral knowledge or the failure to make use of it. I remember that when I came to read the Greek dramatists I was plunged directly into the texts. There was no enlightenment as to how and why the plays were written or how and where they were performed. In fact, for me they were not plays at all; they were exercises in Greek grammar.

I cannot recall the name of my West Indian teacher or which of the islands he came from. Nor can I say how he was able to use this method of instruction without, apparently, any books to which to refer. I have the impression that he was a Jamaican and was educated at one of the excellent colleges there. At any rate, in the whole course of my school work the only other teacher who made a subject as interesting to me as did this little cobbler was Brander Matthews at Columbia. I wonder just what it was that kept him down on a cobbler's bench?

STUDENT: BERNARD M. BARUCH

(1870–1965)

Financier and public servant.

TEACHERS: KATHERINE BLAKE GEORGE N. NEWCOMB

. . . Mother had enrolled us at P.S. 69, then on 54th Street, between Sixth and Seventh avenues. The principal was Mathew Elgas, whom I remember fondly. He escorted me personally to my teacher—Katherine Devereux Blake was her name and more than any other one person she helped overcome the confusion that New York stirred in me. Her first words, as I recall them, were, "Bernard, I am so happy to see you. I am sure the other boys are pleased too."

She sat me in front and seemed to pay no attention to me. But at noon, and again at the end of the day, she asked, "Will some boy volunteer to take Bernard home and call for him until he knows his way to and from school?" A chubby lad, named Clarence Housman, quickly volunteered. Fourteen years later I became his partner in Wall Street.

Katherine Blake gave me the first prize I ever won. A copy of *Oliver Twist*, it still is in my library, bearing the inscription: "Awarded to Bernard Baruch for Gentlemanly Deportment and General Excellence. June 1881."

I kept in touch with her until her death in 1950 and delivered a eulogy to her in John Haynes Holmes' Community Church. I never think of her without feeling how unappreciative our society generally is of our schoolteachers.

It is our teachers—especially those who deal with the very young—who have made the character and conscience of America what it is today. We continue to look to them to instill in future generations a sense of decency and a determination to do one's very best. Yet not so long ago I remember reading that a group of high school students had voted teaching the profession they would like least to enter.

Teachers should be given salaries which will enable them to live comfortably. Their enormous contribution to society should be recognized with public honors. I have urged that "Oscars" be awarded annually to our most deserving teachers. Some such tangible honor is certainly as appropriate as the prizes that are awarded regularly to actors and actresses, writers, ball players, and so many others.

• • •

I was only fourteen years old when I entered the College of the City of New York. This was not, I should hasten to add, evidence of any special precociousness on my part. It was simply that in those days there were no public high schools and one could go directly into college from grammar school if one met the entrance requirements.

• • •

The professor who made the deepest impression on me was George B. Newcomb of the Political Economy Department. He wore gold-rimmed glasses and looked like an old-fashioned Englishman. In a squeaky voice, which he tried to improve by sucking sugar, he used to say, "Those gentlemen who wish to play chess may sit on the back seats. Those gentlemen who wish to hear me may have the front seats."

Although I was a chess player, I always took a front seat and missed little of what the professor said.

Much of my later success can be attributed to what I learned from him. Professor Newcomb never would have agreed with some popular present-day economic theories. He plugged away at the law of supply and demand and taught us to believe in it. It was in his class that I first heard:

"When prices go up two processes will set in—an increased production and a decreased consumption. The effect will be a gradual fall in prices. If prices get too low two processes will set in—decreased production because a man will not continue to produce at a loss and, second, increased consumption. These two forces will tend to establish the normal balance."

Ten years later I became rich by remembering those words.

Professor Newcomb taught not only political economy, but philosophy, logic, ethics, and psychology—all in one course. Today these subjects would be fragmented among several professors. I believe there was considerable advantage in being taught all these subjects by the same man. Too many educators seem to have forgotten that you cannot teach good economics, good politics, good ethics, or good logic unless they are considered together as parts of one whole.

STUDENT: THEODORE DREISER

(1871–1945)

Novelist and journalist.

TEACHER: MILDRED FIELDING

. . . there was for me a most interesting inspirational school life. There were two women teachers in this [Warsaw, Indiana] High School at the time who came to exercise a most hopeful and helpful influence over me, to make for somewhat more of optimism in connection with myself than hitherto had been. One of these was a tall old maid from Malen, Massachusetts, a certain Mildred Fielding, who at thirty-three or thereabouts was for the first time in her life finding herself moderately attractive, and thinking, no doubt, therefore, that the world was not so bad. As I afterwards learned from her, she had had a very hard life. In her youth she had been poor, socially nobody, cursed with an ungainly form, protruding teeth, in short, every physical disadvantage which could afflict a young and otherwise healthy girl. At last she had fought her way up to being a teacher and in addition had had her teeth straightened, her hair properly dressed, had learned to wear appropriate clothes and only now was beginning to reap the fruits of her long struggle. In spite of all her difficulties, she had retained a sweet, gentle and lovable disposition. At thirty-five, her light brown hair, grey-blue eyes, and pink complexion made her seem younger than she was. It was this woman who was destined to come to my aid in a very curious way some two years later. Just then, as director of the High School recitation room, she was in touch with me, my studies in connection with algebra, physical geography, general history, botany, and so on, being recited to and corrected or directed by her.

• • •

Miss Fielding, to my surprise and embarrassed pleasure, frequently assisted me after school with my algebra, with which I had some difficulty. More, and at the same time, she appeared to be aware of our local history, and while this troubled me not a little, at the same time it was coupled with, in her case, a tender and quite obvious solicitude as well as desire to fortify me against any depressing effect our home troubles might be having on me.

Thus, one afternoon, and quite out of a clear sky, in the midst of an explanation in connection with an algebra problem, she paused and said: "Theodore, I want to say something to you. It is not prompted by anything but a real interest in you and your welfare." I instantly shivered with the thought that she was going to tell me I was not sufficiently trained as yet for the work I was undertaking and would need to return to the previous grade. But instead she went on: "I can see that you are not like the other boys and girls here. You are different. You understand well enough where you are interested. It is only where you aren't that you do so poorly. But you mustn't let that worry you. You must study and go on, for your mind will find its way. I know it!" And then looking directly into my eyes, her own lit with a warm, tender, even affectionate, glow, she concluded: "But there is something else. You mustn't mind my saying this, Theodore, because I am fond of you and want you to succeed in life. And you will, if you wish. Please don't mind anything that is said or done in a small town like this, and don't let it hurt you. I was brought up in one, and I know how small people can be and how they talk. But please don't let it affect you. You will soon grow up and go away and then all that has happened here will seem as nothing to you. It is only you that can hurt yourself, not the actions or words or opinions of anyone else. You understand me, Theodore, don't you?"

I was moved almost to tears, and so grateful that though I wished to speak, I could not. Instead I merely looked. But she must have gathered what I felt, for she laid a gentle, caressing hand on my arm and added, smilingly: "Now shall we see if we can solve this?" I tried to follow her, but seeing that I could not, she said: "Well, we'll put it over until to-morrow. You might look it over tonight. It will come to you." And—reluctantly, as it seemed to me—she walked away, and I gathered up my books and hurried out.

But the thrill of it! The bracing, encouraging thrill! Instantly and because of this strong, affectionate support, I felt so much better about everything. Pooh! Warsaw and its people! What of them? Who were they? Had I not just been told that I had a different and good mind and that once I was out in the world I could get along? Supposing our family was talked about—evidently it was, since she chose to refer to it—was that certain to affect me? She seemed to think not, had practically assured me that it could not. I felt so much braver, stronger, walked with an air, a trifle of vanity swelling in me.

• • •

By now I was sixteen years old, old enough to make my own way, I thought. My brothers Paul and Al had already made theirs. My father, recovered, was once more in Terre Haute, and here we were, we four: mother, Trina, Ed and myself. Entering the house I found my mother in the living room.

"Ma, I am going to Chicago!"

"Why, what do you mean? When?" she asked, astonished.

"To-day!"

"What for?"

"I want to get work, if I can. I'm tired of Warsaw. If you'll give me my fare and three dollars, I'll go to-day. I can get something. I know I can. I see lots of places advertised in the papers." I was very sure of what I was saying.

• • •

"Maybe you might," she said, simply, after a time. "Anyhow, it's only three hours away and the others are there." (She meant Eleanor and Ruth.) "You can look them up. I'll give you six dollars, and if you need more, you can write me. Maybe I can help you, or you can come back." (The fare was $1.75.)

"I won't come back," I said—I don't know why, for I had no certainty that I would get anything to do.

• • •

But just as I was beginning to think that the material aspects of my necessities were about as bad as they could be, there arrived on the scene, and at the office of Hibbard, Spencer, Bartlett & Company [a wholesale hardware company], that tall New England spinster of my Warsaw school days—Miss Fielding, if you please—from whom I had parted without a word and had heard nothing of since leaving except that she had accepted a position in Worcester, Massachusetts, the year after I left school. Nevertheless, here she was, called to become principal of an outlying Chicago High School—Irvington, I think—and her proposal after explaining that she had just been over to see my mother and secured my address, was that I resign the work that I was now shirking and spend the next year, or two, at best, at the State University of Indiana. And at her expense, if you please! And in order to discover whether or not I had a peculiar bent or aptitude which I could develop and then follow to success. For she was insistent of her conviction that such was the case. More, that under the circumstances it was my duty to go, since having taught me one year in Warsaw she had not been able to get me out of her mind. And since now she had more money and a good position and was feeling so keenly about this, well . . . therefore.

But imagine my astonishment, as well as my doubts, plus, if you will believe it, not a little shame in regard to my work here—not my idling and discharge but the commonplaceness of it all, if you please, and especially after all that had been said to me in Warsaw in regard to my possibilities. Ah! In consequence, instead of acquiescing with alacrity, as might have been expected, I retreated, pretending to be interested not in the work so much as the prospects of this place, and so, and as usual, made a gauche spectacle of myself, as you may well guess.

But Miss Fielding! Her eyes! Her sympathetic, helpful smile! How clearly I see her looking at me as of yore in Warsaw!

"Now, Theodore," she explained quickly when she saw my puzzled and uncertain look, "I have come here especially to do this, and you must help me. I have the money. I do not need it myself, and it is something I want to do for you and for myself, and you must let me do it. I have thought of you ever since you left Warsaw. I know so much more than you think; I understand you, Theodore, so much better than you think I do. And I need to do this for myself. It is a shame you shouldn't have been permitted to finish your high school work there." (She did not know that I had personally deserted it.) "You are too young, really, to know the importance of finding yourself. A year or two at college, if it doesn't do anything else, will make you think."

She hurried on over many points relative to education and my life which I have forgotten. The principal thing was her intense enthusiasm for me, her determination to make me leave this work, the joy she insisted would be hers in assisting me in this way.

That I speculated much on the fortuitousness and fortune of this is natural. It was such an unexpected and almost spectacular way out of my difficulties. I forgot to say that my father in the interim of the spring months had again returned to Terre Haute and that my mother alone was left to judge of the import of this proposition. As usual, I shifted the responsibility as lightly as I could to her, whereupon Miss Fielding said she would at once return and place the matter before her.

As anyone might have known, it was not difficult to convince my mother. When did she ever balk at any scheme which would give happiness or advancement to her children? As I recall it, she was greatly impressed and even astonished at this windfall in my direction. That a woman so well-placed (for she was by now, as I have said, a principal in one of the outlying high schools of Chicago) should look me up in this fashion was, to say the least, a great tribute to me in her eyes. I think my standing in the family rose at once, and to a very high point. Also I remember pluming myself on my individuality and feeling that there must be something to me after all. Why not? Was not Miss Fielding actually inviting me to her rooms in order to give me some advice, instructing me in the general nature of the work at the State University and the character and personality of one David Starr Jordan, who was then President of this college. More, as she made clear to me at this time, she had resented the, as she put it, unjust disrepute into which our family had fallen in Warsaw. It was all petty and unfair and dangerous to my personal moral and budding talent, if any.

"You need not feel so badly about it, Theodore," she said, although by this time I was not feeling badly about it at all. Quite other things were filling my mind, as you have seen. "I tell you, the world is full of half-concealed shames and tragedies. But they are not really important here, there, or anywhere. What I want you to do is to study and develop your mind. Read philosophy and history. You will see how life works and how mistaken or untrue most beliefs are.

Read Spencer. Read a life of Socrates. Read Marcus Aurelius and Emerson. You have the capacity for rising high in the world, and I want you to do it. Don't let any little beliefs as to family scandals or disgraces lower your personal pride. Your life is yours, and people will take you as an individual, and only so. They will not trouble about your family if you are all that you ought to be."

I felt, for the time being at least, that I was one of the most important youths that ever was.

STUDENT: CLAUDE BOWERS

(1878–1958)

Historian, journalist, biographer and diplomat.

TEACHER: LAURA DONNAN

My happiest memories of those days cluster around the long brick building on Pennsylvania Street, between Michigan and North, known as the Shortridge High School [in Indianapolis]. It had a faculty of extraordinary men and women, and the student body represented every social and financial station—a thoroughly democratic institution. The daughters of the wealthy passed from Shortridge to Vassar, Smith, and Bryn Mawr, and the sons to Harvard, Yale and Princeton.

In one member of the faculty, Laura Donnan, I found one of the greatest women I have ever known, who had a decisive effect on my life. After more than a half a century those who came under her influence speak of her with admiration, appreciation and affection. Her specialty was civil government, and everyone but the dullest emerged from her classroom with the keenest and most lasting understanding of the meaning and obligations of citizenship. She did more to make citizens, and to make them fundamentally American, with a reverence for American institutions and the American way of life, than anyone else I have ever known. She adhered to the Jeffersonian theory that the truth is best served in the arbitrament of debate. If she were living today I am sure she would devote less time to showing that the totalitarian philosophy is wrong than to proving that the philosophy of democracy is right—she would give more time to the positives than to the negatives.

She was vigorous and vivid in her teaching, and her voice, though ordinarily warm and pleasant, had at times a booming quality which made her somewhat formidable though not less feminine. One instinctively felt that she was not only a teacher, she was a Personality. In her classes she encouraged argument, and, since she had powerful convictions and some prejudices, the student trying to curry favor and escape her sarcasm by simulating agreement had her contempt. Having stout convictions of my own in opposition to some of hers, I blurted out precisely what I thought, and, to my amazement at first, I could see that she was immensely pleased. She believed in a robust discussion of controversial subjects. She would have despised the now growing trend toward mildness and conformity in thinking. It was this mutual spirit of combat and independence that made us the closest of friends.

Her interests were unusual for a woman of her day. In her girlhood during the Civil War she had frequented the State House, which was a block from her home, and had listened to the impassioned discussions of the wartime legislators. She had read law under the direction of President Harrison, had lectured on constitutional law at the Law School and had written an excellent class book on our fundamental law.

The old family home where she and two unmarried sisters still lived would have seemed quite in place in the Concord of Emerson, Alcott and Hawthorne. A frame house, plainly and comfortably furnished, it had a library rich in the volumes that live on. I recall busts of Emerson and Lincoln, whom she loved. Being an individualist, she refused to measure her conduct by the tape of fashion. Because she did her own marketing and found it irksome to carry the packages, she bought a boy's toy wagon, and her friends smiled and strangers stared when they saw this woman in her plain gray tailored suit nonchalantly drawing it along the sidewalks. In debates and oratorical contests she was our drillmaster and manager, and woe to the boy who caught a cold on the eve of a contest, since she forced him to take her favorite remedy, hot pepper in capsules, standing sternly by to see them down. To this day I never see pepper on the table without thinking of her.

My prospects were dark during my school days, and her faith in me was a torch. Our close friendship continued throughout her life. When I delivered the keynote address at the 1928 Democratic national convention in Houston, a reporter went to this robust Republican for her comment, and she paid me her highest compliment: "He has always had the courage of his convictions, and we can use more like that today."

After her death former students placed a bust of her by Laura Richards in the new Shortridge High School building as a memorial to a truly great woman who made an indelible impression on the thinking of a great community.

STUDENT: HARRY EMERSON FOSDICK

(1878–1969)

Clergyman, professor and author.

TEACHERS: FRANK S. FOSDICK ARTHUR DETMERS WILLIAM NEWTON CLARKE

My father was a great schoolteacher. To thousands of boys and girls in Buffalo he was affectionately known as ''Pop.'' One of them told me this typical story about him when he was principal of the Masten Park High School.

''Your father was one of the most powerful influences in my life. Once I represented the school in a public-speaking contest. I dreadfully wanted to win. I worked very hard, but lost. They gave me the second prize, and the first prize went to a rival school. When I came down from the platform that night I was one of the most broken-hearted boys you could have found on earth. I couldn't keep the tears back. Your father guessed how I was feeling, so he followed me out of the hall until he caught me alone before I left the building. 'Son,' he said, 'I want to see your shoulders back.' So I squared my shoulders. 'Son,' he said, 'chin up.' 'There,' said your father, 'that's better! Now you can go home.' And,'' added the man, ''in all these years since, I never have been in a tight place without recalling that.''

Thus understanding youth, my father understood his children. Many a time in later years, hearing expounded some new, progressive idea concerning the rearing of children, I have wondered why it was called new, because it was the familiar method of my childhood's home. We were a democratic family from the start. Among my earliest recollections are family conferences where all of us were called together to talk over some problem which concerned the whole household. We youngsters were invited to say what we thought. I never recall feeling that commands were handed down to me by a dictator. My father's typical method in getting something done he wanted done was to ask us what we really thought about it ourselves, and even when I asked him for counsel I was fairly certain to have the question thrown back at me—what did I think myself? So from the beginning we were trained for independence. That was the end and aim of our upbringing—to throw us on our own and enable us to handle ourselves.

• • •

My high school days began with a year under my father's principalship in the "Annex"—the nucleus from which the Masten Park High School later came—and went on to my last three years in Old Central. The teaching was in the classical tradition. My father himself taught Latin and Greek and in that heritage I was reared at home and in school. The most influential teacher I had in high school was Arthur Detmers, who made the classics live so vitally that I gladly gave up Saturdays to the endeavor to make Cicero's orations, when translated, sound like real orations, and Vergil's *Aeneid* sound like real poetry. Beyond his classroom work, however, Arthur Detmers brought a group of us into his own home. How did he ever find the time to do what he did for us! He introduced us to the classics of English literature; he read the best of Walt Whitman to us; and to my amazement I record that he and I read aloud together the whole of Lecky's *History of European Morals*. He was one of the best friends I ever had, and even yet some of the great passages in the English poets carry my recollection gratefully back to him. In high school I began trying to speak in public, but I was a shy, embarrassed youngster on my feet. Elected vice-president of the debating society when the president-elect was absent, I was petrified with stage fright, and taking the chair, could not even say "Thank you." Those, however, were the days of public speaking and debate and, like it or not, we were supposed to be able to stand up and talk. That debating society forced me into public speaking, and before I was through with it, stage fright, while always present, was not the whole of the experience. Once in a while I got something across and liked it.

I was at first a socially awkward boy. A professor of mine once said, in a theological seminary lecture, that an honest man looking back on the things whose recollection makes him cringe, must confess that it is not his real sins he feels most ashamed of but his humiliating gaucheries. I agree. I was clumsy and ill at ease, unsure of the proper thing to do, embarrassed in conversation, sensitive and self-conscious about my awkwardness, and unhappy at not being able to put my best foot forward. Doubtless all youths go through this stage; I suspect that I had more than my share of it.

• • •

Most of all Professor William Newton Clarke, of the [Colgate] Theological Seminary, helped me. He was a religious liberal. His new book, *An Outline of Christian Theology*, had already brought down upon him the invectives of the orthodox. We heard the echoes of the controversy and admired him as a heretic. Other universities gave him honorary degrees, and news of British admiration for his work fanned the flames of our pride. Long before I knew him as a loyal personal friend, he was a powerful influence in my life. Here was an honest man, saying what he really thought, defying the obscurantism of old opinions and daring to phrase the Christian faith in the categories of modern thinking. Every time he walked across the campus he was a living argument that it could be done.

I remember once, as an undergraduate, falling in with him by chance and walking in his company. He soon had me talking about my problems. Troubled about the virgin birth of Jesus, I remarked that I could believe that Jesus was spiritually but not that he was physically divine. "Physically divine?" said Dr. Clarke with a quizzical inflection. "That is nonsense, isn't it?" "Of course it is nonsense," he answered; and then added in effect that if I would start by seeing that any divinity in Jesus must consist in his spiritual quality, I might get somewhere. Looking back on the conventional orthodoxy of those days, I can understand now why the diehards hated him, and why we youngsters turned to him for help.

• • •

Under the influence of such thinkers as Hegel, Lotze and Schleiermacher philosophical idealism powerfully affected American theology in the late nineteenth century. In my early ministry, for example, like many of my generation, I was strongly attracted by Borden P. Bowne's *Personalism*. At the same time Ritschl's emphasis on the historical revelation brought to man in Christ was very appealing, and we were influenced by this "back to Christ" movement, which seemed to promise a middle way between literal Biblicism and metaphysical speculation. Either way, however, the old foundations of Biblical authority were shaken and, consciously or not, a direct appeal to Christian experience became more and more the factual basis for theology.

When I began my year at the divinity school at Colgate all these influences were playing on me, but far from being mainly theoretical my problem was intimately personal.

The major effect which William Newton Clarke had upon me at first was to outflank my intellectual difficulties. He went back behind the forms of doctrine to the basic and abiding experiences of which they were the attempted expression and interpretation. He made essential religion live again for me, real and vital, and let the mental formulations trail along afterward as a matter to be taken up at the mind's leisure. To use his own comparison, he was sure the stars were there, though we had to change our astronomy, and the flowers real, though botany might alter its explanations. He himself was one of the most inspiring teachers I ever sat under. I recall more than once leaving his classroom to seek solitude, that I might gradually come down from the heights to the mundane earth again.

Not all his students were so affected by him. Some were utterly critical of his doctrinal reinterpretations and even contemptuous of what they deemed his intellectual vagueness. Moreover, outside the seminary angry voices in the churches rose against his retention of the professorship, and he once said to me, "They will get me yet." They never did, however. He went from strength to strength. Had it not been for him, I suspect that I should never have been a Christian minister.

I do not mean that I swallowed his opinions whole. He never asked that. Once some of us took him to task for what seemed to us his too labored endeavor, in his book on theology, to save incredible ideas associated with the Trinity. "Well, gentlemen," he said, "sometimes when I read that passage over I think I have said something—and sometimes I don't."

Much that was said in his classroom would now seem outmoded, much of it matter-of-course, some of it strangely conservative, but to me then it was the water of life. All the best meanings of personal religion could be mine again without the crucifixion of the intellect—this assurance he brought me and it was music in my ears. I was sure at last that I would be a minister, not a preacher but a teacher, perhaps of comparative religion.

Some theologians today vehemently condemn the faults of liberal theology, and often they are right about its flaws and failings. There were distortion of perspective, lack of depth, oversimplification, too complaisant optimism, too easy surrender to current categories of modern thought; but such defects, which characterized liberal theology at the turning of the century, were not unperceived by liberals themselves, and always voices from within the liberal camp called for amendment and correction. What present-day critics of liberalism often fail to see is its absolute necessity to multitudes of us who would not have been Christians at all unless we could thus have escaped the bondage of the then reigning orthodoxy. Of course the revolt was not the whole answer! Of course it left out dimensions in Christian faith which would need to be rediscovered! Despite that, however, it offered to a generation of earnest youth the only chance they had to be honest while being Christian.

As for men such as Dr. Clarke, their revolt, like that of Jesus against the orthodoxy of his time, was in the interest of a deeper, more vital, more transforming Christian experience than literalism, legalism and authoritarianism could supply. The result for many of us was not alone a new theology but a new spiritual life.

STUDENT: CARL SANDBURG

(1878–1967)

Poet, journalist and author.

TEACHER: PHILIP GREEN WRIGHT

One professor had many facets, angles, windows. Mathematics he taught, from plane geometry to quaternions and higher. The galaxies of the starry heavens were a majestic poem to him, and he could be sentimental or practical teaching astronomy. *Financial History of the United States* was a class textbook he taught from and we saw he knew far more in that field than the book. He was later to write books to help the federal government on *Sugar in Relation to the Tariff* and *The Tariff on Animal and Vegetable Oils*. In English and American literature he knew more than anyone on the campus about creative writing and how to get it out of the students if they had it in them. You got only a half credit in his ''Daily Themes'' class but it paid off. He had us read *Pastels in Prose* by French writers such as Baudelaire and Mallarme—and a book of short pieces by Turgenev—and discuss how a mood or a story could be told in a few well-chosen words. We wrote our pieces on one or two sheets, the professor picked a few to read aloud, and we would comment, analyse, and point out where they were good, bad, or so-so. In no other class did I see such keen interest, such lively faces, and hear such independent opinions and ideas spoken. I saw students learn and grow in writing, some of them flowering, under the guidance of forty-year-old Professor Philip Green Wright, M.A.

Boston born, his father was a musician, his grandfather Elizur Wright a radical abolitionist, editor of the *Quarterly Anti-Slavery Magazine*, translator and publisher of a two-volume edition of *Fables of La Fontaine* which he sold from door to door. Later the published findings of Elizur Wright showing fraud, theft, perjury, and bribery in life insurance practice brought several companies to hire him to work out tables "which would show total reserves required for safety." As a one-man lobbyist, and later as Commissioner of Insurance in Massachusetts, he brought life insurance forms and improvements in that state and over the country in general. Though not exactly the "Father of Life Insurance," as Elizur Wright was sometimes called, it was responsibly written that he "probably had more to do with the developments of sound standards for life insurance than any other man in its history." His wife Susan bore him eighteen children, six dying in infancy, most of the others living on into exceptional careers.

The remarkable grandfather Elizur had parallels in his grandson Philip Green. Both ran close in feeling to radicals and extremists, yet both were sharks at intricate arithmetic, experts in mathematics and business economics. The findings of the grandson in the field of tariff had a competency like that of the grandfather in life insurance. In a book of poems, *The Dreamer*, Philip Green Wright under the title of "The Captain of Industry" portrayed an American businessman, the smaller industrialist, his problems, his anxieties about making free private enterprise pay a profit while keeping friendly human relations with his workers—a completely sympathetic and understanding portrait. Alongside this was "The Socialist," a portrayal through monologue of a moderate revolutionary who wanted changes made in the distribution of wealth. Professor Wright couldn't go along with the main analysis of the capitalist system made by Karl Marx; that system would prove more resilient and changeful than as Marx saw it. He did accept as correct the reports of Marx and Engels on the human misery and degradation put upon the working class by insensate capitalist overlords. He was closer to the English poet and craftsman William Morris than to Marx. I heard him read his poem "The Cry of the Underlings," in which those underlings in a deep and bitter anger foretell a reckoning to come. A wide-ranging man he was. I have seen him in ten minutes change from the darkest pessimism about the human race to unlimited hope and the brightest promises you could think of.

His humor could be profound and again lackadaisical, as when he told of one Bostonian saying to another, "The fog this morning has a foul odor, I can't understand it"—and the other, "Someone must have lifted the lid off the Chamber of Commerce." He liked to tell of the professor of mathematics whose wife took him to his first symphony performance; as they were leaving, he said, "I get the idea, it all dovetails and coincides, doesn't it?" Or of another professor of mathematics, "That symphony was all very interesting but I don't see that it demonstrates anything." And the author after hearing a concerto, "It sounded to me like a long opinion."

He turned his hand to musical comedy in *The Cannibal Converts*, performed in the Galesburg Auditorium by Lombard students, libretto by Wright, music by Ruth Nash, eldest daughter of President Nash. In line with the new national policy of taking on colonies, preferably islands, a Lombard crew voyaged the Pacific, landed on cannibal islands, and after songs and negotiations converted the natives to change their diet and come to Lombard and learn to be civilized. I can't remember a word of what I said or sang as the cannibal king, but I did keep one verse that I have gone on singing ever since for its words and tune:

Joyously fly, little rover,
Spread thy glad wings and be free,
Free as the air fresh and piney,
Spindrift the combers are flinging,
Free, free as the fetterless sea.

Professor Wright enjoyed the Gilbert and Sullivan operas and would quote Gilbert: "Do you know what it is to yearn for the Indefinable and yet to be brought face to face, daily, with the Multiplication Table?"

In classes Professor Wright at times would stand gazing over and beyond all faces and then come up with something new, pat, and pertinent to what had gone before. He was lean and spare of body, erect and graceful in movements, almost acrobatic in the way he could move back and forth in a demonstration in mathematics, covering a long blackboard with figures and equations, once smiling and telling a class as he finished, "And the beauty of it is that it is of no use whatsoever." From him I first heard the Phi Beta Kappa toast, "Here's to higher mathematics: may it never be of use to any one."

He spoke with a Boston accent somewhat modulated to the midwest. The overall beard of his face gave way to a stubbily trimmed mustache. His mouth and eyes could change from the keenly aware to dreams and speculations beyond the horizon. His singing voice was so-so, but when he sat up to the piano those in the know could tell whether he was playing Mozart, Chopin, or Liszt. In the windowed basement of his house he put in type and printing presswork and binding. He named it The Asgard Press, after the Norse "Home of the gods and slain heroes."

Philip Green Wright had earned his way through Tufts college by teaching at a seminary, and with summer work as postmaster, ticket agent, and printer at a hotel in the White Mountains. After his M. A. at Harvard he worked as a civil engineer and a life insurance actuary, coming to Lombard in 1892. He had luck in getting as a life partner Elizabeth Quincy Sewall of St. Paul, Minnesota, also a grandchild of Elizur Wright. She had an appreciation of his work habits, his putterings and experiments. She bore him three sons who went on to careers of rare distinction, Quincy in international law, Sewall in zoology, Theodore in aircraft engineering.

In a big front room of the Wright house on Sunday nights in the winter months a dozen or so boy and girl students in English and writing would meet to hear one of the group read from a modern talked-about author such as Maeterlinck, Ibsen, Kipling. Then followed an always lively free-for-all discussion. If you read from favorite authors of yours, you found out their faults. I tore to shreds, or tried to, such enthusiasms as there were about the vogue of the historical novel, in such books as *When Knighthood Was in Flower* by the Indianapolis lawyer, Charles Major. I read my favorites. I heard after reading George Ade in *Fables in Slang* that he was not a deep thinker and lacked noble motives. I read from Richard Whiting's novel of London slums, *Number Five John Street*, and heard that it was too dreary and sounded like socialist propaganda. I read from Elbert Hubbard's *The Philistine* and heard that he was a poser and wore his hair long, topped with a ten-gallon hat, to advertise himself. Such criticisms were made half in fun, and we all felt we were getting knowledge and impressions worthwhile not covered in college classes, at the same time having a gay party. Professor Wright guided the discussions and kept them from getting heavy or stodgy. The party began about 7:30. About 9 o'clock "Betty" (Mrs. Wright) would serve to each of us a cup of chocolate with Nabisco wafers, and the talk would go on till nearly 10 o'clock with enough time for the girls to get back to the Ladies' Hall by that hour.

In my last college year Professor Wright organized "The Poor Writers' Club," saying we were poor, and we were writers, so why not? The professor was writing poetry, and so were Athol Brown and myself (of a sort), and the lean, redheaded and brown-eyed Howard Lauer was writing clever skits for *The Lombard Review* in the manner of Bill Nye. Lauer signed himself "Friday" because in Lawrence, Kansas, he had done many smart political chores for Congressman Justin DeWitt Bowersock and was known as "Bowersock's Man Friday." Lauer wrote about funny and near scandalous happenings in and around the college, often taking up the question of who was this skulking anonymous "Friday" who didn't dare to come out into the open. He stood high in classes; after graduation he went to California and was a leading figure in organizing the California Teachers' Federation which became a reckonable force in California politics and state finances. In The Poor Writers' Club we showed our written stuff to each other, talked about what makes a poor writer better, and shared a fellowship worth the time.

Philip Green Wright had gifts and gave us of what he had with never a hint or assumption to us younger ones of a superior and richly stored mind. I had learned a little about Leonardo da Vinci and gave Professor Wright the nickname of "The Illinois Prairie Leonardo." I had four years of almost daily contact with him and visited with him in later years as often as possible. And there was never a time when he didn't deepen whatever of reverence I had for the human mind and the workings of a vast mysterious Universe.

STUDENT: HELEN KELLER

(1880–1968)

Author, lecturer, social reformer and humanitarian.

TEACHER: ANNE MANSFIELD SULLIVAN

The most important day I remember in all my life is the one on which my teacher, Anne Mansfield Sullivan, came to me. I am filled with wonder when I consider the immeasurable contrasts between the two lives which it connects. It was the third of March 1887, three months before I was seven years old.

On the afternoon of that eventful day, I stood on the porch, dumb, expectant. I guessed vaguely from my mother's signs and from the hurrying to and fro in the house that something unusual was about to happen, so I went to the door and waited on the steps. The afternoon sun penetrated the mass of honeysuckle that covered the porch, and fell on my upturned face. My fingers lingered almost unconsciously on the familiar leaves and blossoms which had just come forth to greet the sweet southern spring. I did not know what the future held of marvel or surprise for me. Anger and bitterness had preyed upon me continually for weeks and a deep languor had succeeded this passionate struggle.

Have you ever been at sea in a dense fog, when it seemed as if a tangible white darkness shut you in, and the great ship, tense and anxious, groped her way toward the shore with plummet and sounding-line, and you waited with beating heart for something to happen? I was like that ship before my education began, only I was without compass or sounding-line, and had no way of knowing how near the harbour was. "Light! give me light!" was the wordless cry of my soul, and the light of love shone on me in that very hour.

I felt approaching footsteps. I stretched out my hand as I supposed to my mother. Some one took it, and I was caught up and held close in the arms of her who had come to reveal all things to me, and, more than all things else, to love me.

The morning after my teacher came she led me into her room and gave me a doll. The little blind children at the Perkins Institution had sent it and Laura Bridgman had dressed it; but I did not know this until afterward. When I had played with it a little while, Miss Sullivan slowly spelled into my hand the word "d-o-l-l." I was at once interested in this finger play and tried to imitate it. When I finally succeeded in making the letters correctly I was flushed with childish pleasure and pride. Running downstairs to my mother I held up my hand and made the letters for doll. I did not know that I was spelling a word or even that words existed; I was simply making my fingers go in monkey-like imitation. In the days that followed I learned to spell in this uncomprehending way a great many words, among them *pin, hat, cup* and a few verbs like *sit, stand* and *walk.* But my teacher had been with me several weeks before I understood that everything has a name.

One day, while I was playing with my new doll, Miss Sullivan put my big rag doll into my lap also, spelled "d-o-l-l" and tried to make me understand that "d-o-l-l" applied to both. Earlier in the day we had had a tussle over the word "m-u-g" and "w-a-t-e-r." Miss Sullivan had tried to impress it upon me that "m-u-g" is *mug* and that "w-a-t-e-r" is *water*, but I persisted in confounding the two. In despair she had dropped the subject for the time, only to renew it at the first opportunity. I became impatient at her repeated attempts and, seizing the new doll, I dashed it upon the floor. I was keenly delighted when I felt the fragments of the broken doll at my feet. Neither sorrow nor regret followed my passionate outburst. I had not loved the doll. In the still, dark world in which I lived there was no strong sentiment or tenderness. I felt my teacher sweep the fragments to one side of the hearth, and I had a sense of satisfaction that the cause of my discomfort was removed. She brought me my hat, and I knew I was going out into the warm sunshine. This thought, if a wordless sensation may be a thought, made me hop and skip with pleasure.

We walked down the path to the well-house, attracted by the fragrance of the honeysuckle with which it was covered. Some one was drawing water and my teacher placed my hand under the spout. As the cool stream gushed over one hand she spelled into the other the word *water*, first slowly, then rapidly. I stood still, my whole attention fixed upon the motions of her fingers. Suddenly I felt a misty consciousness as of something forgotten—a thrill of returning thought; and somehow the mystery of language was revealed to me. I knew then that "w-a-t-e-r" meant the wonderful cool something that was flowing over my hand. That living word awakened my soul, gave it light, hope, joy, set it free! There were barriers still, it is true, but barriers that could in time be swept away.

I left the well-house eager to learn. Everything had a name, and each name gave birth to a new thought. As we returned to the house every object which I touched seemed to quiver with life. That was because I saw everything with the strange, new sight that had come to me. On entering the door I remembered the doll I had broken. I felt my way to the hearth and picked up the pieces. I tried vainly to put them together. Then my eyes filled with tears; for I realized what I had done, and for the first time I felt repentance and sorrow.

I learned a great many new words that day. I do not remember what they all were; but I do know that *mother, father, sister, teacher* were among them—words that were to make the world blossom for me, "like Aaron's rod, with flowers." It would have been difficult to find a happier child than I was as I lay in my crib at the close of that eventful day and lived over the joys it had brought me, and for the first time longed for a new day to come.

• • •

I had now the key to all language, and I was eager to learn to use it. Children who hear acquire language without any particular effort; the words that fall from others' lips they catch on the wing, as it were, delightedly, while the little deaf child must trap them by a slow and often painful process. But whatever the process, the result is wonderful. Gradually from naming an object we advance step by step until we have traversed the vast distance between our first stammered syllable and the sweep of thought in a line of Shakespeare.

At first, when my teacher told me about a new thing I asked very few questions. My ideas were vague, and my vocabulary was inadequate; but as my knowledge of things grew, and I learned more and more words, my field of inquiry broadened, and I would return again and again to the same subject, eager for further information. Sometimes a new word revived an image that some earlier experience had engraved on my brain.

I remember the morning that I first asked the meaning of the word, "love." This was before I knew many words. I had found a few early violets in the garden and brought them to my teacher. She tried to kiss me; but at that time I did not like to have any one kiss me except my mother. Miss Sullivan put her arm gently round me and spelled into my hand, "I love Helen."

"What is love?" I asked.

She drew me closer to her and said, "It is here," pointing to my heart, whose beats I was conscious of for the first time. Her words puzzled me very much because I did not then understand anything unless I touched it.

I smelt the violets in her hand and asked, half in words, half in signs, a question which meant, "Is love the sweetness of flowers?"

"No," said my teacher.

Again I thought. The warm sun was shining on us.

"Is this not love?" I asked, pointing in the direction from which the heat come, "Is this not love?"

It seemed to me that there could be nothing more beautiful than the sun, whose warmth makes all things grow. But Miss Sullivan shook her head, and I was greatly puzzled and disappointed. I thought it strange that my teacher could not show me love.

A day or two afterward I was stringing beads of different sizes in symmetrical groups—two large beads, three small ones, and so on. I had made many mistakes and Miss Sullivan had pointed them out again and again with gentle patience. Finally I noticed a very obvious error in the sequence and for an instant I concentrated my attention on the lesson and tried to think how I should have arranged the beads. Miss Sullivan touched my forehead and spelled with decided emphasis, "Think."

In a flash I knew that the word was the name of the process that was going on in my head. This was my first conscious perception of an abstract idea.

For a long time I was still—I was not thinking of the beads in my lap, but trying to find a meaning for "love" in the light of this new idea. The sun had been under a cloud all day, and there had been brief showers; but suddenly the sun broke forth in all its southern splendour.

Again I asked my teacher, "Is this not love?"

"Love is something like the clouds that were in the sky before the sun came out," she replied. Then in simpler words than these, which at that time I could not have understood she explained: "You cannot touch the clouds, you know; but you feel the rain and know how glad the flowers and the thirsty earth are to have it after a hot day. You cannot touch love either; but you feel the sweetness that it pours into everything. Without love you would not be happy or want to play."

The beautiful truth burst upon my mind—I felt that there were invisible lines stretched between my spirit and the spirits of others.

From the beginning of my education Miss Sullivan made it a practice to speak to me as she would speak to any hearing child; the only difference was that she spelled the sentences into my hand instead of speaking them. If I did not know the words and idioms necessary to express my thoughts she supplied them, even suggesting conversation when I was unable to keep up my end of the dialogue. This process was continued for several years; for the deaf child does not learn in a month, or even in two or three years, the numberless idioms and expressions used in the simplest daily intercourse.

The hearing child learns these from constant repetition and imitation. The conversation he hears in his home stimulates his mind and suggests topics and calls forth the spontaneous expression of his own thoughts. This natural exchange of ideas is denied to the deaf child. My teacher, realizing this, determined to supply the kinds of stimulus I lacked. This she did by repeating to me as far as possible, verbatim, what she heard, and by showing me how I could take part in the conversation. But it was a long time before I ventured to take the initiative, and still longer before I could find something appropriate to say at the right time.

The deaf and the blind find it very difficult to acquire the amenities of conversation. How much more this difficulty must be augmented in the case of those who are both deaf and blind! They cannot distinguish the tone of the voice or, without assistance, go up and down the gamut of tones that give significance to words; nor can they watch the expression of the speaker's face, and a look is often the very soul of what one says.

• • •

The next important step in my education was learning to read.

As soon as I could spell a few words my teacher gave me slips of cardboard on which were printed words in raised letters. I quickly learned that each printed word stood for an object, an act, or a quality. I had a frame in which I could arrange the words in little sentences; but before I ever put sentences in the frame I used to make them in objects. I found the slips of paper which represented, for example, "doll," "is," "on," "bed" and placed each name on its object; then I put my doll on the bed with the words *is, on, bed* arranged beside the doll, thus making a sentence of the words, and at the same time carrying out the idea of the sentence with the things themselves.

One day, Miss Sullivan tells me, I pinned the word *girl* on my pinafore and stood in the wardrobe. On the shelf I arranged the words, *is, in, wardrobe*. Nothing delighted me so much as this game. My teacher and I played it for hours at a time. Often everything in the room was arranged in object sentences.

From the printed slip it was but a step to the printed book. I took my "Reader for Beginners" and hunted for the words I knew; when I found them my joy was like that of a game of hide-and-seek. Thus I began to read. Of the time when I began to read connected stories I shall speak later.

For a long time I had no regular lessons. Even when I studied most earnestly it seemed more like play than work. Everything Miss Sullivan taught me she illustrated by a beautiful story or a poem. Whenever anything delighted or interested me she talked it over with me just as if she were a little girl herself. What many children think of with dread, as a painful plodding through grammar, hard sums and harder definitions, is to-day one of my most precious memories.

I cannot explain the peculiar sympathy Miss Sullivan had with my pleasures and desires. Perhaps it was the result of long association with the blind. Added to this she had a wonderful faculty for description. She went quickly over uninteresting details, and never nagged me with questions to see if I remembered the day-before-yesterday's lesson. She introduced dry technicalities of science little by little, making every subject so real that I could not help remembering what she taught.

We read and studied out of doors, preferring the sunlit woods to the house. All my early lessons have in them the breath of the woods—the fine, resinous odour of pine needles, blended with the perfume of wild grapes. Seated in the gracious shade of a wild tulip tree, I learned to think that everything has a lesson and a suggestion. "The loveliness of things taught me all their use." Indeed, everything that could hum, or buzz, or sing, or bloom, had a part in my education—noisy-throated frogs, katydids and crickets held my hand until, forgetting their embarrassment, they trilled their reedy note, little downy chickens and wildflowers, the dogwood blossoms, meadow-violets and budding fruit trees. I felt the bursting cotton-bolls and fingered their soft fiber and fuzzy seeds; I felt the low soughing of the wind through the cornstalks, and silky rustling of the long leaves, and the indignant snort of my pony, as we caught him in the pasture and put the bit in his mouth—ah me! how well I remember the spicy, clovery smell of his breath!

Sometimes I rose at dawn and stole into the garden while the heavy dew lay on the grass and flowers. Few know what joy it is to feel the roses pressing softly into the hand, or the beautiful motion of the lilies as they sway in the morning breeze. Sometimes I caught an insect in the flower I was plucking, and I felt the faint noise of a pair of wings rubbed together in a sudden terror, as the little creature became aware of a pressure from without.

Another favourite haunt of mine was the orchard, where the fruit ripened early in July. The large, downy peaches would reach themselves into my hand, and as the joyous breezes flew about the trees the apples tumbled at my feet. Oh, the delight with which I gathered up the fruit in my pinafore, pressed my face against the smooth cheeks of the apples, still warm from the sun, and skipped back to the house!

Our favourite walk was to Keller's Landing, an old tumble-down lumber-wharf on the Tennessee River, used during the Civil War to land soldiers. There we spent many happy hours and played at learning geography. I built dams of pebbles, made islands and lakes, and dug river-beds, all for fun, and never dreamed that I was learning a lesson. I listened with increasing wonder to Miss Sullivan's descriptions of the great round world with its burning mountains, buried cities, moving rivers of ice, and many other things as strange. She made raised maps in clay, so that I could feel the mountain ridges and valleys, and follow with my fingers the devious course of rivers. I liked this too; but the division of the earth into zones and poles confused and teased my mind. The illustrative strings and the orange stick representing the poles seemed so real that even to this day the mere mention of temperate zone suggests a series of twine circles; and I believe that if any one should set about it he could convince me that white bears actually climb the North Pole.

Arithmetic seems to have been the only study I did not like. From the first I was not interested in the science of numbers. Miss Sullivan tried to teach me to count by stringing beads in groups, and by arranging kindergarten straws I learned to add and subtract. I never had patience to arrange more than five or six groups at a time. When I had accomplished this my conscience was at rest for the day, and I went out quickly to find my playmates.

In this same leisurely manner I studied zoology and botany.

Once a gentleman, whose name I have forgotten, sent me a collection of fossils—tiny mollusk shells beautifully marked, and bits of sandstone with the print of birds' claws, and a lovely fern in bas-relief. These were the keys which unlocked the treasures of the antediluvian world for me. With trembling fingers I listened to Miss Sullivan's descriptions of the terrible beasts, with uncouth, unpronounceable names, which once went tramping through the primeval forests, tearing down the branches of gigantic trees for food, and died in the dismal swamps of an unknown age. For a long time these strange creatures haunted my dreams, and this gloomy period formed a somber background to the joyous Now, filled with sunshine and roses and echoing with the gentle beat of my pony's hoof.

Another time a beautiful shell was given me, and with a child's surprise and delight I learned how a tiny mollusk had built the lustrous coil for his dwelling place, and how on still nights, when there is no breeze stirring on the waves, the Nautilus sails on the blue waters on the Indian Ocean in his "ship of pearl." After I had learned a great many interesting things about the life and habits of the children of the sea—how in the midst of dashing waves the little polyps build the beautiful coral isles of the Pacific, and the foraminifera have made the chalk-hills of many a land—my teacher read me "The Chambered Nautilus," and showed me that the shell-building process of the mollusks is symbolical of the development of the mind. Just as the wonder-working mantle of the Nautilus changes the material it absorbs from the water and makes it a part of itself, so the bits of knowledge one gathers undergo a similar change and become pearls of thought.

Again, it was the growth of a plant that furnished the text for a lesson. We bought a lily and set it in a sunny window. Very soon the green, pointed buds showed signs of opening. The slender, fingerlike leaves on the outside opened slowly, reluctant, I thought, to reveal the loveliness they hid; once having made a start, however, the opening process went on rapidly, but in order and systematically. There was always one bud larger and more beautiful than the rest, which pushed her outer covering back with more pomp, as if the beauty in soft, silky robes knew that she was the lily-queen by right divine, while her more timid sisters doffed their green hoods shyly, until the whole plant was one nodding bough of loveliness and fragrance.

Once there were eleven tadpoles in a glass globe set in a window full of plants. I remember the eagerness with which I made discoveries about them. It was great fun to plunge my hand into the bowl and feel the tadpoles frisk about, and to let them slip and slide between my fingers. One day a more ambitious fellow leaped beyond the edge of the bowl and fell on the floor, where I found him to all appearance more dead than alive. The only sign of life was a slight wriggling of his tail. But no sooner had he returned to his element than he darted to the bottom, swimming round and round in joyous activity. He had made his leap, he had seen the great world, and was content to stay in his pretty glass house under the big fuchsia tree until he attained the dignity of froghood. Then he went to live in the leafy pool at the end of the garden, where he made the summer nights musical with his quaint love-song.

Thus I learned from life itself. At the beginning I was only a little mass of possibilities. It was my teacher who unfolded and developed them. When she came, everything about me breathed of love and joy and was full of meaning. She has never since let pass an opportunity to point out the beauty that is in everything, nor has she ceased trying in thought and action and example to make my life sweet and useful.

It was my teacher's genius, her quick sympathy, her loving tact which made the first years of my education so beautiful. It was because she seized the right moment to impart knowledge that made it so pleasant and acceptable to me. She realized that a child's mind is like a shallow brook which ripples and dances merrily over the stony course of its education and reflects here a flower, there a bush, yonder a fleecy cloud and she attempted to guide my mind on its way, knowing that like a brook it should be fed by mountain streams and hidden springs, until it broadened out into a deep river, capable of reflecting in its placid surface, billowy hills, the luminous shadows of trees and the blue heavens, as well as the sweet face of a little flower.

Any teacher can take a child to the classroom, but not every teacher can make him learn. He will not work joyously unless he feels that liberty is his, whether he is busy or at rest; he must feel the flush of victory and the heart-sinking of disappointment before he takes with a will the tasks distasteful to him and resolves to dance his way bravely through a dull routine of textbooks.

My teacher is so near to me that I scarcely think of myself apart from her. How much of my delight in all beautiful things is innate, and how much is due to her influence, I can never tell. I feel that her being is inseparable from my own, and that the footsteps of my life are in hers. All the best of me belongs to her—there is not a talent, or an aspiration or a joy in me that has not been awakened by her loving touch.

STUDENT: CALVIN COOLIDGE

(1882–1933)

Attorney; Massachusetts State Senator, Lieutenant Governor and Governor; Vice President and 29th President of the United States.

TEACHERS: GEORGE SHERMAN M. BELLE CHELLIS ANSON D. MORSE CHARLES E. GARMAN

During most of my course George Sherman was the principal [of Black River Academy] and Miss M. Belle Chellis was the first assistant. I owe much to the inspiration and scholarly direction which they gave to my undergraduate days. They both lived to see me President and sent me letters at the time, though they left the school long ago. It was under their teaching that I first learned of the glory and grandeur of the ancient civilization that grew up around the Mediterranean and in Mesopotamia. Under their guidance I beheld the marvels of old Babylon, I marched with the Ten Thousand of Xenophon, I witnessed the conflict around beleaguered Troy which doomed that proud city to pillage and to flames, I heard the tramp of the invincible legions of Rome, I saw the victorious galleys of the Eternal City carrying destruction to the Carthaginian shore, and I listened to the lofty eloquence of Cicero and the matchless imagery of Homer. They gave me a vision of the world when it was young and showed me how it grew. It seems to me that it is almost impossible for those who have not traveled that road to reach a very clear conception of what the world now means.

It was in this period that I learned something of the thread of events that ran from the Euphrates and the Nile through Athens to the Tiber and thence stretched on to the Seine and the Thames to be carried overseas to the James, the Charles and the Hudson. I found that the English language was generously compounded with Greek and Latin, which it was necessary to know if I was to understand my native tongue. I discovered that our ideas of democracy came from the agora of Greece, and our ideas of liberty came from the forum of Rome. Something of the sequence of history was revealed to me, so that I began to understand the significance of our own times and our own country.

• • •

During my first two years at Amherst I studied hard but my marks were only fair. It needed some encouragement from my father for me to continue. In junior year, however, my powers began to increase and my work began to improve. My studies became more interesting. I found the course in history under Professor Anson D. Morse was very absorbing. His lectures on medieval and modern Europe were inspiring, seeking to give his students not only the facts of past human experience but also their meaning. He was very strong on the political side of history, bringing before us the great figures from Charlemagne to Napoleon with remarkable distinctness, and showing us the influence of the Great Gregory and Innocent III. The work of Abelard and Erasmus was considered, and the important era of Luther and Calvin thoroughly explored.

In due time we crossed the Channel with William the Conqueror and learned how he subdued and solidified the Kingdom of England. The significance of the long struggle with the Crown before the Parliament finally reached a position of independence was disclosed, and the slow growth of a system of liberty under the law, until at last it was firmly established, was carefully explained. We saw the British Empire rise until it ruled the seas. The brilliance of the statesmanship of the different periods, the rugged character of the patriotic leaders, of Anselm and Simon de Montfort, of Cromwell and the Puritans, who dared to oppose the tyranny of the kings, the growth of learning, the development of commerce, the administration of justice—all these and more were presented for our consideration. Whatever was essential to a general comprehension of European history we had.

But it was when he turned to the United States that Professor Morse became most impressive. He placed particular emphasis on the era when our institutions had their beginnings. Washington was treated with the greatest reverence, and a high estimate was placed on the statesmanlike qualities and financial capacity of Hamilton, but Jefferson was not neglected. In spite of his many vagaries it was shown that in saving the nation from the danger of falling under the domination of an oligarchy, and in establishing a firm rule of the people which was forever to remain, he vindicated the soundness of our political institutions. The whole course was a thesis on good citizenship and good government. Those who took it came to a clearer comprehension not only of their rights and liberties but of their duties and responsibilities.

• • •

It always seemed to me that all our other studies were in the nature of a preparation for the course in philosophy. The head of this department was Charles E. Garman, who was one of the most remarkable men with whom I ever came in contact. He used numerous text books, which he furnished, and many pamphlets that he not only had written but had printed himself on a hand press in his home. These he pledged us to show to no one outside the class, because, being fragmentary, and disclosing but one line of argument which might be entirely demolished in succeeding lessons, they might involve him in some needless controversy. It is difficult to imagine his superior as an educator. Truly he drew men out.

Beginning in the spring of junior year his course extended through four terms. The first part was devoted to psychology, in order to find out the capacity and the limits of the human mind. It was here that we learned the nature of habits and the great advantage of making them our allies instead of our enemies.

Much stress was placed on a thorough mastery and careful analysis of all the arguments presented by the writers on any subject under consideration. Then when it was certain that they were fully understood they were criticized, so that what was unsound was rejected and what was true accepted. We were thoroughly drilled in the necessity of distinguishing between the accidental and the essential.

The proper method of presenting a subject and an argument was discussed. We were not only learning about the human mind but learning how to use it, learning how to think. A problem would often be stated and the class left to attempt to find the solution unaided by the teacher. Above all we were taught to follow the truth whithersoever it might lead. We were warned that this would oftentimes be very difficult and result in much opposition, for there would be many who were not going that way, but if we pressed on steadfastly it was sure to yield the peaceable fruits of the mind. It does.

Our investigation revealed that man is endowed with reason, that the human mind has the power to weigh the evidence, to distinguish between right and wrong and to know the truth. I should call this the central theme of his philosophy. While the quantity of the truth we know may be small it is the quality that is important. If we really know one truth the quality of our knowledge could not be surpassed by the Infinite.

We looked upon Garman as a man who walked with God. His course was a demonstration of the existence of a personal God, of our power to know Him, of the Divine immanence, and of the complete dependence of all the universe on Him as the Creator and Father "in whom we live and move and have our being." Every reaction in the universe is a manifestation of His presence. Man was revealed as His son, and nature as the hem of His garment, while through a common Fatherhood we are all embraced in a common brotherhood. The spiritual appeal of music, sculpture, painting and all other art lies in the revelation it affords of the Divine beauty.

The conclusions which followed from this position were logical and inescapable. It sets man off in a separate kingdom from all the other creatures in the universe, and makes him a true son of God and a partaker of the Divine nature. This is the warrant for his freedom and the demonstration of his equality. It does not assume all are equal in degree but all are equal in kind. On that precept rests a foundation for democracy that cannot be shaken. It justifies faith in the people.

No doubt there are those who think they can demonstrate that this teaching was not correct. With them I have no argument. I know that in experience it has worked. In time of crisis my belief that people can know the truth, that when it is presented to them they must accept it, has saved me from many of the counsels of expediency. The spiritual nature of men has a power of its own that is manifest in every great emergency from Runnymede to Marston Moor, from the Declaration of Independence to the abolition of slavery.

In ethics he taught us that there is a standard of righteousness, that might does not make right, that the end does not justify the means and that expediency as a working principle is bound to fail. The only hope of perfecting human relationship is in accordance with the law of service under which men are not so solicitous about what they shall get as they are about what they shall give. Yet people are entitled to the rewards of their industry. What they earn is theirs, no matter how small or how great. But the possession of property carries the obligation to use it in a larger service. For a man not to recognize the truth, not to be obedient to law, not to render allegiance to the State, is for him to be at war with his own nature, to commit suicide. That is why "the wages of sin is death." Unless we live rationally we perish, physically, mentally, spiritually.

A great deal of emphasis was placed on the necessity and dignity of work. Our talents are given us in order that we may serve ourselves and our fellow men. Work is the expansion of intelligent action for a specified end. It is not industry, but idleness, that is degrading. All kinds of work from the most menial service to the most exalted station are alike honorable. One of the earliest mandates laid on the human race was to subdue the earth. That meant work.

If he was not in accord with some of the current teachings about religion, he gave to his class a foundation for the firmest religious convictions. He presented no mysteries or dogmas and never asked us to take a theory on faith, but supported every position by facts and logic. He believed in the Bible and constantly quoted it to illustrate his position. He divested religion and science of any conflict with each other, and showed that each rested on the common basis of our ability to know the truth.

To Garman was given a power which took his class up into a high mountain of spiritual life and left them alone with God.

In him was no pride of opinion, no atom of selfishness. He was a follower of the truth, a disciple of the Cross, who bore the infirmities of us all. Those who finished his course in the last term of senior year found in their graduating exercise a real commencement, when they would begin their efforts to serve their fellow men in the practical affairs of life. Of course it was not possible for us to accept immediately the results of his teachings or live altogether in accordance with them. I do not think he expected it. He was constantly reminding us that the spirit was willing but the flesh was *strong*, but that nevertheless, if we would continue steadfastly to think of these things we would be changed from glory to glory through increasing intellectual and moral power. He was right.

To many my report of his course will seem incomplete and crude. I am not writing a treatise but trying to tell what I secured from his teaching, and relating what has seemed important in it to me, from the memory I have retained of it, since I began it thirty-five years ago. He expected it to be supplemented. He was fond of referring to it as a mansion not made with hands, incomplete, but sufficient for our spiritual habitation. What he revealed to us of the nature of God and man will stand. Against it "the gates of hell shall not prevail."

As I look back upon the college I am more and more impressed with the strength of its faculty, with their power for good. Perhaps it has men now with a broader preliminary training, though they then were profound scholars, perhaps it has men of keener intellects though they then were very exact in their reasoning, but the great distinguishing mark of all of them was that they were men of character. Their words carried conviction because we were compelled to believe in the men who uttered them. They had the power not merely to advise but literally to instruct their students.

STUDENT: RAYMOND B. FOSDICK
(1883–1972)

Attorney, administrator, Undersecretary General of the League of Nations and President of the Rockefeller Foundation.

TEACHER: WOODROW WILSON

Three days after I entered Princeton . . . , I met Woodrow Wilson. It was entirely by accident. I saw him approaching me on the walk across the front campus, and I recognized him from his pictures. At Colgate it was an ironclad custom for undergraduates to take their hats off to the president, and I assumed, erroneously, that the same tradition held at Princeton. I therefore doffed my hat to him. He smiled and took off his hat to me. Then he stopped and said:

"You're new here, aren't you?"

"Yes, sir," I replied

"And I see you are not a freshman," he continued, because I was not wearing the prescribed freshman cap.

I told him I was entering as a junior, and I answered two or three of his questions about Colgate. He chatted in a friendly manner for a minute or two, and then, as we parted, he said:

"I wish you would drop in to see me."

This was my introduction to Princeton, and I am sure that no welcome was ever so stimulating to a lonely and somewhat bewildered student coming to an institution in which he did not know a soul. I assumed that Mr. Wilson meant what he said, and a week or two later I called on him at his house, just as we were accustomed to do at Colgate. It was the beginning of a long and occasionally intimate association which lasted until his death over twenty years later.

Wilson on first appearance was not what would be called a handsome man. Indeed he was curiously homely. He had what he himself described as a "horse face"—a long, thin and generally unsmiling visage with strong jaws. He had also an extraordinarily keen gaze, which could sometimes be disconcerting. But his eyes were nevertheless his best feature; they could light up with humor and kindliness, and his whole face would soften as it reflected his thoughts. His figure was tall and lithe, and he held himself erect and walked with a brisk pace. When I first met him he was forty-seven years old, and the mark of leadership was on his face and in his whole bearing.

What I remember initially about him at Princeton was the way he conducted chapel. Attendance at college chapel in my time was compulsory—five days a week and once on Sunday—and the whole business, rooted in Calvinistic traditions, was heartily disliked by the students. Once when a group of undergraduates approached Wilson on the question of making chapel attendance optional, he replied with mock gravity: "Why, gentlemen, it *is* optional. If you wish to go to chapel you may." But when Wilson himself conducted the chapel exercises, as he did once or twice a week, he brought an atmosphere of reverence and sincerity which subdued even the students of Nassau Hall of my boisterous generation. He had a magnificent, resonant voice, and I can still recall his incomparable reading of the scriptures—his favorite nineteenth Psalm, for example: "The heavens declare the glory of God; and the firmament showeth his handiwork"; or the thirteenth chapter of I Corinthians: "And now abideth faith, hope, charity, these three." When these old words came ringing through the chapel, carried by the magnetism of Wilson's voice, I do not say that the students were spellbound, but they were significantly silent.

His prayers were even more compelling. They generally had to do with the hope that we young men might be worthy and effective tools in the hands of an omnipotent will. They were always extemporaneous, but no matter what the occasion, he invariably concluded them with the section from the Episcopalian prayer book which begins: "Almighty and most merciful Father, we have erred and strayed from thy ways like lost sheep," and which ends with the sentence: "And grant O most merciful Father, that we may hereafter live a godly, righteous and sober life, to the glory of the holy Name."

In trying to understand the personality of Woodrow Wilson we have to remember that first and foremost he was a deeply religious man. With the exception of Gladstone, probably no man in supreme power in the life of any nation was so profoundly imbued by the Christian faith. He came from a Calvinistic background, and he was sturdily and mystically Christian. He believed that God was working out His purposes in this world, and once he made up his mind that a particular course of action represented the will of God, nothing could shake him loose from it. "God save us from compromise," he used to say; or again: "Let's stop being merely practical and find out what's right." I remember when I last saw him, in his house on S Street in Washington, a few weeks before he died, we discussed the recent progress that the League of Nations had been making. With tears rolling down his face he said: "You can't fight God!" To him the underlying principle of the League of Nations represented the fulfillment of a preordained purpose, and if he took any pride in the situation at all, it was that he had been an instrument—however faulty—in carrying out the will of God.

That this aspect of his character frequently made him appear unyielding and stubborn cannot be denied. That it was one of the great sources of his strength is equally true. He was a man to whom the realities of the life of the spirit were very real, and those of us who heard his occasional lay sermons before the Philadelphian Society in Princeton will never forget the subdued but intense tones of his voice in those evening hours, as with quiet eloquence he upheld the priority of spiritual values in the lives of men.

Of course he was one of the great public speakers of his generation. I would be inclined to say that he was the greatest orator I have ever heard, although the word orator in our day has taken on a somewhat invidious meaning—sound and fury, signifying nothing. But there was no trace of the rotund or of bombast in Wilson's method of speaking, no forensic attitudes, no histrionic gestures. Indeed he employed few gestures, the only one I can recall being the use of the forefinger of his right hand pointed at his audience. His power lay in the precision of his mind, in the matchless lucidity of his argument, and in his passionate sincerity. His influence on his listeners was almost hypnotic, and he could fairly bring them to their feet with a stirring phrase. I remember one night after his election to the White House, but before he had taken office, he spoke at a dinner in New York City. I do not recall what the occasion was, but in referring to some evil influences or threatening figures in public life he electrified his audience by the grim comment in measured accents: "We'll hang them on a gibbet higher than Haman's."

His addresses were almost invariably extemporaneous, although he prepared his outlines with care. Once when he was asked by some undergraduates to make a speech he inquired how long it should be. "It doesn't matter," he was told. "If you want me to talk for ten minutes, I need two weeks to prepare. If you want me to speak for half an hour I need a day. If you have no time limit I am ready right now." And yet he never memorized an address, and he seldom used notes. The words seemed to flow naturally and logically with uninterrupted cadence.

I heard Lloyd George at the top of his form in the budget debates in the House of Commons in 1909. I heard Asquith and Lord Balfour on several occasions, and William J. Bryan as well, particularly in his later days. I heard Senator Beveridge and other great speakers of their time. In sheer ability and power it seems to me that Wilson towered above them all. He was a scholar in action, a prophet touched by fire, with unmatched strength to persuade and move the hearts of his listeners.

This ability to express himself in cogent, vivid phrase was one of the reasons, I suspect, why he was so outstanding as a teacher. I have never seen his equal in a classroom, whether the room was a lecture hall, crowded with four or five hundred students, or a curtained-off cubicle for a hastily improvised seminar, or, best of all, his study in Prospect, the President's home in Princeton, with three or four of us asking him questions. More than any other man I have ever met he seemed to personify the dignity and power of ideas. He made the life of the intellect attractive. It was through him that we became aware of our inheritance of the rational tradition that was born in ancient Greece—a tradition of candid and fearless thinking about the great questions of liberty and government, of freedom and control.

Wilson's regular courses were in jurisprudence and in constitutional government, given on the top floor of old Dickinson Hall to a class of perhaps five hundred students. He always started his lectures with the salutation: "Good morning, gentlemen." He generally had a page of notes on the lectern in front of him—notes written in shorthand, for he was a master of shorthand—but he seldom appeared to refer to them. Occasionally he would interrupt his lecture with the remark: "Now gentlemen, I suggest you take this down," and he would dictate slowly and succinctly some idea he had been developing. I still have my old notebooks which I kept in his classes, and I find they contain such sentences as these:

> The associated life out of which law springs produces many things: natural ties, ties of habit or affection, ties of interest, a developed set of rules of social morality. Law takes up whatever is in this way completed—whatever has been made ready and reduced to a uniform rule of conduct—and provides it with a compulsive sanction.

Is it any wonder that a man who taught this kind of doctrine should, sixteen years later, describe the proposed prohibition law as unworkable and send it back to the Congress with a stern veto? Or take this from my notebook, obviously the outline of an idea far more extensively treated:

> Morality is a great deal bigger than law. The individual morality is the sense of right or wrong of one man. The social morality must strike an average. This is where reformers make their tragic mistake. There can be no compromise in individual morality; but there *has* to be a compromise, an average, in social morality. There is indeed an element of morality in the very fact of compromise on *social* undertakings.

Here Wilson was posing a difficult question: how to draw a rational line between the individual conscience and social action. The question has plagued the minds of thoughtful men from the days of Plato; and with Wilson's own passionate convictions and fighting spirit, it proved to be the major problem which he had to face again and again.

I can still see his strong, long-jawed, animated face and hear the cadences of his amazing extemporary eloquence. No matter how he began them, his sentences always came out in perfect form. Occasionally when he plunged headlong into an involved sentence structure, I would think to myself: "There's a sentence he can't extricate himself from"; but I was always wrong. Not only were his sentences works of art, but his argument was presented with a convincing skill and an intellectual brilliance which held his students spellbound, so that frequently they broke into applause and stamped their feet at the end of his lectures—an almost unheard of occurrence in the conservative traditions of Princeton.

It was not his regular lectures, however, but in his informal and sometimes casual contacts with the students that he made his deepest impressions—his occasional talks at Whig Hall, one of the two debating societies on the campus; the more or less informal seminars at which his attendance, because of his administrative duties, was necessarily irregular; and particularly the occasional meetings with small groups in his own home. On some of these evenings his brother-in-law, Stockton Axson, read Browning or Wordsworth to us. Wilson was fond of poetry and read it himself with great effect.

I recall on one occasion—just what it was I don't remember—the dramatic earnestness with which he described the Covenanter movement in Scotland in 1638—the forbidding Sunday morning in Greyfriars churchyard, under the shadow of Edinburgh Castle, when the grim and determined citizens signed their names to the Covenant on a flat tombstone just outside the door. Years later, because I had never forgotten his description of it, I went to the churchyard to see for myself the setting and background of the incident. To Wilson it was one of the outstanding events in the long struggle for liberty. It was here that freedom of conscience took root; this was a stepping stone by which the past made its way into a future of wider justice. We who had the privilege of listening to him when he was in this kind of mood always came away feeling that we had been in the presence of someone upon whom had fallen the mantle of the old prophets of liberty.

In Wilson's system of social philosophy, Locke and Bagehot seemed to be the high priests, and in his lectures he quoted them constantly. To some he may have given the impression that he was interested in theory to the exclusion of everything else. But he had a way of illustrating his theory by graphic references to the present; and by indirection he introduced us to a new world of reality in which ideas were put to practical ends. It was through him that many of us received our first impressions of the color and significance of contemporary events. Our academic work largely centered on Latin, Greek and mathematics. It was the wisdom of the past that preoccupied us. We now entered a realm in which the current Russian-Japanese war was a matter of deep concern, and the question of efficient government on both the local and national level was of intriguing interest.

Of course Wilson had a lighter and gayer side which we students seldom saw, and it was not until later, when I got to know him better, that I realized how significant a part of his personality it was. He was a superb raconteur, with an amazing fund of anecdotes and stories. Indeed his dialect stories, told in Scotch, Irish or Negro accents, were often side-splitting, and a few of them I recall even today. Any kind of foolish verse or limerick had a strong appeal to him, and he could recite scores of them. He had, too, a lively wit, and some of his retorts are still cherished in the memory of his friends. For example, the mother of one of his students urged him to make Princeton a coeducational institution.

"Why?" he asked.

"To remove the false glamor with which the two sexes see each other," she replied.

"My dear madam," Wilson shot back, "that is the very thing we want to preserve at all costs!"

In his later years, certainly, he did not hesitate, on informal occasions, to employ a picturesque kind of slang if it suited his purpose; and he could come out with a good healthy "damn" if the occasion required it. But I never heard him go beyond this in the way of expletives, and I doubt if he did. Always he was restrained by a natural fastidiousness, an innate temperance of taste.

I have frequently been asked whether during my student days Wilson was a liberal in his political and social thinking. The word liberal, of course, is capable of wide definition, but I cannot say that at that time he was in any sense a militant progressive. He seemed to be more of a Federalist than a Democrat, more of a Hamiltonian than a Jeffersonian, and I suspect that at this point in his career he had a kind of intellectual impatience with the practical processes of democracy. For example, he was opposed at that time, and even later, to woman suffrage. "I do not believe in it," he used to say, "but I never argue against it, for there *are* no logical arguments against it." Wilson's awakening to a new social and political awareness came, I am sure, after I graduated. But to the students of my time the word "liberal" or "conservative" had no particular significance. It was enough for us that Wilson challenged our ability to think and led us to some appreciation of the place and power of ideas in the life of men.

I speak only as a single student at Princeton of over fifty years ago. For me Wilson lit a lamp which has never been put out. All my life I have remembered him as the inspiring teacher who introduced us to the kingdom of the mind, and held up before our eyes what Whitehead later called "an habitual vision of greatness."

STUDENT: ELEANOR ROOSEVELT
(1884–1962)
Humanitarian, diplomat, columnist, author and 31st First Lady of the United States.

TEACHERS: MLLE. SOUVESTRE MLLE. SAMAIA

There had been much discussion as to where I should go to school. Finally it was decided to send me to Mlle. Souvestre's school, "Allenswood," at a little place called South Fields, not far from Wimbledon Common and by the tube, which corresponds to our subway, a short distance from London.

The reason Mlle. Souvestre's school was chosen was that my father's sister, Mrs. Cowles, had gone to her school years before at Les Ruches, outside of Paris. To be sure, that had been before the Franco-Prussian War. The siege of Paris had been such an ordeal that Mlle. Souvestre had left France and moved to England.

Naturally, she was considerably older than when Auntie Bye studied under her, but at least there was a personal tie, and I think the family felt that as I was to be left alone at school when Auntie Tissie returned to the United States it would be pleasanter to feel that the head mistress had a personal interest in me.

We went to Claridge's Hotel in London, and I spent only one night there. My first impression of London was rather bewildering. There were quiet little back streets and alleyways, but the main thoroughfares were appallingly crowded with traffic. London seemed to me a most tremendous city, for you could go for hours in any direction and still apparently be in the heart of a great city.

The next day Tissie took me out to see Mlle. Souvestre, and I was left there with the promise that I would spend Christmas with her in London. I felt lost and very lonely when she drove away.

I unpacked, and found my room-mate, Marjorie Bennett, a very shy, gentle girl who was a little bit younger than I was, quite ready to show me around and tell me about rules, etc. There were a great many rules, and the first one was that all had to talk French, and if they used an English word they had to report themselves at the end of the day. A girl stood in the dining room door as we went in to supper and we told her the horrid truth, as far as we could remember it. This always seemed to me a rather ridiculous rule, as we all knew quite well we could not be accurate, but perhaps it made us remember that French was the language we were supposed to converse in.

• • •

Mlle. Souvestre, older and white-haired and obliged to take a certain amount of care of her health, never came to breakfast, but we were well watched over by Mlle. Samaia, a very tiny and dynamic woman who adored Mlle. Souvestre and waited on her hand and foot, ran all the business end of the school, and gave our Italian lessons to those of us who took Italian.

To be in Mlle. Samaia's good graces you had to show practical qualities. The girls who were singled out by her to hold positions of trust were dependable, could usually do almost anything with their hands, and had the ability to manage and lead their fellow students.

It took me a long time to get into her good graces, for I was a good deal of a dreamer and, in any case, American, which to her was an unknown quantity.

Mlle. Souvestre, on the contrary, had a very soft spot for Americans and liked them as pupils. This was not surprising, because a number of her pupils turned out to be rather outstanding women. Auntie Bye, for instance, was one of the most interesting women I have ever known.

• • •

As it was, Mlle. Souvestre and Mlle. Samaia stand out as the two most important people in this period, with Mlle. Souvestre far and away the most impressive and fascinating person.

Mlle. Souvestre was short and rather stout, and had snow-white hair. Her head was beautiful, with clear-cut, strong features, a very strong face and broad forehead. Her hair grew to a peak in front and waved back in natural waves to a twist at the back of her head. Her eyes looked through you, and she always knew more than she was told.

• • •

School life was fairly uneventful, but in the world outside great excitement reigned. I had hardly been conscious of our own Spanish War in 1898, even though I had heard a great deal about the sinking of the "Maine" and about Uncle Ted and his Rough Riders; my grandmother and her family lived so completely out of the political circles of the day and took very little interest in public affairs. Maude and Pussie, however, had friends who went to the war and we would scan the list of casualties or deaths, but on the whole this war did not bring sorrow to enough homes or last long enough to mean real privation to the people of the country. I remember the general horror when one young man who had been a prominent figure in New York society died in a Florida camp, and the joy and excitement when Uncle Ted came back and went to Albany as Governor of New York.

One read in the papers, of scandals and of battles, but it was all on a fairly small scale. This war of ours had hardly touched my daily life.

In England, however, the Boer War, which lasted from 1899 to 1902, was of a more serious nature, and the tremendous feeling in the country at large was soon reflected in the school. There was great confidence at first in rapid victory, then months of anxiety and dogged "carrying on" in the face of unexpected and successful resistance from the Boers.

There was a considerable group in England and in other countries that did not believe in the righteousness of the English cause, and Mlle. Souvestre was among this group. She was pro-Boer, and was not in the habit of hiding her feelings. She was, however, always fair, and she realized that it would be most unfair to the English girls to try to make them think as she did. With them she never discussed the rights and wrongs of the war. Victories were celebrated in the gym and holidays were allowed, but Mlle. Souvestre never took part in any of the demonstrations. She remained in her library, and there she gathered around her the Americans and the foreign girls, of which there were a great number. I remember a Russian girl, who was very attractive to me, a Dutch girl, a Swedish girl, and one or two girls from South America. These she felt at liberty to keep with her and to them she expounded her theories on the rights of the Boer or small nations in general in their own countries and their freedom. Those long talks were very interesting, and echoes of them still live in my mind when certain subjects come up for discussion today.

She told us she was an atheist, primarily because she could not comprehend a God who would think of bothering about such insignificant things as individual human beings, and doctrines of religion which preached reward for good behavior and punishment for bad she considered food for small minds. Right should be done for right's sake and not for reward or through fear of punishment, and only the weak needed religion. I often thought of what my dear, religious grandmother would have thought had she been able to listen to some of the doctrines which Mlle. Souvestre propounded. I do not know what effect it had on the others, but, as far as I was concerned, I think it did me no harm. Mlle. Souvestre shocked me into thinking, and that on the whole was very beneficial.

• • •

Mlle. Souvestre introduced me to her guests occasionally, and in this way I met many interesting people. For instance, Beatrice Chamberlain had been her pupil, and when she came out to visit, because of her American mother Mlle. Souvestre introduced me to her. Whenever I read her name or that of her father in the newspapers after that it gave me a thrill, because I had really seen and talked with her. This is one way of giving youth an interest in the "news."

• • •

Mlle. Souvestre taught me also on these journeys with her that the way to make young people responsible is to throw real responsibility on them. She was an old lady and I was sixteen. The packing and unpacking for both of us was up to me once we were on the road. I looked up trains, got the tickets, made all the detailed arrangements necessary for comfortable traveling. Though I lost some of my self-confidence and ability to look after myself in the early days of my marriage, when it was needed again, later on it came back to me more easily because of these trips with Mlle. Souvestre.

• • •

The summer was now approaching, and I knew that I must go home for good. Mlle. Souvestre had become one of the people whom I cared most for in the world, and the thought of the long separation seemed very hard to bear. I would have given a great deal to have spent another year on my education, but to my grandmother the age of eighteen was the time that you "came out," and not to "come" was unthinkable.

Luckily, when I actually left I felt quite sure that I would return before long, but I realize now that Mlle. Souvestre, knowing her infirmities, had very little hope of seeing me again. She wrote me very lovely letters, which I still cherish. They show the kind of relationship which had grown up between us, and give an idea of the very fine person who certainly exerted the greatest influence, after my father, on this period of my life.

STUDENT: FRANCIS BIDDLE

(1886–1968)

Lawyer, judge, U.S. Attorney General and author.

TEACHERS: AMORY GARDNER GEORGE SANTAYANA

Amory Gardner was an original and talented scholar—eccentric and unorthodox, just what Groton needed. He and his older brother had been brought up by his aunt, the famous Mrs. Jack Gardner, who spent her life scrimping to found, and, with the help of Bernard Berenson, build up the museum on the Fenway in Boston. The two boys, whose parents had died when they were small, were immensely rich. They were both high-strung and nervous. It is related that Amory Gardner used to get so stirred when he played bridge, which he greatly loved, that he had to get up and hold his heart to quiet his excitement; and that when he was racing his yacht, the cup defender *Mayflower*, he went below to avoid too great a strain. He read when he walked, and rode rather absent-mindedly. Groton was the love of his life, on which he lavished generosity. He built the beautiful Gothic chapel and the ''Pleasure Dome'' where on Sunday afternoons the boys trooped over to drink a sweet and sticky substance known as ''google,'' and eat sponge cake.

Now and then a distinguished stranger would visit the ''Pleasure Dome.'' Once Mr. G, as we called him, brought over Nancy Langhorne, who was then Mrs. Robert Gould Shaw of Boston, before she married Lord Astor. I had the good luck to be there when she arrived. It had been a dismal day, and the impulse to break the crushing solemnity of the boys stirred her. In a moment she was in the midst of a circle, holding her skirts high (for those days) over pretty ankles, abandoning herself to the tap-tap-tap of a "breakdown," while we clapped our hands to the flow of the rhythm, and Mr. G looked on smiling, not at all sheepishly. . . . We were thrilled, and that spark of gaiety lifted our hearts out of the long, dreary, bleak, featureless Sunday. On Sunday boys were not allowed to play any game, golf or tennis or fives, nor could they skate or coast or toboggan down Joy's Hill. They could take walks and write to their parents. Newspapers were forbidden. It was rumored that the Rector was "absolutely furious" when he heard about Nancy Shaw's performance, and that he gave Mr. G a terrific lecture.

Mr. G's eccentricities, particularly in teaching, were accounted for by his contempt for the commonplace and the average. He was convinced that it was not enough to drill boys and "learn 'em," but that they must be stirred with a glimpse of the richness and wonder of a world culture which was alien to the cramped and tepid background of the average member of the well-to-do American middle class. His methods were a continual protest against the complacent assumptions and large healthy generalities of the headmaster, whom he greatly loved and clearly understood. Mr. G was not easily shocked himself—not by novelty, or impropriety, or breaches in custom, or even by the exercise of thinking—and believed that it was good for boys to be continually shaken up in his class, because they were so seldom excited in any other. I think he would have stood on his head if he had thought it necessary to keep the boys' attention or drive in a point. He made us feel ashamed of being ignorant barbarians. We did not know our fundamentals, he insisted, like Mother Goose, or—and he liked to come back to this:

AB ab, call me a cab,
IB ib, tie on my bib,
OB ob, don't be a slob.

A lot of Mr. G's beliefs about education must have been heresy to the Old Man, as we sometimes called the Rector. Mr. G believed in the broadest possible base of culture, and put the humanities behind and before any specialization. Teachers of physics and chemistry should know a good deal about Homer, Beethoven, Dante, and Velasquez, just as those who instructed in the classics and history should have some familiarity with business, trigonometry, "how long it takes a hen's egg to hatch . . . . " Even at school, he wrote, a boy devours ideas "because they are new and totally different from the point of view here," so that masters should not shut their eyes to facts, or forget that in vocation life, if it is not broader, always seems broader. . . .

He shared the Rector's concern over the detail of tradition—pancakes on Shrove Tuesday and hot cross buns on Good Friday—because Groton was the resultant of a thousand little manners and customs and traditions. But the flavor, he insisted, of the whole thing, its personality, could not be put into words. Mr. Peabody was content with the black and white of alternatives. Mr. Gardner knew that life—and youth—was subtler than that.

• • •

I cannot say clearly that one course influenced me, that another did not. I know that [at Harvard] Santayana opened a new world of understanding. If Mr. Peabody had ever read him and taken the trouble to understand him, he would not have thought of him as the destroyer of faith. I am inclined to think that my experience of the lectures tended to deflect the reaction of skepticism with which Groton had left me. It was perhaps ironic but probably inevitable that a rational skeptic should have taught me the limits of reason, the value of symbols, and the reality of mysticism, even if only as a state of mind.

Santayana was a modern, but believed that "for any wide and honest imagination the supernatural must figure as an idea in the human mind." He was not a mocker. A Roman Catholic, he accepted the beauty of that Church not merely as a link with the tradition of the past, or for its aesthetic value, but because its symbols revealed mysteries which he respected, beyond the realm of rational description. He was a poet who was never able to write poetry. In his preface to his collected poems he says that his excuse for writing them was merely the human excuse which every new poet has for writing about spring.

His lectures brought his listener a felt sense of the epochs in which the poets lived, and the impulses which dominated each. For each was typical of his age, and taken together they summed up all European philosophy. Lucretius, he told us, was interested in the birth and composition of things, and his poetry is of things themselves, with their own movement and life. He has abandoned fairyland because he has discovered nature—*always infinite and at hand*—and history, and the actual passions of man, and the tribes of animals, who when the sunshine floods the serene sky feel the mighty impulse of Venus in their hearts. His materialism is not without aspiration—the freedom and the happiness of men on earth. A thousand years later Dante sees the "raptures of a perfect conformity with the will of God" as the ultimate. He is the poet of supernaturalism. And finally, when another five hundred years has gone, Goethe, representing the Teutonic races, the modern man with "too much vitality and too little maturity," talks of the driving demon of man's inmost self. This is romanticism, the Faust presents *experience in its immediacy, variety, and apparent groundlessness*. . . . Much later I remembered that Goethe had said somewhere that the young man should take care what he asks for in his youth, for in his age he shall have it.

If Santayana's style was harmonious, it had the dispassion of an observant intellect rather than any extravagance of the heart. Through [Benjamin Apthorp Gould] Fuller [Harvard philosopher], who knew him well, I saw something of him while I was an undergraduate, and this impression was confirmed. Fuller would ask two or three of us to spend a weekend at Sherborne, where we rode his hunters and talked with Santayana. Then he seemed to me remote and effeminate—he would climb through fences with some difficulty; and, first refusing a cocktail, would accept it as an afterthought, remarking that his doctor had told him he must take one now and then. Pierre La Rose said that Santayana was cat Latin—you must stroke him downward, the pleasing way, but never against the fur. He did not seem quite human. He was the embodiment of an idea without sustaining flesh. He wore a beard at the time, and never was without a walking stick, even to cross the Yard. He had written *The Sense of Beauty* and *The Life of Reason*, and was to leave Harvard four years later, before he was fifty, having put away just enough money (he believed) to live simply (as a philosopher should) in his beloved Avila—he had been born in Madrid—shaking from his feet the hated dust of Boston, never to return.

STUDENT: BENJAMIN E. MAYS

(1895–1984)

Teacher, pastor, dean, author and Morehouse College President.

TEACHERS: ELLEN WALLER
NELSON C. NIX

In later years, my wife was shocked when she first saw the Brickhouse School, for she had expected to see a real brick building. It was named the Brickhouse School after a large brick house nearby owned by a white man. It was a frame, one-room building with a wood stove in the center of the room, with boys seated on one side and girls on the other. The school ran for four months, from the first of November through February. . . .

It was a happy day for me when I entered the Brickhouse School at the age of six. I discovered on that eventful day that I knew more than any of the other children who were entering school for the first time. Susie, my oldest sister, had taught me to say the alphabet, to count to a hundred, and to read a little. Since I was the only one in the beginners' class who could do these things, I was praised and highly complimented by the surprised teacher. As we put it, she "bragged on me." The next church Sunday, the second Sunday in November, my teacher sought my parents and told them, with other people standing around, "Bennie is smart." From that moment on, I was the star of that one-room school. The experience made a tremendous impression on me, so much so that I felt I had to live up to my teacher's expectations. I became Exhibit A when visitors came around and I was called upon to recite, which I was always eager to do. I dearly loved the spelling class, where the best speller stood at the head of the class. If the boy or girl at the head of the class missed a word, the one who spelled the word correctly moved to the head of the class. I had been so impressed with myself that first day that I always strove thereafter to occupy the first place in class. I loved school so well that when the weather was bad and Mother kept me home I would weep. The student who was out of school a day had to go to the foot of the class, even though he had been standing at the head. When it did happen that I had to go to the foot for being absent, I took great delight in working my way up from the foot to the head.

I fell in love with my teacher, and I am sure I studied hard to please her as well as to learn. My first teacher was Ellen Waller, daughter of Tom Waller, the wealthy Negro farmer. Miss Waller was a high school graduate from Benedict College in Columbia, South Carolina. Very few Negroes went to college from my county. I can think of only four, before my time, who went to college and received degrees. A fair number went to high school and were graduated.

• • •

It did my soul good in 1911 to find at [South Carolina] State College [at Orangeburg] an all-Negro faculty and a Negro president. They were good teachers, holding degrees from Benedict College, Biddle University (now Johnson C. Smith), Lincoln University in Pennsylvania, Fisk University, and other colleges. President Robert Shaw Wilkinson was a graduate of Oberlin. His wife, Marian Birnie Wilkinson, was one of the finest women I have ever known. She fought racial injustice and discrimination, and the white merchants who sold to the school paid her the unusual tribute of calling her *Mrs.* Wilkinson. She had a proud carriage, and I enjoyed seeing her walk across the campus. The inspiration which I received at State College was and is of incalculable value.

All my teachers were lavish with their praise and encouragement, primarily I suppose because I studied hard and made good grades. Perhaps the one who inspired me the most was Professor Nelson C. Nix. He had an interesting way of challenging the students. When virtually the whole class was stuck on a problem in mathematics, Nix would say, "You boys can't work these problems? The white boys at the University of South Carolina are eating these problems up!'' All the forces in my environment had been designed to make me accept the fallacy that the quality of my mind was different from that of white boys; but Nix challenged us with his talk about the white boys at the University of South Carolina once too often for me. He said it one day just after he had returned a test paper to me marked ''100.'' After class I asked Professor Nix how much more than 100 would the white boys at the University of South Carolina make on the test. His patting me on the back and saying, ''Ah, my boy, they wouldn't beat *you*!'' did not quite reassure me. The very fact that Nix kept saying it made me wonder sometimes if he himself did not believe there was a difference in mentality between black and white.

Professor Nix had an A.B., and I believe a degree in theology from Benedict College. I believe he had not earned an M.A. in mathematics, but he knew high school mathematics and he was a good teacher. He had studied at least one summer at the University of Chicago, and, from the proud and proprietary way he talked about the university one could believe that he had earned a Ph.D. there. It was he who made me want to attend the University of Chicago someday. One summer, working out of Grand Central Station in New York as a Pullman porter, I was delighted to be assigned to a car to Chicago. While there, I took the streetcar and rode to the South Side to see the University of Chicago. I was impressed. I wrote a card to a classmate, Mattie Mae Fitzgerald, telling her that someday I would be a student at the University of Chicago. This prophecy came true on January 3, 1921, when I enrolled there.

STUDENT: NORMAN VINCENT PEALE

(1898–)

Clergyman and author.

TEACHER: GEORGE REEVES

When I was a young boy, I attended the old Williams Avenue school in Norwood, Ohio. The teacher of the fifth grade was professor George Reeves. In those days, teachers, even those below university rank, were referred to with a dignity regretfully absent today. Mr. Reeves is stamped indelibly upon my memory. He was a large man, weighing over 220 pounds and of good height. He had a stern look, which covered up a kind heart. He was, in a sense, a character, which seems to be a term applied to any "different" type of person. But Mr. Reeves would do things that were unforgettable. For example, occasionally he would write on the blackboard in large letters the word "CAN'T." Then, dusting the chalk off his fingers, he would look at the class and ask, "What shall I do now?"

We knew what he wanted and changed back, "Knock the 't' off the 'can't'" which he proceeded to do forthwith with a sweeping gesture. Then he would say, "Let that be a lesson to you—you can if you think you can." Following this, he would point his big forefinger and growl, "And don't you ever forget it either."

Doubtless some modern instructors would lift an eyebrow at such pedagogy. But it must have had some teaching effect, for one student at least remembers the lesson after more than half a century. I bless the name of George Reeves, for he started a trend of thought working in the mind of a shy little boy. I am sure he had an influence upon my development of the positive thinking principle. He lodged in my mind the essence of an idea: The way one thinks has a powerful effect upon one's ability to perform effectively. Of course, I did not realize it at the time, but since the incident never faded from memory it follows that it had a pervasive and continuing influence in my growing experience.

STUDENT: MARTIN LUTHER KING, SR.

(1899–1984)

Pastor and Civil Rights Leader.

TEACHER: MRS. LOW

On those farms in Georgia when I was growing up, a child was always looked upon first as a worker, then as a youngster. The large family was a rule much more than it was an exception. Many hands were needed to complete the hard, constant work that was so central to life in the country. As a result, school became a luxury around Stockbridge. I don't remember going for more than three months during any single year. An old shack had served for more years than anyone could remember as the school for Negro kids, and there was one teacher for all of us, young ones and older alike. The wife of Floyd Chapel's preacher, Mrs. Low, taught us, working as hard as one person could to bring us an education in that cold and damp little building. We had no books, no materials to write with, and no blackboard for her to use in instructing us. But I loved going, particularly when we began learning numbers, which always had a fascination for me.

Mama was very encouraging so far as my schooling was concerned. Although she'd never learned to read or write herself, there was a great sense of the value of learning within her. She was just the opposite of my father in this respect. He never saw the value of education. And he made going to school difficult for me by insisting I carry out all my chores early in the morning before I left the house, during those periods, mainly in the winter, when Mrs. Low taught her classes. So I got up early, fed chickens and pigs when we had them, carried water, got firewood. I saved my favorite chore for last—currying the mule. I loved animals, and so this part of the work was something I actually looked forward to, even with my eyes still half shut on all those chilly, dark winter mornings. It was a mule, in a roundabout way, that gave me one of my very first true tests of self-confidence at school. All the other kids teased me constantly. They'd see me currying our mule near our shed first thing every morning, and by the time I reached the school yard, the guys who knew me would be chanting stuff like, "Here come the fool, he smells just like a mule!" And I put up with it. The mule did have a way of clinging to me long after I'd left him. But one day when I'd had enough of all this chanting, when they'd even gotten some of the girls to join in, which *really* upset me, I just yelled back: "Hey, I may smell like a mule, but I sure don't think like one!"

They shut up. No more chants were heard for a good while. It was at school, small and broken down as it was, that I learned of the world beyond the farm. Mrs. Low told stories as a way of keeping our attention, and she was very good at it. My imagination just began to soar when she talked about big cities and even *bigger* countries, trains that traveled across the whole country, not just past Stockbridge on the way to Macon. I wanted to go to one of those cities and stay. I memorized all the places she talked about. And when she talked about numbers and planets, and other times in history, I learned everything by heart. I'd walk around saying the multiplication tables, doing long division as I made it up, humming the lessons, saying them over and over as I ran through the woods playing or just walking home from school. Soon all I was thinking about was leaving the country, becoming a teacher myself, or a builder, or a railroad engineer—anything that would get me away.

Sometimes I shared those dreams with Mama. She'd laugh and tell me not to run off and leave without telling her first. It was hard to think about it all, though, wanting to go away from there and find another kind of life. How could I go and leave my mother behind?

"Michael," she'd say, "if you have to leave this place, you just go right on and leave, you hear?" When the time comes, and you're grown, don't you worry about anything. Go on and live your life, son."

How could I do both, though, I'd find myself thinking. Make Mama happy, and myself, too? And then I'd think. *When you get older, these things work themselves out in some grown-up way.* I knew they'd work themselves out for me, too, just as Mama said: *When the time comes . . .*

STUDENT: REXFORD G. TUGWELL

(1891–1979)

Economist, professor, Governor of Puerto Rico, FDR's Brain Trust, public servant and author.

TEACHER: MARION GEMMEL

There were indeed some notable instructors [at Masten Park High School in New York state]. If they had had easier schedules and consequent leisure for the cultivation of their subjects, they would have become scholars as useful as those I afterward met in universities. As it was, their energies had to be devoted to imparting such elementary knowledge as would meet the Regents requirements. Still, a few students, those who showed promise, were always given special attention. The one who established between herself and me the traditional relationship of student and mentor was Marion Gemmel. I owed her the same debt I hope some students afterward owed me. Such debts are never paid. But at least I often thought of her at times when my own students seemed unreasonably demanding. When I did I was ashamed of flagging.

It was through Marion Gemmel that I first began to understand some of the norms of life, to work backward and forward along the lines of evolution, to appreciate the mutual adjustments among living plants and animals and their environment. But these were a kind of dividend. Her first concern with her students was that they should see how marvelously animals and plants were made. From this they could understand why it had happened. And she was especially meticulous in demanding that they should discover how. She used to repeat over and over again that it was the how we must know. If we knew about that, everything else would come more easily.

The lesson in this was, of course, that observation of behavior was not enough. It was all very well to watch how living things behaved, to count and classify, and to build up statistics. But unless the mechanisms were analyzed, it was impossible to be certain that the data did not conceal more than they revealed. For a student who seemed to grasp the principles she hoped would be discovered by analysis, she would take pains and find time. She did for me. I had my own microscope and table in a corner. I often worked there when I should have been doing something else.

• • •

I carried over from my biology one strongly felt analogy. There must be specialized connective and managerial tissue in the municipal organ. This was, for me, an important thought, one I came back to often in later years. That capricious and self-centered individuals are capable of producing something which would function with regularity in the general interest must be because there were those who specialized in planning, articulation, conjuncture, administration. These would be individuals too. But they would be different, much as the apparently similar cells of a body are different and, as they mature, develop into specialized members. I did not see how all this came about, but I knew it must be so. This was the *why* of my biology lesson. The *how* I had still to discover, but I knew that I wanted to discover it.

• • •

I had had a glimpse, in Miss Gemmel's biology teaching, of something to hold to. The marvelous adaptations of organic life, showing themselves finally in structure, had their counterparts in social groups. I even saw that one old difficulty was becoming less a puzzle. Darwin had been unable to explain certain phenomena of evolution except by accepting the family as the evolutional unit. Natural selection must work through groups as well as individuals. In a way I had arrived at an idea which would for me be a lasting foundation for my own thinking. There was more that I did not know than I could guess at, many gaps, many unanswered questions; but the transfer of my interest from individuals to groups was satisfactorily accomplished. The social sciences were the area of inquiry for me.

STUDENT: FULTON OURSLER

(1893–1952)

Author, editor and reporter.

TEACHER: PROFESSOR SNEIDER

It was in my new "advanced" school that I got my first taste of learning and the grave beauty of scholarship. Ever since, I have spent a lifetime trudging after knowledge.

On the first step of Latin and of German, I was taught by a man whose sarcastic voice, impish eyes and tender spirit I shall never forget. His name was Professor Sneider, and he was the greatest teacher I was ever to know. It was his job to pound new languages—German and Latin—into our unaccustomed brains, and he had his own methods of doing it. The way to the soul of any speech, he told us, was through its poems and songs: "You can learn to feel instinctively its syntax, its irregular verbs, the rhythm of its personality, the nature of its idioms, by singing and reciting its folk music. I shall repeat—*noch einmal*—write it down and memorize the theory; in this world we ought to know what we are about."

From the blackboards of those School Number 91 classrooms, we learned to sing in noble chorus the stately and somber measures of "Gaudeamus Igitur" and "Adeste Fideles" and a score of the loveliest of lieder: "Roeslein auf der Heiden," "Klaus ist in den Wald Gegangen" and, of course, "Die Lorelei." I had little more than one school year with Professor Sneider—I left before the second Christmas, in my fourteenth year, and never went back—but in that short time, he gave me the feeling that all the wonderful treasures of two languages were mine to take; that in their mysterious vistas I would be a welcome settler. He put into my hands a copy of *Robin-*

son Crusoe printed in *deutsche Buchstaben* and said to me: "Read it, translate it, then compare what you have with Defoe's original. Go through the whole thing and you will know the German language."

In that same year, Professor Sneider unrolled before us a procession of German composers. Not satisfied with teaching us about Bach, Beethoven, Mendelssohn, and Schubert—whose sad life he acted out for us, pretending to cadge a meal at a restaurant table and writing music on the back of a menu card—he rushed on to Chopin, Handel and Brahms. He would drop the third German declension to explain the anatomy of sonata, symphony and concerto, and the rare and precious ecstasies to be looked for in chamber music, and something of the intricacies of harmony and composition. Back with a guilty start he would leap to a quiz on vocabulary.

"Karl!" That was what he called me. "Tell me the meaning of *Pferd*."

I would get red and wriggle and glare prayerfully into space. With a snort, Professor Sneider would straddle a chair and hop halfway across the room.

"What am I doing," he would shriek, swinging his arm as if he had a whip and clamping his ankles as if he wore spurs.

"Riding."

"Riding what?" he howled.

"A horse!"

"*Ach*! *Wunderbar*! You know it perfectly now. A *Pferd* is a horse. Baxter Trussell! Define the word *tod*."

Baxter didn't know either. Upon which Professor Sneider would swing his golden beard from one side to another, and gasp for breath, and wave his red hands with their golden hairs, and fall to the floor, where he would lie in a frozen, unmoving attitude until one of the girls in the class began to cry.

"What am I now?"

"Dead!" cried Baxter.

Up sprang the professor like an actor ready to take a bow. "*Tod* means dead. *Donnerwetter*! Prepare better for tomorrow."

The day was not far off when I would no longer be his pupil. When, instead, as a cub reporter, I would be sent to cover the deliberations of the Board of School Commissioners, and there sit making notes while the new principal of Number 91 recommended his dismissal. Some said he was a drunkard, others said he was mad, and most of his fellow teachers were frightened of him. But I, who can never forget that I might never have heard of Publius Verginius Maro, or Quintus Horatius Flaccus, or so much more of beauty and delight, stayed after the board finished its business and spoke as a witness and a testimony for the only professor I ever was to have. (The wonder of it was that they did not turn him out; he served other boys and girls for some years afterward, and, I think, died in harness.)

That seventh year of schooling was the only time I ever enjoyed the dream of going to college. That was because Professor Sneider talked about it at least once a week—he told us we were all there in his class because we were advanced and exceptional; we were the ones who could get the most benefit out of higher education. This made the topic a lively one, and many of the boys talked of where they were to go, four years hence. Fred Eigulhardt declared there was no other college in America like Lehigh, and thrashed Leon Tarbacker who stood up for Saint John's in Annapolis.

But my dream did not last long; at home my plans were dashed with a plain dose of mathematics. We had barely enough to live on, and Mother's hopes were centered on the day when I could leave home and go to work and ease thc family burden. The sooner the better.

STUDENT: NORMAN ROCKWELL

(1894–1978)

Illustrator.

TEACHER: JULIA M. SMITH

My favorite memory of those days is of Miss Julia M. Smith, my eighth-grade teacher. She taught me what little I know about geography, arithmetic, grammar, et cetera. But I remember her mostly because she encouraged me in my drawing: every year she asked me to draw a Christmas picture on the blackboard in colored chalks; in history class I drew Revolutionary soldiers and covered wagons; in science, birds, lions, fish, elephants. That meant a lot to me; it was sort of a public recognition of my ability. I guess . . . No, I *know* she saw where I was headed and, because she was a fine teacher, helped me along. God bless her.

Forty-odd years later I received a letter from a woman who was taking care of Miss Smith (she had been married and her name was now Mrs. Ottley; but I've never been able to think of her as anyone but Miss Smith) somewhere in upstate New York. Miss Smith, the woman wrote, was going blind but every time one of my covers appeared on the *Post* she would ask her friend to describe it to her. Then she'd tell about how I used to be her pupil, how I used to draw on the blackboard at Christmastime. And she'd asked her friend to write the note to me just to see if I remembered those old times. I wrote back, asking the woman to tell Miss Smith that she had been my favorite teacher and that I remembered her very well because she'd done me so much good.

The letter and others which followed brought back my school days. I recalled how devoted and kind Miss Smith had been. Then I thought of how hard-working and underpaid schoolteachers were. And after I'd mulled all this over for a while I decided to do a *Post* cover of a schoolteacher—sort of a tribute to Miss Smith and all the other schoolteachers.

Well, I don't know how the general public liked the cover but it was very unpopular with the schoolteachers. I got all kinds of letters saying very indignantly, "We're not like *that*!" A superintendent of schools in Texas wrote that there was not one teacher in all Texas as plain-looking as the one I'd painted. I hadn't felt that way at all. I'd just wanted to portray a patient, hard-working, devoted person. I thought if I made her a beautiful girl I wouldn't get my feeling across. Even after forty-three years of painting *Post* covers I can't tell what the reaction to a cover will be.

STUDENT: MARK VAN DOREN

(1894–1972)

Poet, professor, editor, critic and author.

TEACHERS: MR. BOWDITCH ARTHUR TIETJE MEILETUS FLANINGAM STUART SHERMAN

Those school years passed as one; or so it now seems. Teachers who were undoubtedly different from one another become in my memory a composite person whom it was my perpetual desire to please. Miss Fenner, Miss Lloyd, Miss Radebaugh, Mr. Lawrence and the rest—I would walk beside my father, holding his hand perhaps, and tell him how wonderful each one of them was. He always listened, and seemed glad that I approved of them; though my adjectives could have conveyed to him little of their true characters, assuming that I knew those characters at all. To me a teacher, purely by virtue of his profession, was wonderful to begin with and could not lose distinction by anything he did or said. If I was a docile child, which is to say a child who wanted to be taught, the chief reason could have been the necessity I felt that my teachers should like me. And since among other things this meant my doing my work as well as possible, I did do it as well as possible; and so I learned. The admission sounds smug, but I must make it because it is true.

• • •

High school and university, for all of their importance to any future I might have, were then but incidents in what seemed a present that would never end. They occupied nine years of the fifteen I lived in Urbana, and during the last of those years I wrote my first book: proof, if any was required, that I had ceased to be a stammering child. Yet even so my memories of school, of home, of town, of farm run all together in one timeless, even placeless pattern, so that to separate any one set of them from the others is more difficult; it is unreal. As student then, as teacher since, I have never found that books and studies, however much I loved them, filled the world. I have loved as many things outside as in.

I do remember, though, the first day I went with Frank to the Thornburn High School, on the north side of Urbana near the Boneyard and the interurban tracks. I was twelve, I still wore short pants, and doubtless I seemed an infant to the sophomore who sat on a wooden fence and said to me: "Mark, do you think you can do the work?" I was at once convinced that I could not, so that I went on in as one doomed to humiliation. I did go in, however, as I had not done at Hope; and soon enough had lost my fears. For one thing, I began to study Latin, and through this to understand grammar and syntax better than I had before, or rather to understand them for the first time, and to think of them, as I have ever since, as beautiful things so basic to the mind that if they are not known, nothing is known. German did this for me too, though Latin was the more attractive language, with something elegant in it like the mathematical idiom I learned from Mr. Bowditch, a soft-voiced old man—at least I thought him old—who taught plane and solid geometry, and then for a climax trigonometry. Mr. Bowditch, as strict as he was gentle, conveyed to me a lively sense that mathematics is grammar and rhetoric no less than logic is language too, and a way of reporting upon the mind's adventure through the world.

These things prepared me as nothing else could have done to move among the mysteries of my own language. And here it was my good fortune to have for a teacher Arthur Tietje, a hawk-faced, not very robust man whom it was a discipline to hear talk, and who when he criticized my compositions went so directly and swiftly to every weakness in them that I could wince at the prospect of his reading me at all, though I could rejoice too when he commended a paragraph. For some reason I have never forgotten his writing on the blackboard a sentence of mine in which I had tried the trick of alliteration: "He joyously jumped across the stream." Tietje explained to the class that alliteration could be done both well and badly; in this case it had been done badly, for the result was a silly phrase; "jumped joyously" would have been a little better, but another pair of words might have been better still.

Then there was the day when Meiletus Flaningam, an old friend of the family whom my father, then a member of the school board, had brought down from Potomac to be principal of the high school (his first name had been given to Paul for a middle name, now never used), came into our English class where *Macbeth* was being read. He electrified us by talking about the whole play as if it were a single thing instead of a series of things—of scenes—which under another teacher, a well-intentioned woman who this day was ill, we had been studying for weeks as if there were little connection between them. Lete, as we privately called the principal, was of course not prepared to do what the teacher would have done; so he drew upon his knowledge of Shakespeare generally. He said that *Macbeth* was a tragedy; told us what a tragedy was; spoke of Shakespeare's other great tragedies, *Hamlet, Othello*, and *King Lear*; distinguished each one of them from *Macbeth* by describing the passion that obsessed its hero; and ended by scarcely having to talk about *Macbeth* at all, at any rate to me, because now I understood and felt the play, and somehow knew that I would never in my life encounter a greater poet than this one who understood everything about grief, jealousy, pride, and ambition. Before that day I had wondered if my father was right in bringing Lete to Urbana. Now I could have no further doubts. In forty minutes he created a world—perhaps *the* world—and I was never to forget it. This was powerful teaching; it assumed maturity in us who listened; it spoke to that maturity; and in so far as such a thing can be done to a boy of thirteen, it made me a reading man.

• • •

As for English, I began now to read by myself: Robert Louis Stevenson in prose, for example, and Wordsworth in verse. These were my first enthusiasms. I thought Stevenson a master; and as for Wordsworth, whenever I could I shut myself in a room to intone

"Tintern Abbey" aloud—very much aloud, for sometimes the family heard me, though nobody complained. Meanwhile, however, I had come under the spell of the finest teacher I was ever to know, and his subject was Shakespeare. Stuart Sherman, with whom Carl had struck up a close friendship during his last year in Urbana [at the University of Illinois], now became my idol. He had a gift which I since realized is rare among teachers: he thought while he talked. And since his mind was rich, he was always discovering new depths in his own understanding. This happened before our very eyes; we could see it in his face, which was remarkably revealing and mobile, just as we could hear it in his voice, an excellent reading voice, too, so that many of Shakespeare's dramatic effects were delivered to us without loss. But the main thing was Sherman's mind, at once a critical and a creative instrument; he gave it all to Shakespeare, and Shakespeare responded as he ever will to those who bring him their whole selves. Nor did the talk have reference to art in a precious or finical sense. Its final reference was to human life as Shakespeare had explored it: a bottomless subject, nor did Sherman seem to think he could exhaust it in the few things there was time to say. To the extent that he was aware of my presence in the class he may have thought of me merely as a neighbor boy who had stayed one night with his infant son while he and his wife went with Carl to see *Antony and Cleopatra* in a local theater. As he walked out of the door he pointed to a plate of bananas on the hall table and said to me: "Young man, when we come home I don't want to see a single one of those." Nor did he. I had an adolescent's appetite. And it was long a family joke that when Carl spoke next morning at home of my having eaten a dozen bananas in three hours, I protested angrily: "There were only eleven!" But now as many as five years had passed; and Sherman, less aware of that than I was, may not have realized how much of him I was understanding.

STUDENT: WILLIAM O. DOUGLAS

(1898–1980)

Teacher, attorney, professor, author, Associate Justice of the Supreme Court of the United States and naturalist.

TEACHERS: LOUISE DEGRAFF
SUSAN ANTHON
C. A. PALMER
LUCILLE JAMES
ELIZABETH PRYOR
LILLIAN WHEELER
ROSE M. BOENING
DR. BENJAMIN H. BROWN
DR. WILLIAM R. DAVIS

The Columbia [Washington] Grade School was across the alley from our home. I attended it for eight years. And I went through the high school located some six blocks distant on South Seventh Avenue. They were excellent schools, so far as teachers and library facilities were concerned. I have been grateful, many times since then, that they were to shape my early life.

• • •

Louise DeGraff, in my eighth grade, taught American history with emphasis on the economic system. We did not learn much about depreciation or depletion or the relation of wages to profits. But we got some glimmering of the problems of costs and profits and the historic place of business in the American scheme. Miss De-Graff neither made business a graven image to worship nor did she make us think it was suspect. Rather, she taught what business was and some basic things about its anatomy and how it had helped shape the American destiny. I was to learn about the robber barons later. Under Louise DeGraff, I made my first distillation of facts; and from her I received, I think, my first lesson in the nice distinction between the relevant and the irrelevant in any analysis.

Yakima High School, which I entered in the fall of 1912, was a joy. A. C. Davis was then principal; Susan Anthon (later a columnist for the Yakima *Daily Republic*) taught botany; C. A. Palmer, physics; Lucille James and Elizabeth Pryor, English; Lillian Wheeler, Latin; and Rose M. Boening, history. As a newspaperwoman, Susan Anthon came to represent a conventional point of view, yet she pleasantly tolerated me in later years. As a teacher, she introduced me to a new world of flora, where I discovered that many flowers, trees, and shrubs of the Pacific Northwest had marched all the way from Asia to become established here. From Mr. Palmer we learned about some of the phenomena of physics in our daily lives. From Lucille James, I acquired a love of Latin and gained such proficiency that I could converse or orate in that tongue by the time I was a senior. From her also, and from Elizabeth Pryor, I discovered great tides of history in our literature and learned something of their meaning.

Miss Pryor also taught public speaking and debate; in retrospect, I marvel at her ability to take a slightly crippled, nervous, frightened young man and give him poise and stage presence. I became such an excellent orator under her tutelage that I was selected for the school finals in my sophomore year. I had a beautiful oration and I practiced it to perfection. When the big night arrived, I walked onto the platform with the two other contestants, sure of victory. The others spoke first, increasing my confidence. But as I was being introduced, my mind went blank. I could remember only the first sentence of my speech. I stood in the spotlight, saying it over and over again, each time with more emphasis. The rest was utterly gone. I had learned to speak only from memory, not yet knowing how to extemporize. After what seemed an eternity, I gave up, tears welling to my eyes. I left the platform in utter humiliation, disappeared into the darkness of the night and did not return home for hours. By the end of another year, however, Elizabeth Pryor had not only restored my confidence but also introduced me to the rough and tumble of debate—a contest that I greatly enjoyed.

Lillian Wheeler and Rose M. Boening were also inspirations. Miss Wheeler made Latin a thing of beauty, and she tidied up our minds, making perfectionists of us. Miss Boening, in history, emphasized not *what* happened but *why* it happened. She made the question *why?* ring in our ears. America now turned on a different axis for me, as ambition, greed, self-sacrifice, lust for power, face-saving, all these and many more motives gave new dimensions to the history in our texts. Years later I was to discover Thorstein Veblen and John Dewey, Underhill Moore and Karl Llewellyn at Columbia, Robert M. Hutchins, Thurman Arnold, and Charles E. Clark at Yale, asking the same questions about law. I have always thought that Miss Boening of Yakima started my bent toward what was later dubbed "sociological jurisprudence."

Mr. Palmer, the physics teacher, coached track as well. By the time I was a junior, my slightly impaired physical condition had pretty well gone, so I went out for track. I chose the mile run as my specialty. I never came in better than third and I never quite broke five minutes. Years later Paavo Nurmi of Finland became my hero when he set the world's mark at 4:10:4. Once when I was in Helsinki, I walked the city over trying to locate him to express my admiration, but I never did meet up with him. When Roger Bannister of England broke the four-minute barrier in 1954, I was amazed. When in 1962 Peter Snell of New Zealand ran it in 3:54:4 I was dumbfounded. And when in 1967 Jim Ryun lowered the outdoor mile to 3:51:1, I gave up wondering. My own five-minute time was to me the outer limit of endurance.

• • •

I went to Whitman College, Walla Walla, Washington, in the fall of 1916 because Whitman gave me a scholarship. Most of my high school friends were going to the University of Washington in Seattle, but there was a program at the time whereby the valedictorians of certain public high schools across the state—and I was one—were offered full tuition scholarships of one hundred dollars a semester to Whitman.

• • •

At Whitman, I came under the influence of two powerful professors—Dr. Benjamin H. Brown, who taught physics and geology, and Dr. William R. Davis, who taught English. Daddy Brown, as we knew him, lived at the cosmic level, not the ideological one. Russia had gone Red in the Revolution of 1917, but Daddy Brown knew that come spring, the fields of Russia would be alive with the brilliance of wildflowers. Creeds and dogma come and go, but planetary life goes on undisturbed. He taught us man's small role in the universe, the immensity of the Glacial Age, the magnitude of the Pleistocene, and so on. He taught us to observe the winds and the rocks. Rocks became round by rolling, and that was all we needed to find old watercourses. Wind carried dust. Who loses dust? Who gets it? Solve that, and you know what lands are becoming poorer, what lands richer. That lesson was useful to me years later in North Africa.

Daddy Brown had an earth's weighing machine in the basement of Billings Hall. A select few of us were allowed to weigh the earth. The job could be done only after 2:00 A.M. or before 4:00 A.M. when there was no traffic on the street. By two o'clock the nighthawks were home, and no milk vans started on their way until four. No vibrations reached the delicate machine. Precisely how it worked I do not know, but one time, we were all able to say, "We only missed the weight of the earth by six hundred pounds."

Life after death? The loveliest image Daddy Brown could draw was illustrated by a skull he had unearthed near an apple tree. The root of the tree had grown through the eyes of the skull, sucking up into the tree the entire brain of the deceased. "How wonderful to become an apple tree!" he exclaimed. "Can you think of anything more choice for an afterlife?"

Father would have been shocked, but I shared Daddy Brown's feelings.

Dr. Davis, like Elizabeth Pryor at Yakima High, taught literature as a mirror of history, sociology, economics, politics. His counterpart at the University of Washington was Vernon Louis Parrington, whose *Main Currents in American Thought,* published after I finished Whitman, in addition to Veblen's *Absentee Ownership,* were, in my estimation, classics.

Davis was an inspirational man who had a knack of worming his way into another's life. In a few years he became indispensable to me. He was, indeed, a second father. If I had a speech to make, Davis heard me rehearse it at the crack of dawn in the outdoor college amphitheater. If I had a personal problem, he was my confessor. As a result, Davis became so powerful in my life, that when I graduated, I had almost decided to make English literature my career.

STUDENT: BRUCE CATTON

(1899–1978)

Historian and journalist.

TEACHER: GEORGE R. CATTON

The last of the logs were still drifting down the Boyne River when Father concluded that he had had enough. He had tried his hand at making money, and it had lasted just long enough to convince him that he was at a dead end—not because the money was hard to get, but because this was not in the least what he wanted to do. I did not know anything about such matters at the time, but later I understood that although he had been fairly successful—as far as anyone could be successful, selling shares in the future in a town whose inevitable decline was clearly visible even before the crest had been reached—he discovered quickly enough that he was woefully miscast, and I believe that down inside he felt mildly guilty for having so much as tried it. He carried with him, from his youth to the day of his death, the notion that man is born to a splendid debt—that he owes, to some force beyond the circling stars, the duty of spending himself to the uttermost for something beyond his own well-being. This conviction is a hard thing to live with; or perhaps it is a very easy thing, because its imperatives are at least distinct and living seems much more important than making a living; in any case, it rarely leaves a man in doubt about what he ought to do. So when the trustees of Benzonia Academy notified him that they would like to make him principal of that shaking, imperfect and probably doomed institution he accepted without hesitation. We moved back to Benzonia in the summer of 1906, and at the age of fifty Father began a new career: George R. Catton, head man of a shaky preparatory school.

Now in a sense; if he became responsible for the survival, growth and development of this enterprise the task at least lay in the general field of education, and he had been in that field nearly all of his life. Yet it was a field in which he was almost fantastically unfitted to serve, as far as formal preparation was concerned, and he probably could have got into it nowhere on earth except in the frontier society of the Michigan lumber country at that particular stage in its development. Father was an educator, but technically he was almost wholly uneducated. He had never been so much as graduated from high school, and to the end of his days he was never enrolled in a college. He was a self-taught teacher, lifting himself by his own bootstraps, somehow managing to lift others along with him. He prepared young people to go to college; which is to say that he gave them the training, the broadened outlook and the habits of study they would need if they were to do college work. More than this, he made them want to go to college, and persuaded a surprising number of them that even a student without any financial resources whatever could go on and win a college degree if he tried hard enough. (Summertimes you could work and lay by a little money; at college you could earn your board and room, by waiting on table, tending furnaces or doing other odd jobs; once convince the college authorities that you were really in earnest, and they usually would find some way to smooth the path for you.) Perhaps that was the core of his teaching—the idea that you can be whatever you want if you really want it. All that matters is your choice of goal. Be careful what goal you choose, because some day you may reach it. He fitted in perfectly at Benzonia Academy. At a time when the state as a whole was waging war on the visible surrounding wilderness this school saw itself as waging war on the wilderness of ignorance, whose tangled undergrowth was also visible out in the clearings the lumbermen were creating. The sense of mission was powerful. The forests were being destroyed for a purpose: so that men and women could have better lives after the forests had been removed. That the physical obstacles to achievement were being taken away was interesting but not particularly important. What mattered was to teach men and women that the obstacles to their mental and spiritual development could be destroyed. Man could control his future, but that control did not in the least depend on improved machinery or mechanical progress. According to Holy Writ, the kingdom of Heaven lay within; a man who hoped to enter the kingdom had to blaze a trail through his own heart, and to do that was the whole point of human existence.

It sounds quaint and faraway now. To suppose that man's real antagonist is himself rather than his environment is to turn workaday standards upside down. We know how to conquer the environment—or at least we would, if it would just stay conquered, once beaten—but how do you defeat that inner antagonist? With education, transmitted by an uneducated man through a school which had not a tenth of the resources it needed? At this distance that seems an odd way to build the road to the future. Yet the desperate and dangerous chaos of today *is* the future toward which men seventy years ago were moving. Perhaps the road actually chosen was a trifle odd too. I do not know much about Father's early life. His parents came to the United States from a farm in Yorkshire, England, a decade or more before the Civil War, and he was born on a farm near Constantine, Michigan, down near the Indiana border, in 1856. I can remember only one story about his childhood, a story so slight that it means nothing; as a nine-year-old he was working in a field one spring morning when a man on horseback came pelting along the road, reined up by the fence, and told him to run to the house at once and tell his father and mother that General Lee had surrendered the Army of Northern Virginia. Father ran in with the news, the horseman galloped off, and that is all there is to the story. Of the rest of his boyhood I know nothing whatever, except that his home was full of piety and held the improvement of a man's mind and spirit in high regard. Apparently it was sheer poverty that kept Father from getting an education. What formal training he got seems to have come from the public school system of Constantine; I believe he had a little time in high school there, but he was not able to remain and finish the course. At an early age he was out on his own, earning a living . . . by teaching school.

He knew perfectly well, of course, that a schoolteacher, even in the informal grade schools of that day, needed more education than he had been able to get, so he set to work to educate himself. It must have been a laborious process. He bought a Latin grammar, and probably copies of Caesar and Cicero as well, and taught himself Latin; aided, possibly, by some rudiments picked up during his brief stay in high school. He studied English grammar and composition, and applied himself with especial enthusiasm to the study of history. But bit by bit he ground it out, led on in part by nothing more exalted than the need to keep at least one jump ahead of the students he was teaching, but driven also by the consuming desire to broaden his mental horizons and develop his powers. In the end, he succeeded. His speech, his outlook and his habits of thought were those of an educated man. He was an extremely good teacher—by the testimony of those who studied under him—and a competent school administrator, and in the end it developed that he was ideally suited for the tasks the academy offered him. But his earnest, persuasive, repeated advice to earnest students—go on to college even if you haven't a cent in your pockets, show them that you can do the work and make them take you—must have come from the heart.

STUDENT: LOUIS ARMSTRONG

(1900–1971)

Musician, singer, composer, orchestra leader, and recording artist.

TEACHER: PETER DAVIS

New Orleans celebrates the period from Christmas through the New Year jubilantly, with torch light processions and firing off Roman candles. In those days we used to shoot off guns and pistols or anything loud so as to make as much noise as possible. Guns, of course, were not allowed officially, and we had to keep an eye on the police to see that we were not pulled in for toting one. That is precisely what happened to me, and as a matter of fact that is what taught me how to play the trumpet.

I had found that .38 pistol in the bottom of Mayann's [Mother's] old cedar trunk. Naturally she did not know that I had taken it with me that night when I went out to sing.

First I must explain how our quartet used to do its hustling so as to attract an audience. We began by walking down Rampart Street between Perdido and Gravier. The lead singer and the tenor walked together in front followed by the baritone and the bass. Singing at random we wandered through the streets until someone called to us to sing a few songs. Afterwards we would pass our hats and at the end of the night we would divvy up. Most of the time we would draw down a nice little taste. Then I would make a bee line for home and dump my share into mama's lap.

Little Mack, our lead singer, later became one of the best drummers in New Orleans. Big Nose Sidney was the bass. Redhead Happy Bolton was the baritone. Happy was also a drummer and the greatest showman of them all, as the old-timers will tell you. As for me, I was the tenor. I used to put my hand behind my ear, and move my mouth from side to side, and some beautiful tones would appear. Being young, I had a high voice and it stayed that way until I got out of the orphanage into which I was about to be thrown.

As usual we were walking down Rampart Street, just singing and minding our own business, when all of a sudden a guy on the opposite side of the street pulled out a little old six-shooter pistol and fired it off. Dy-Dy-Dy-Dy-Dy-Dy.

"Go get him, Dipper," my gang said.

Without hesitating I pulled out my stepfather's revolver from my bosom and raised my arm into the air and let her go. Mine was a better gun than the kid's and the six shots made more noise. The kid was frightened and cut out and was out of sight like a jack rabbit. We all laughed about it and started down the street again, singing as we walked along.

Further down on Rampart Street I reloaded my gun and started to shoot again up into the air, to the great thrill of my companions. I had just finished firing my last blank cartridge when a couple of strong arms came from behind me. It was cold enough that night, but I broke out into a sweat that was even colder. My companions cut out and left me, and I turned around to see a tall white detective who had been watching me fire my gun. Oh boy! I started crying and making all kinds of excuses.

"Please, mister, don't arrest me. . . . I won't do it no more. . . . Please. . . . Let me go back to mama . . . I won't do it no more."

It was no use. The man did not let me go. I was taken to the Juvenile Court, and then locked up in a cell where, sick and disheartened, I slept on a hard bed until the next morning.

I was frightened when I woke. What were they going to do to me? Where were they going to send me? I had no idea what a Waifs' Home was. How long would I have to stay there? How serious was it to fire off a pistol in the street? Oh, I had a million minds, and I could not pacify any of them. I was scared, more scared than I was the day Jack Johnson knocked out Jim Jeffries. That day I was going to get my supply of papers from Charlie, who employed a good many colored boys like myself. On Canal Street I saw a crowd of colored boys running like mad toward me.

I asked one of them what had happened.

"You better get started, black boy," he said breathlessly as he started to pull me along. "Jack Johnson has just knocked out Jim Jeffries. The white boys are sore about it and they're going to take it out on us."

He did not have to do any urging. I lit out and passed the other boys in a flash. I was a fast runner, and when the other boys reached our neighborhood I was at home looking calmly out of the window. The next day the excitement had blown over.

But to return to the cell in which they had kept me all night for celebrating with my stepfather's old .38 revolver . . . was opened about ten o'clock by a man carrying a bunch of keys.

"Louis Armstrong?" he asked.

"Yes, sir."

"This way. You are going out to the Colored Waifs' Home for Boys."

When I went out in the yard a wagon like the Black Maria at the House of Detention was waiting with two fine horses to pull it. A door with a little bitty grilled window was slammed behind me and away I went, along with several other youngsters who had been arrested for doing the same thing I had done.

The Waifs' Home was an old building which had apparently formerly been used for another purpose. It was located in the country opposite a great big dairy farm where hundreds of cows, bulls, calves and a few horses were standing. Some were eating, and some prancing around like they wanted to tell somebody, anybody, how good they felt. The average square would automatically say those animals were all loco, to go running like that, but for me they wanted to express themselves as being very happy, gay, and contented.

When I got out of the wagon with the other boys the first thing I noticed was several large trees standing before the building. A very lovely odor was swinging across my nostrils.

"What flowers are those that smell so good?" I asked.

"Honeysuckles," was the answer.

I fell in love with them, and I'm ready to get a whiff of them any time.

The inmates were having their lunch. We walked down a long corridor leading to the mess hall where a long line of boys was seated eating white beans without rice out of tin plates. They gave me a rooky greeting saying, "Welcome, newcomer. Welcome to your new home.'' I was too depressed to answer. When I sat down at the end of the table I saw a plate full of beans being passed in my direction. In times that I didn't have a care in the world I would have annihilated those beans. But this time I only pushed them away. I did the same thing for several days. The keepers, Mr. and Mrs. Jones and Mr. Alexander and Mr. Peter Davis, saw me refuse these meals, but they did not say anything about it. On the fourth day I was so hungry I was first at the table. Mr. Jones and his colleagues gave me a big laugh. I replied with a sheepish grin. I did not share their sense of humor; it did not blend with mine.

The keepers were all colored. Mr. Jones, a young man who had recently served in the cavalry, drilled us every morning in the court in front of the Waifs' Home, and we were taught the manual of arms with wooden guns.

Mr. Alexander taught the boys how to do carpentry, how to garden and how to build camp fires. Mr. Peter Davis taught music and gave vocational training. Each boy had the right to choose the vocation which interested him.

Quite naturally, I would make a bee line to Mr. Davis and his music. Music has been in my blood from the day I was born. Unluckily at first I did not get on very well with Mr. Davis because he did not like the neighborhood I came from. He thought that only the toughest kids came from Liberty and Perdido Streets. They were full of honky-tonks, toughs and fancy women. Furthermore, the Fisk School had a bad reputation. Mr. Davis thought since I had been raised in such bad company I must also be worthless. From the start he gave me a very hard way to go, and I kept my distance. One day I broke an unimportant rule, and he gave me fifteen hard lashes on the hand. After that I was really scared of him for a long time.

Our life was regulated by bugle calls. A kid blew a bugle for us to get up, and to go to bed and to come to meals. The last call was the favorite with us all. Whether they were cutting trees a mile away or building a fire under a great kettle in the yard to scald our dirty clothes, the boys would hot foot it back to the Home when they heard the mess call. I envied the bugler because he had more chances to use his instrument than anyone else.

When the orchestra practiced with Mr. Davis, who was a good teacher, I listened very carefully, but I did not dare to go near the band though I wanted to in the worst way. I was afraid Mr. Davis would bawl me out or give me a few more lashes. He made me feel he hated the ground I walked on, so I would sit in a corner and listen, enjoying myself immensely.

The little brass band was very good, and Mr. Davis made the boys play a little of every kind of music. I had never tried to play the cornet, but while listening to the band every day I remembered Joe Oliver, Bolden and Bunk Johnson. And I had an awful urge to learn the cornet. But Mr. Davis hated me. Furthermore I did not know how long they were going to keep me at the Home. The judge had condemned me for an indefinite period which meant that I would have to stay there until he set me free or until some important white person vouched for me and for my mother and father. That was my only chance of getting out of the Waifs' Home fast. So I had plenty of time to listen to the band and wish I could learn to play the cornet.

Finally, through Mr. Jones, I got a chance to sing in the school. My first teacher was Miss Spriggins. Then I was sent to Mrs. Vigne, who taught the higher grades.

As the days rolled by, Mr. Davis commenced to lighten up on his hatred of me. Occasionally I would catch his eye meeting with mine. I would turn away, but he would catch them again and give me a slight smile of approval which would make me feel good inside. From then on whenever Mr. Davis spoke to me or smiled I was happy. Gee, what a feeling—that coming from him! I was beginning to adapt myself to the place, and since I had to stay there for a long time I thought I might as well adjust myself. I did.

Six months went by. We were having supper of black molasses and a big hunk of bread which after all that time seemed just as good as a home cooked chicken dinner. Just as we were about to get up from the table Mr. Davis slowly came over and stopped by me.

"Louis Armstrong," he said, "how would you like to join our brass band?"

I was so speechless and so surprised I just could not answer him right away. To make sure I had understood him he repeated his question.

"Louis Armstrong, I asked if you would like to join *our* brass band."

"I certainly would, Mr. Davis. I certainly would," I stammered.

He patted me on the back and said:

"Wash up and come to rehearsal."

While I was washing I could not think of anything but of my good luck in finally getting a chance to play the cornet. I got soap in my eyes but didn't pay any attention to it. I thought of what the gang would say when they saw me pass through the neighborhood blowing a cornet. I already pictured myself playing with all the power and endurance of a Bunk, Joe or Bolden. When I was washed I rushed to rehearsal.

"Here I am, Mr. Davis."

To my surprise he handed me a tambourine, the little thing you tap with your fingers like a miniature drum. So that was the end of my beautiful dream! But I did not say a word. Taking the tambourine, I started to whip it in rhythm with the band. Mr. Davis was so impressed he immediately changed me to the drums. He must have sensed that I had the beat he was looking for.

They were playing *At the Animal's Ball,* a tune that was very popular in those days and which had a break right in the channel. When the break came I made it a real good one and a fly one at that. All the boys yelled "Hooray for Louis Armstrong." Mr. Davis nodded with approval which was all I needed. His approval was all important for any boy who wanted a musical career.

"You are very good, Louis," he said. "But I need an alto player. How about trying your luck?"

"Anything you like, Mr. Davis," I answered with all the confidence in the world.

He handed me an alto. I had been singing for a number of years and my instinct told me that an alto takes a part in a band same as a baritone or tenor in a quartet. I played my part on the alto very well.

• • •

As time went on I commenced being the most popular boy in the Home. Seeing how much Mr. Davis liked me and the amount of time he gave me, the boys began to warm up to me and take me into their confidence.

One day the young bugler's mother and father, who had gotten his release, came to take him home. The minute he left Mr. Davis gave me his place. I took up the bugle at once and began to shine it up. The other bugler had never shined the instrument and the brass was dirty and green. The kids gave me a big hand when they saw the gleaming bright instrument instead of the old filthy green one.

I felt real proud of my position as bugler. I would stand very erect as I would put the bugle nonchalantly to my lips and blow real mellow tones. The whole place seemed to change. Satisfied with my tone Mr. Davis gave me a cornet and taught me how to play *Home, Sweet Home*. Then I was in seventh heaven. Unless I was dreaming, my ambition had been realized.

Every day I practiced faithfully on the lesson Mr. Davis gave me. I became so good on the cornet that one day Mr. Davis said to me:

"Louis, I am going to make you leader of the band."

I jumped straight into the air, with Mr. Davis watching me, and ran to the mess room to tell the boys the good news. They all rejoiced with me. Now at last I was not only a musician but a band leader! Now I would get a chance to go out in the streets and see Mayann and the gang that hung around Liberty and Perdido Streets. The band often got a chance to play at a private picnic or join one of the frequent parades through the streets of New Orleans covering all parts of the city, Uptown, Back o' Town, Front o' Town, Downtown. The band was even sent to play in the West End and Spanish Fort, our popular summer resorts, and also at Milenburg and Little Woods.

The band's uniform consisted of long white pants turned up to look like knickers, black easy-walkers, or sneakers as they are now called, thin blue gabardine coats, black stockings and caps with black and white bands which looked very good on the young musicians. To stand out as the leader of the band I wore cream colored pants, brown stockings, brown easy-walkers and a cream colored cap.

In those days some of the social clubs paraded all day long. When the big bands consisting of old-timers complained about such a tiresome job, the club members called on us.

"Those boys," they said, "will march all day long and won't squawk one bit."

They were right. We were so glad to get a chance to walk in the street that we did not care how long we paraded or how far. The day we were engaged by the Merry-Go-Round Social Club we walked all the way to Carrolton, a distance of about twenty-five miles. Playing like mad, we loved every foot of the trip.

The first day we paraded through my old neighborhood everybody was gathered on the sidewalks to see us pass. All the whores, pimps, gamblers, thieves and beggars were waiting for the band because they knew that Dipper, Mayann's son, would be in it. But they had never dreamed that I would be playing the cornet, blowing it as good as I did. They ran to wake mama, who was sleeping after a night job, so she could see me go by. Then they asked Mr. Davis if they could give me some money. He nodded his head with approval, not thinking that the money would amount to very much. But he did not know that sporting crowd. Those sports gave me so much that I had to borrow the hats of several boys to hold it all. I took in enough to buy new uniforms, and new instruments for everybody in the band. The instruments we had been using were old and badly battered.

This increased my popularity at the Home, and Mr. Davis gave me permission to go to town by myself to visit Mayann. He and Mr. and Mrs. Jones probably felt that this was the best way to show their gratitude.

• • •

The Waifs' Home was surely a very clean place, and we did all the work ourselves. That's where I learned how to scrub floors, wash and iron, cook, make up beds, do a little of everything around the house. The first thing we did to a newcomer was to make him take a good shower, and his head and body were carefully examined to see that he did not bring any vermin into the Home. Every day we had to line up for inspection.

Anyone whose clothes were not in proper condition was pulled out of line and made to fix them himself. Once a week we were given a physic, when we lined up in the morning, and very few boys were sick. The place was more like a health center or a boarding school than a boys' jail. We played all kinds of sports, and we turned out some mighty fine baseball players, swimmers and musicians. All in all I am proud of the days I spent at the Colored Waifs' Home for Boys.

STUDENT: AARON COPLAND
(1900–)
Composer.

TEACHERS: RUBIN GOLDMARK
NADIA BOULANGER

As near as I can calculate, it must have been during the winter of 1915-16 when I was just fifteen that I came to the daring decision to spend my life as a musician. It was so startling an idea that I dared not share it with anyone. By this time my brother Ralph was at Columbia University, studying to become a lawyer even though he was not at all of the right temperament to be a successful one. My other brother Leon followed Pa into the store. But a musician? Music is so uncertain, so few reach the top, and how does one support a family on so shaky a basis? And where did you get such an idea anyway? I asked myself all these things if only because I realized I would hear them from my father sooner or later. But deep down I knew that reasonableness had nothing to do with it. The urge toward spending a life in music was irresistible.

• • •

In 1916 I was still lacking a finished composition. I sent for a mail-order harmony course, but when I could not complete a *Capriccio* for violin and piano in 1916, I realized that in order to develop I needed a real teacher of harmony and counterpoint. Once again, my parents were good enough to agree to pay for lessons if I found the teacher. Not knowing any harmony teachers myself, I naturally asked

Mr. Wolfsohn if he could recommend someone. He did—Rubin Goldmark, whose studio was at 140 West 87th Street in Manhattan. I telephoned for an appointment and at the agreed time approached the brownstone house with a certain trepidation. As I mounted the outdoor steps I noticed a sign in the first-floor window that read: Dr. Goldmark. That's reassuring, I thought to myself; if he earned a doctorate in music, he *must* be good. The maid who answered the doorbell ushered me into an anteroom and said that Dr. Goldmark would see me shortly. I waited as patiently as I could—so much depended on this visit. After what seemed like a long time, the double doors finally opened and a portly gentlemen motioned me to enter. When we were seated he said, "Well, what's the matter with you?" "Nothing," I replied. "I just want to study harmony." "In that case," he said, "you want to see my brother Rubin on the third floor."

Rubin Goldmark, as it turned out, proved to be an excellent teacher in the fundamentals of musical composition. He was born in New York and came from a musical family—his uncle, Karl Goldmark, was the famous Austro-Hungarian composer of opera in mid-nineteenth-century Vienna. Rubin Goldmark had studied composition at the Vienna Conservatory, and later in New York with Dvořák. The lessons he gave were clearly presented and stayed close to the subject under discussion. He used Richter's *Manual of Harmony* and *Modern Harmony in Its Theory and Practice* by Foote and Spalding. Goldmark had a dry wit, and had earned a well-deserved reputation as an after-dinner speaker at musical gatherings. If a student made a real boner, he was invited by Goldmark, with a twinkle in his eye, to become a member of his "Schlemiel" Club. I studied with him for four years, from the winter of 1917 to the spring of 1921. The one drawback—a serious one from my standpoint—was that he had little if any sympathy for the advanced musical idioms of the day, and frankly admitted the fact. I remember seeing on his piano in 1921 a copy of Charles Ives' extraordinary *"Concord" Sonata*. I immediately asked if I could borrow the music, but Goldmark said, "You stay away from it. I don't want you to be contaminated by stuff like that." I didn't see the piece again, actually, until ten years had gone by. Moreover, I never remember his discussing the subject of nationalism or folklorism, and he certainly never suggested them to me as possible influences. Other talented musicians, George Gershwin, Leopold Godowsky II, and Frederick Jacobi studied with Goldmark during my time with him, but I had little contact with them. I don't believe I met Gershwin then, and I saw Jacobi and Godowsky only a few times. I suffered from a sense of musical isolation during those years. Nevertheless, I have always been grateful to Goldmark for the solid basic training he was able to impart, and which accounted, I believe, for the high regard in which he was held. When the Juilliard School of Music was founded in 1924, he was named head of the Department of Composition.

After my initial winter of study we both agreed that I might do well to find a new piano teacher. My own idea was that I had absorbed about as much as I could from Mr. Wolfsohn. Goldmark advised a New York pianist named Victor Wittgenstein. I spent two winters as his student, hoping to gain some insight into the performance of a more contemporary piano repertoire, without any memorable results. Wittgenstein considered me to be something of a musical radical, and in that sense, perhaps, too much for him to handle. In any event, I moved on from Wittgenstein to a well-known pedagogue, Clarence Adler, and remained with him from the winter of 1919 to the spring of 1921. Mr. Adler was a cultivated and sensitive musician with broad tastes, known for the beautiful tone he drew from the instrument. From time to time his pupils gathered at his studio to perform for their friends and for one another. At one such occasion, I played the Ravel *Sonatine*. The piece was considered so unconventional as to need explanatory remarks from me. It was my first talk about a musical "modernist." Without being aware of it, I was embarking here for the first time on the role of musical commentator, which has afforded me pleasure and income ever since.

• • •

I had read in the magazine *Musical America* of a plan by the French government to establish a summer school for American musicians in the Palace of Fontainebleau, a short distance from Paris. This was said to be a gesture of appreciation to America for its friendship during World War I. I was in such a rush to enroll that I was the first student to sign up and be accepted. Actually, I was one out of nine awarded scholarships. My parents were less than enthusiastic, but it was known that any well-educated musician had to have the European experience.

• • •

Walter Damrosch was the American founder of the school at Fontainebleau. The director in France was Francis Casadesus (the uncle of Robert and Jules, who was then about my age and who became my friend during that summer). Saint-Saëns held the honorary position of general director. In later years, Fontainebleau attracted some very fine students, among them pianists Beveridge Webster, who enrolled as a teenager in 1922, and John Kirkpatrick, who was there for several summers in the twenties. But the student body that first summer of 1921 at Fontainebleau was not my dream of what a student body might be. The degree of scholarly interest was rather mild, I would say. The Americans were there partly because the school was in France, and to some, it was a pleasant way of spending a vacation in a foreign land. But after all, I also went there because I was concerned about going to France all alone, not knowing a living soul. Most of the ninety-one students like myself had never been to France, and we thought of it as an easy way of making contact with French culture, especially musical culture. But the students were friendly and called me "George" because of the fame of the pianist and Debussy specialist George Copeland. It was, as Duchamp had warned, a rather conventional school, except for the presence there of Nadia Boulanger.

• • •

Djina Ostrowska was older than the rest of us, and had come to study with the French harp virtuoso, Marcel Grandjany, who was a member of the faculty at the Paris Conservatoire. (In the thirties Ostrowska became second harpist with the New York Philharmonic, the only woman in the orchestra at that time.) It was she who first began talking to me about Nadia Boulanger, enthusing about a harmony teacher at the school. I had several years of harmony, so, of course, I wasn't interested in further harmonic studies. It was old stuff to me. I had worked on harmony, counterpoint, and composition with Rubin Goldmark for four years. It's perfectly possible that I might never have had any contact with Nadia Boulanger at the Fontainebleau school if it were not for the enthusiasm of Ostrowska, urging me to visit Mademoiselle's harmony class. "Just go and see the way she does it.'' I said to her, ''I've had three years of harmony. I'm not interested in harmony classes.'' But she repeatedly urged, ''Just go and see the way she does it.'' So I allowed myself to be persuaded.

I no longer recall what Mademoiselle Boulanger was doing that day, harmonically speaking, that was so striking, although I remember that the subject was *Boris Godunov.* Her sense of involvement in the whole subject of harmony made it more lively than I ever thought it could be. She created a kind of excitement about the subject, emphasizing how it was, after all, the fundamental basis of our music, when one really thought about it. I suspected that first day that I had found my composition teacher. Later in the summer, I was rather surprised and flattered when Mademoiselle invited me with a group of her students to come to the other side of Paris for tea at her summer home in Gargenville. It felt like special attention. So I went, and that day I made the decision to study with her after returning to Paris in the fall.

• • •

The time had come to continue my studies. On 26 October I went to 36 rue Ballu to talk to Nadia Boulanger about composition lessons. As the small elevator lifted me to her fourth-floor apartment, I began to have second thoughts. I knew of no other American who had ever studied advanced composition with her. In fact, I had never heard of any composer who had studied with a woman. History, for some unexplained reasons, had not yet produced a great woman composer. How was this going to sound to the folks back home? Standing alone in Mademoiselle Boulanger's imposing presence—the long dark skirt, pince-nez glasses—I was conscious of the stark differences between us: a gawky twenty-year old from Brooklyn and the self-assured ''older woman'' who regularly dined with the intellectual Parisian heroes. She glanced at the sonata written for Goldmark and then asked to hear one of my other compositions. I played a short piece rooted in the jazz idiom, so modern that Goldmark earlier had confessed he didn't know what to say about it. Mademoiselle, as all her students called her, simply said, ''Yes. Come. We will start tomorrow.''

So began the decisive musical experience of my life, for Nadia Boulanger turned out to be one of the great music teachers of her time. I wrote home: "Now be prepared for a surprise. My teacher is not as you suppose—a man, but a woman of about 40 [she was actually 34], one of the best known musicians in France, a teacher of harmony at the Paris Conservatoire. She understands the kind of modern music I like to write, so that she was the teacher I was looking for. It has been all arranged and I have a lesson on Saturday morning of each week. . . . " To soften the surprise, I added: " . . . she charges only 60 frcs. (about $4.20) a lesson, which compared with the $6.00 I paid Goldmark is not so expensive. . . . "

Two other Americans found Mademoiselle at about the same time—Melville Smith and Virgil Thomson. They came to Boulanger for organ lessons, and Virgil for counterpoint as well. I believe that I was the first to study advanced composition with her. Many years later, Virgil wrote that every town in the United States could boast of two things: a five-and-ten-cent store and a Boulanger student. As it turned out, he was not far from the truth. Over the years, Mademoiselle taught a host of gifted young men and women, composers and conductors of contemporary music, teachers, writers, and performers. Twentieth-century music was nurtured in her old-fashioned salon. "The composition of music cannot be taught," she used to say—then went ahead and taught it anyway. She knew everything about music—what came before Bach, Stravinsky's latest works, what came after Stravinsky, and everything in between. Technical skills—counterpoint, orchestration, sight-reading—were in the range of her work day. She was profoundly committed to music. In her eyes, one *had* to be wholly committed. Technical mastery was to be rigorously pursued and absorbed, and essentials implanted early. There wasn't anything she couldn't do in a technical sense—read all the various music clefs with ease, play orchestral scores at the piano—all the things that are desirable for a young musician to know, she was able to do easily. She knew that unerring musicianship had to become a reflex so that the mind could be free for the art of composition. "To study music, we must forget them." And then she might quote Stravinsky, "If everything would be permitted to me, I would feel lost in this abyss of freedom."

No one ever came to a Boulanger class late more than once; her disapproval could be annihilating. Nor was her praise lavishly given. When Mademoiselle called something good, it was a red-letter day. She never missed student concerts and could be seen applauding with the rest of the audience, but the next day she would enumerate every flaw in the performance. She could look at a score and "hear" the music in her head, understanding at once what the composer was attempting. Mademoiselle could always find the weak spot in a piece you suspected was weak, but had hoped she would not notice. She could also tell you *why* it was weak. Her critical facility was unerring. Known to be difficult with those she considered untalented, she felt it her duty to be brutally honest and uncompromising. There must have been some unhappy scenes in that studio at times! I must say that I never witnessed that side of Boulanger's nature, although I do recall having to read torturously through Mahler orchestra scores at the piano with Mademoiselle insisting I go on to the end without stopping, no matter how slowly; this was a routine requirement of her score-reading classes.

But it was wonderful for me to find a teacher with such openness of mind, while at the same time she held firm ideas of right and wrong in musical matters. The confidence she had in my talents and her belief in me were at the very least flattering and more—they were crucial to my development at this time of my career. Mademoiselle had the sensitivity of the finest musician and the matchless gift of conveying her understanding with such enthusiasm that it made me try harder, which was all she really wanted. Having divined the depth of talent with which each of her students was endowed, she simply proposed to develop it to the full. She had an unusual method of rating her students; the poorest ones were taught on Monday. On each successive day in the week the quality improved, so that by Saturday she was teaching her best students. Then, in each category, she put the poorest students earliest each day, so everyone knew that those who came late on Saturday were Mademoiselle's favorites. I do not know exactly how she taught others; some must have sat at the organ that dominated the far end of the spacious living room of that legendary apartment. For my lessons, we both sat at one of the grand pianos, and at her command, I would prop my most recent composition on the music stand and play it for her. She did not lecture, but she would ask, over and over, "What do you *hear*?" And constantly searching my own heart and mind, I would play on, ending the hour exhausted, exhilarated.

It might not seem so at first, but perhaps it was an advantage that Nadia Boulanger was not herself a regularly practicing composer. Teaching came first for her; it was not something she *had* to do in order to free herself for something else. To what extent Mademoiselle had serious ambitions as a composer has never been entirely established. Born 16 September 1887 as Nadia Juliette Boulanger, she came from a musical milieu. Her father, Ernest Boulanger, was a composer and singing teacher at the Paris Conservatoire, and her mother, formerly the Princess Mychetsky, had been his pupil. Nadia had a few short pieces published and had aided pianist Raoul Pugno in the orchestration of an opera. Mainly she was credited with the training of her gifted younger sister, Lili, who won the first Prix de Rome ever accorded a woman composer. Lili fell ill and died at the age of twenty-four in 1918, and Nadia mourned her the rest of her life. She told me that her dedication to teaching was in Lili's memory and therefore a sacred trust.

Mademoiselle was a very devout Catholic. Her students would sometimes joke that if you wrote a work with religious words for her, you were made. But Nadia considered personal beliefs a private matter. In all the time I knew her, I never recall any remark or discussion about religion. A biographer has accused Boulanger of anti-Semitism, and then to cover any conflicting opinion, such as my own, the writer claimed: "Her self-control was so remarkable that apparently none of her Jewish students ever noticed any tinge of anti-Semitism in her behavior." Nadia's strength and self-control were indeed admirable, but being without family, she relied on her friends in times of personal need and support. She and I became close friends, and there were other Jewish students who were Nadia's friends. It is impossible that one of us would not have noticed anti-Semitism in her behavior. Especially during the war years we were very much aware of such things. I feel certain that anti-Semitism was not part of Nadia Boulanger's personality. I also find puzzling the descriptions of Nadia as masculine and dour. I must assume that they come from persons who saw her only in later years. As a young woman, she gave off a kind of reserved warmth, and there was an old-fashioned womanliness about her that was charming. She wore low-heeled, "sensible" shoes, long black skirts, and glasses, but these seemed to contrast pleasantly with her bright intelligence and lively temperament. In later years, as she became smaller and thinner, Nadia was quasi-nunlike in her appearance. Her voice was distinctive—it was very low and remained extraordinary resonant throughout her long life.

It soon became clear that the teaching aspect of our relationship was not the only valuable thing for me. One must not forget that

Mademoiselle's intelligence went beyond the subject of music. She was a superior person, knowledgeable about literature and other arts. Altogether, you had the warmth of her personality, the extensive musical knowledge, and a first-class intellect. The feeling in her Paris studio was of being at the center of what was going on in the artistic life of Paris. You weren't merely studying an art that happened in the past. It was all alive, and being created around you. It was not at all unusual to find the latest score of Stravinsky on her piano, still in manuscript, or those of Albert Roussel, Milhaud, or Honegger. I discovered Mahler through Mademoiselle. How she got on to him I don't know, but she had the score for *Das Lied von der Erde* in 1922, and we pored over it together—especially the orchestration. On Wednesday afternoons she held class meetings for her students, *dechiffrage* classes, where new works were read at the piano by some bright student. They would be discussed and enthused about, or dismissed. At other times we sang Monteverdi and Gesualdo madrigals, which were virtually unperformed at that time. Also, the latest literary and artistic works were examined: Kafka, Mann, Gide, Pound. Those Wednesday afternoons became an institution. After two hours or more of music, tea and cakes were served. The musical greats came to Mademoiselle's Wednesday teas—pianists, singers, and composers—as well as students and journalists. I met Stravinsky there, Milhaud, Poulenc, and Roussel. I saw Ravel and Villa-Lobos, and on one occasion I shook hands with Saint-Saëns. He played the piano and he played well, though he was in his eighties. I came to know Nadia's French students: Jean Françaix, Annette Dieudonné, and Marcelle de Manziarly. Nadia's mother always presided over the tea table, her hand shaking, but never spilling a drop. I never heard Nadia boast about her mother being of the aristocracy as has been stated in some writing about her. Madame was an ebullient type who seemed to take pleasure in shocking visitors with her outspoken language. She was very much in evidence and at times younger in behavior that her daughter. Nadia was quite proper, while her mother was rather Rabelaisian at times; their roles often seemed oddly reversed to me.

When I first knew Nadia, she was already teaching harmony at the Paris Conservatoire (later she became professor of composition); she also taught organ and counterpoint at the Ecole Normale de Musique, and in summers she drove twice a week from her home in Gargenville to teach at Fontainebleau. She was second organist at the Church of the Madeleine and served on several important boards, among them the score-reading and program committees for the Société Musique de Indépendants (SMI), which sponsored contests of contemporary music for little-known and unpublished composers. It was not long after our lessons began that Mademoiselle suggested a performance of my music at a December SMI concert. My songs, "Pastorale" and "Old Poem," were sung by the American tenor Charles Hubbard with Boulanger at the piano. That was my first experience of hearing my music performed by others while I sat in the audience. The concert was favorably reviewed the next day in the Paris *Herald.* Later that season, on 10 January 1922, Hubbard performed the songs again in a recital at the Salle des Agriculteurs.

I can still remember the eagerness of Nadia's curiosity concerning my rhythms in these early works, particularly the jazz-derived ones. Before long we were exploring polyrhythmic devices together—their difficulty of execution intrigued her. Mademoiselle was confident that I could write in larger forms. Within a short time she was able to extract from a composer of two-page songs and three-page piano pieces a full-sized ballet lasting over thirty minutes. At the period when I was her pupil, Boulanger had one all-embracing principle, namely, the desirability of aiming first and foremost at the creation of what she called "la grande ligne" in music. Much was included in that phrase: the sense of forward motion, of flow and continuity in the musical discourse; the feeling for inevitability, for the creating of an entire piece that could be thought of as a functioning entity. Boulanger had an acute sense of contrast and balance. Her teaching, I suppose, was French in that she stressed clarity of conception, textures, and elegance in proportion. Much has happened in music since those years, and perhaps Boulanger's theories seem outdated; but in the early twenties her musical ideas and her confidence in my ability to apply them meant a great deal as a composer.

It must have been cause for profound satisfaction for Nadia that she guided the musical destiny of so many of this country's fine composers: in France, Marcelle de Manziarly, Jean Françaix, and Igor Markevitch; in England, Lennox Berkeley: in America, Walter Piston, Roy Harris, Marc Blitzstein, David Diamond, Elliott Carter, Irving Fine, Harold Shapero, Louise Talma, Arthur Berger, Easley Blackwood, and others, many of whom came to Nadia through my recommendation. We were called the "Boulangerie." I have lost track, if I ever knew, how that got started, but Nadia used the term herself in a letter to me as early as 1925. Honors and awards were bestowed on Nadia Boulanger during her lifetime, but we have no reward in this country commensurate with her contribution to our musical development. I am certain that she had the reward she most coveted—the deep affection and respect of her many pupils. Even those who were critical of her had respect for her profound musical knowledge and devotion to her art and to her students. She wanted them to do well, not out of vanity for herself, but out of the depth of her caring for them. Of course, Boulanger's insistence on discipline and reliance on traditional formulae was not right for everyone. Roy Harris said that except for the strongest musicians it was dangerous to study with Boulanger, because her *own* personality and talents were so strong.

My relationship with her began in 1921 as student to teacher and grew into an enduring friendship. She always helped me in every way she possibly could, and we were never out of touch with each other for long. Even now, I think of Nadia as still there in that legendary apartment on the rue Ballu where she lived for over seventy years. From my very first lessons, I sensed something special there.

Edward Tyrell Channing
"He fulfilled the aspiration attributed to Increase Mather when he wished to become president of Harvard College: to mould not merely the teaching, but the teachers. . . ."
Thomas Wentworth Higginson
Courtesy of The Harvard University Portrait Collection

Santee Sioux
"Religion was the basis of all Indian training."
Ohiyesa, a.k.a. Charles A. Eastman
Courtesy of The Newberry Library, Chicago

Samuel Davies
". . . his mode of teaching inspired me with a love of knowledge. . . ."
Benjamin Rush
Courtesy of University Archives, Princeton University

Samuel K. Hoshour
"He had dropped a light into my understanding and caught me."
Lew Wallace
Courtesy of Butler University Archives

MARK HOPKINS
" What do you think about it?'— was the key to his success as a teacher."
Bliss Perry

Courtesy of William College Archives and Special Collections

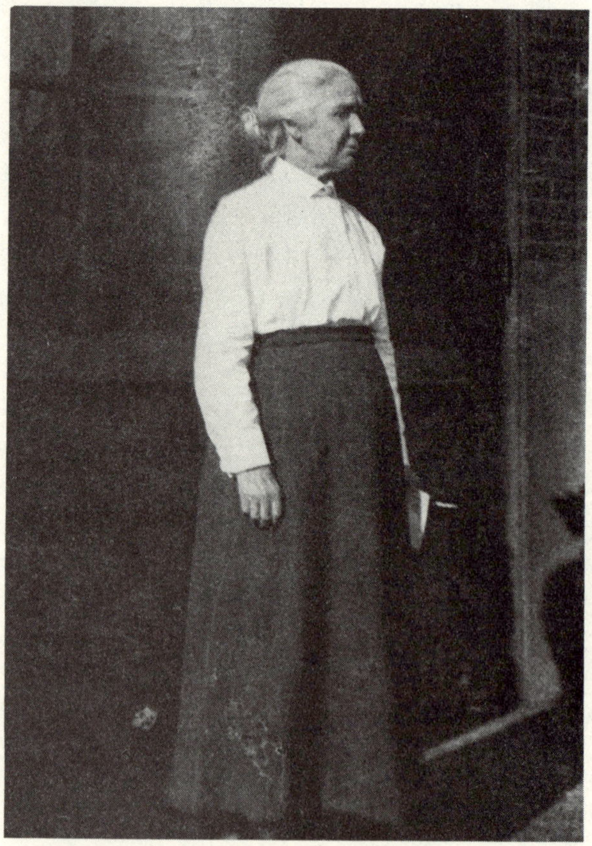

LAURA DONNAN
"She believed in a robust discussion of controversial subjects."
Claude Bowers

Courtesy of the Shortridge High School Collection; Indiana Historical Society Library

PHILIP GREEN WRIGHT
". . . there was never a time when he didn't deepen whatever of reverence I had for the human mind and the workings of a vast mysterious Universe."
Carl Sandburg
Courtesy of Knox College, Galesburg, Illinois

FRANK S. FOSDICK
"My father was a great schoolteacher . . . from the beginning we were trained for independence."
Harry Emerson Fosdick
Courtesy of *The Buffalo News*

ANNE MANSFIELD SULLIVAN
"The most important day I remember in all my life is the one on which my teacher, Anne Mansfield Sullivan, came to me."
Helen Keller
Courtesy of the Perkins School for the Blind, Watertown, Massachusetts

WOODROW WILSON
"His power lay in the precision of his mind, in the matchless lucidity of his argument, and in his passionate sincerity."
Raymond B. Fosdick

Courtesy of University Archives, Princeton University

CHARLES E. GARMAN
"We looked upon Garman as a man who walked with God."
Calvin Coolidge
Courtesy of the Amherst College Archives

AMORY GARDNER
"He read when he walked . . . He made us feel ashamed of being ignorant barbarians."
Francis Biddle
Courtesy of Groton School Archives

FRANZ BOAS
"Boas was a surprising and somewhat frightening teacher."
Margaret Mead
Courtesy Department Library Services American Museum of Natural History

NELSON C. NIX
"He had an interesting way of challenging the students."
Benjamin E. Mays
Courtesy of South Carolina State College Library

MARION GEMMEL
"She used to repeat over and over again that it was the how we must know."
Rexford G. Tugwell
Courtesy of Smith College Archives, Smith College

GIUSEPPE BOGHETTI

"Mr. Boghetti was a strict teacher. He expected you to do a lot of homework."

Marian Anderson

Courtesy The Music Collection of The New York Public Library at Lincoln Center. Astor, Lenox and Tilden Foundations Photo by: Kubey-Rembrandt

NADIA BOULANGER

"Teaching came first for her; it was not something she had *to do in order to free herself for something else."*

Aaron Copland

Courtesy Library of Congress

PETER DAVIS

"From the start he gave me a very hard way to go. . . ."

Louis Armstrong

Courtesy of the William Ransom Hogan Jazz Archive, Tulane University

FELIX FRANKFURTER

"Frankfurter was a dedicated teacher, generous with his time, sympathetic to the aspirations of youth."

Alger Hiss

Courtesy of the Harvard University Archives
Photo by: Harris and Ewing

THADDEUS C. TERRY

"He humiliated. He taunted. He ridiculed—but how he taught!"

Louis Nizer

Courtesy of Columbia University School of Law

GRACE BIDLACK
"The gods . . . had given her the power to teach young boys. . . . She spent her natural life doing just that. I never met a human being with more single-minded purpose."
MacKinlay Kantor

Courtesy of Webster City (Iowa) Community School District

MARY GRAVES
"Her influence was felt outside the school. . . . she stood for culture."
B. F. Skinner

Courtesy of The Monday Club, Susquehanna, Pennsylvania

Anna Von Helmholtz Phelan
"She took each of us with total seriousness. . . ."
Harrison E. Salisbury
Courtesy of the Star/Tribune, Minneapolis-St. Paul

Oscar W. Firkins
"Being in Firkins' classes was like being admitted to a secret society."
Harrison E. Salisbury
Courtesy University of Minnesota Archives

Bernard De Voto

"More than a writer, he was also a gifted teacher. . . ."

George W. Ball

Courtesy of the Department of Special Collections, Stanford University Libraries

Ella Toëdt

"She said, 'I believe in you, you are going to sing.' "

Burl Ives

Courtesy The Music Collection of The New York Public Library at Lincoln Center. Astor, Lenox and Tilden Foundations

LORENA DULING

"Her standards were very high and of course inflexible, her authority was total. . . ."
Eudora Welty

Courtesy of Mississippi Department of Archives and History

AGNES BOYLE O'REILLY HOCKING

"She did not tell us about poetry; she made us live its life."

May Sarton

Courtesy of Richard Hocking

ROBERT PEARSON

"The most important goal, he said, is 'the service of others.' And, he added, the most vital ingredient in a useful and satisfying career is 'imagination.'"

George McGovern

Courtesy of Mitchell (South Dakota) School District No. 17-2

EARL REED SILVERS

"For he inspired love, loyalty, obedience by the simplest of formulas: he gave love, loyalty, and obedience in return."

Earl Schenck Miers

Courtesy of Earl Reed Silvers, Jr.

JULIA COLEMAN
". . . my exposure to classical literature, art, and music was insured by this superlative teacher."
Jimmy Carter
Courtesy of the *Columbus Ledger-Enquirer*, Columbus, Georgia

HUGH CUNNINGHAM
"His idea of teaching journalism was to get you away from the classroom."
Dan Rather
Courtesy of Hugh Cunningham Photo by: Fred Ward

Ruth King

"She took me seriously, which is something that no one, not even I myself, had ever done."

Daniel K. Inouye

Courtesy of McKinley High School, Honolulu, Hawaii

Louis Warsoff

"A blind political science professor, Louis Warsoff, became interested in me. . . . He was one of the first white men whom I ever really knew and trusted."

Shirley Chisholm

Courtesy of Brooklyn College of The City University of New York

Antonia Brico

"I sensed . . . that she would drive me until I longed to live up to my own."

Judy Collins

Courtesy of *The Denver Post*

FRANCIS CARSON TIDYMAN
"For her the language held holy force, and she shuddered at any squander of it."
Ivan Doig
Courtesy of John and Thomas C. Tidyman

LUCILE SIZELOVE
"In her eyes, all were equal. Every pupil received equal treatment, equal opportunity, equal sternness, equal compassion."
John C. Board

STUDENT: ZORA NEALE HURSTON

(1901–1960)
Author.

TEACHER: DWIGHT O. W. HOLMES

How then did I get back to school? I just went. I got tired of trying to get the money to go. My clothes were practically gone. Nickeling and dimering along was not getting me anywhere. So I went to the night high school in Baltimore and that did something for my soul.

There I met the man who was to give me the key to certain things. In English, I was under Dwight O. W. Holmes. There is no more dynamic teacher anywhere under any skin. He radiates newness and nerve and says to your mind, "There is something wonderful to behold just ahead. Let's go see what it is." He is a pilgrim to the horizon. Anyway, that is the way he struck me. He made the way clear. Something about his face killed the drabness and discouragement in me. I felt that the thing could be done.

I turned in written work and answered questions like everybody else, but he took no notice of me particularly until one night in the study of English poets he read Kubla Khan. You must get him to read it for you sometime. He is not a pretty man, but he has the face of a scholar, not dry and set like, but fire flashes from his deep-set eyes. His high-bridged, but sort of bent nose over his thin-lipped mouth . . . well, the whole thing reminds you of some old Roman like Cicero, Caesar or Virgil in tan skin.

That night, he liquefied the immortal brains of Coleridge, and let the fountain flow. I do not know whether something in my attitude attracted his attention, or whether what I had done previously made him direct the stream at me. Certainly every time he lifted his eyes from the page, he looked right into my eyes. It did not make me see him particularly, but it made me see the poem. That night seemed queer, but I am so visual-minded that all the other senses induce pictures in me. Listening to Coleridge's poem for the first time, I saw all that the writer had meant for me to see with him, and infinite cosmic things besides. I was not of the work-a-day world for days after Mr. Holmes's voice had ceased.

This was my world, I said to myself, and I shall be in it, surrounded by it, if it is the last thing I do on God's green dirt-ball.

But he did something more positive than that. He stopped me after class and complimented me on my work. He did something else. He never asked me anything about myself, but he looked at me and toned his voice in such a way that I felt he knew all about me. His whole manner said, "No matter about the difficulties past and present, step on it!"

STUDENT: MARGARET MEAD
(1901–1978)
Anthropologist and author.

Teacher: FRANZ BOAS

I entered my senior year [at Barnard College] committed to psychology, but I also took a course on psychological aspects of culture given by William Fielding Ogburn, one of the first courses in which Freudian psychology was treated with respect. I had also to choose between the two most distinguished courses open to seniors—a philosophy course given by William Pepperell Montague and the course in anthropology given by Franz Boas. I chose anthropology.

I had absorbed many of the premises of anthropology at home as they lay back of what my mother had learned at Bryn Mawr under Caseby and what both my parents had learned from Veblen. I was accustomed to regard all the races of man as equal and to look at all human cultures as comparable. What was new to me was the vista that was opened up by discussions of the development of men from their earliest beginnings. The reconstructions of Stone Age men with bundles of sticks in their arms had a tremendous power to move me, as they evoked a sense of the millennia it had taken man to take the first groping steps toward civilization and of how many thousands of years the slender flakes from the cores men made into hammerstones had lain unused in paleolithic workshops.

Boas was a surprising and somewhat frightening teacher. He had a bad side and a good side of his face. On one side there was a long dueling scar from his student days in Germany—an unusual pursuit for a Jewish student—on which his eyelid drooped and teared from a recent stroke. But seen from the other side, his face showed him to be as handsome as he had been as a young man. His lectures were polished and clear. Occasionally he would look around and ask a rhetorical question which no one would venture to answer. I got into the habit of writing down an answer and nodding when it turned out to be right. At the end of the semester I and another girl whom I did not know but whose name rhymed with mine were excused from taking the examination for "helpful participation in class discussion."

Ruth Benedict was Boas' teaching assistant. She was tentative and shy and always wore the same dress. She spoke so hesitatingly that many students were put off by her manner, but Marie Bloomfield and I were increasingly fascinated. On Museum trips we would ride down and back on the Broadway street car with her. Her comments humanized Boas' formal lectures, so she would remark how like a communist state the Inca Empire had been or satirize the way the Crow Indians invested in visions. She invited Marie and me to the graduate seminar, where we were embarrassed by her shy, inarticulate report on John Dewey's *Human Nature and Conduct*. But we kept on going to the seminar. By the end of the first term I had decided to attend everything Boas taught, as Ruth Benedict said he might retire at the end of the year. I also propagandized the course so thoroughly at Barnard that it doubled in size the second semester and this made it possible for Boas to persuade the Barnard administration to appoint an instructor rather than paying Columbia for each student.

By spring I was actively considering the possibility of entering anthropology, but I was already launched on my Master's essay in psychology. Then one day, when I was at lunch with Ruth Benedict and was discussing with her whether to go into sociology, as Ogburn wanted me to do, or into psychology, as I had already planned to do, she said, "Professor Boas and I have nothing to offer but an opportunity to do work that matters." That settled it for me. Anthropology had to be done *now*. Other things could wait.

The choice of where I went to the field and what problem I would work on was not mine alone to make. The final decision rested with Boas, and he wanted me to study adolescence.

He had reached one of those watersheds that occur in the lives of statesmen-scientists who are mapping out the whole course of a discipline. He felt that sufficient work had gone into demonstrating that people borrowed from one another, that no society evolved in isolation, but was continually influenced in its development by other peoples, cultures, and other, differing, levels of technology. He decided that the time had come to tackle the set of problems that linked the development of individuals to what was distinctive in the culture in which they were reared. In the summer of 1924, when Ruth Bunzel said she wanted to go to Zuni, he suggested that she work on the role of the individual artist. Now he wanted me to work on adolescence, on the adolescent girl, to test out, on the one hand, the extent to which the troubles of adolescence, called in German *Sturm und Drang* and *Weltschmerz,* depended upon the attitudes of a particular culture and, on the other hand, the extent to which they were inherent in the adolescent stage of psychobiological development with all its discrepancies, uneven growth, and new impulses.

Scientists who are building a new discipline have to keep in mind the necessary next steps. In Boas' case, there were two additional considerations: first, the materials on which the new science depended were fast vanishing, and forever. The last primitive people were being contacted, missionized, given new tools and new ideas. Their primitive cultures would soon become changed beyond recovery. Among many American Indian groups, the last old women who spoke a language that had developed over thousands of years were already senile and babbling in their cups; the last man who had ever been on a buffalo hunt would soon die. The time to do the work was *now.* And secondly, there were few sources of funds and very few people to do the work. In 1924 there were four graduate students in anthropology at Columbia and a mere handful in other universities. He had to plan—much as if he were a general with only a handful of troops available to save a whole country—where to place each student most strategically, so that each piece of work would count and nothing would be wasted and no piece of work would have to be done over.

Boas had a keen eye for the capabilities of his students, although he confounded them by devoting his time to those he found least promising. As long as a student was doing well, he paid almost no attention to him at all. This was a loss. For good students it meant little person-to-person contact with Boas, and in some cases it led to serious errors in a student's self-estimate. With the exception of an occasional course taught by an outsider from another institution, Boas taught everything. This meant that I saw him in classes every day. But I had only a few rare interviews with him. The first was when I told him that I wanted to do graduate work in anthropology and he advised me to go to Harvard. The second took place when I chose my thesis subject and he suggested that I compare different cultures within an area: I could work on Siberia (that would mean learning Chinese and Russian), or on the Low Countries (for which I would have to have a command of French, Dutch, German, and medieval Latin), or on Polynesia (''which you could do with only French and German''). I chose Polynesia. I gave a seminar report on one section of my work, and when I turned in my dissertation I was told to add another paragraph or so to the introduction. That was all. But now there was the question of field work.

Boas was profoundly human in his concern for students who had no money to live on. There was no question of rewarding those who did good work by giving them grants or appointments. Those who had enough money he did nothing for. The few jobs that were at his disposal went to those who needed them most. But research was a different matter. He assigned problems to those who could handle them, alone or with his help. In a way it was an ideal world where

> . . . no one shall work for money and no one shall work for fame,
> But each for the joy of working, and each, in his separate star,
> Shall draw the Thing as he see It for the God of Things as They are!

It was said that in those last years of his teaching he was softening. We heard stories of how, in earlier years, he would assign a topic to be reported on within a couple of weeks in a language the student did not read. The generation of our elders—Kroeber, Lowie, Goldenweiser, Radin, Sapir, and others—had had a hard time. But he treated us rather like grandchildren, and we called him ''Papa Franz.'' Still, he was very definite about what he wanted done.

I was equally definite. I wanted to go to Polynesia, the area on which I had read so extensively. He thought it was too dangerous, and recited a sort of litany of young men who had died or been killed while they were working outside the United States. He wanted me to work among American Indians.

I wanted to study culture change, a subject that was not yet on his agenda, although it was soon to be. He wanted me to study adolescence.

Today a student would chafe against the restrictions with which we had to contend. Even then, some of my older contemporaries did chafe when Boas wanted them to work on the problems he thought came next, instead of following their own interests, like will-o'-the-wisps, wherever they led. But going to the field at all depended on his approval, for the only way to do it was to get one of the newly inaugurated graduate fellowships.

I was determined to go to Polynesia, but I was willing to compromise and study the adolescent girl, especially as the technology I had hoped to use in studying change had proved to be disappointingly inadequate. So I did what I had learned to do when I had to work things out with my father. I knew that there was one thing that mattered more to Boas than the direction taken by anthropological research. This was that he should behave like a liberal, democratic, modern man, not like a Prussian autocrat. It was enough to accuse him obliquely of exercising inappropriate authority to have him draw back. So I repeated over and over that by insisting that I work with American Indians he was preventing me from going where I wanted to work. Unable to bear the implied accusation that he was bullying me, Boas gave in. But he refused to let me go to the remote Tuamotu Islands; I must choose an island to which a ship came regularly—at least every three weeks. This was a restriction I could accept.

From that point on Boas gave me his firm support. He fully backed up my application for the National Research Council fellowship I needed in order to do the field work, and he resisted Sapir's argument that I was not strong enough to survive in the field. His concern and the grounds on which he stood by his decision, once he had made up his mind, came out clearly in the letter he wrote Ruth Benedict a few weeks before I left for the field:

> My dear Ruth:
>
> Sapir had a long talk with me about Margaret Mead. You know that I myself am not very pleased with this idea of her going to the tropics for a long stay. It seems to my mind, however, and it has seemed to my mind ever since I prevented her going to the Tuamotu, that it would be much worse to put obstacles in her way that prevented her from doing a piece of work on which she had set her heart, than to let her run a certain amount of risk. . . . Of course, I know that Margaret is high strung and emotional, but I also believe that nothing would depress her more than the inability on account of her physical makeup and her mental characteristics to do the work she wants to do. In my opinion an attempt to compel her now to give up the trip—and that is all Sapir has in mind—would be disastrous. Besides it is entirely against my point of view to interfere in such a

> radical way with the future of a person for his or her own sake,—unless there is actual disease that needs control. Of course, Sapir takes that point of view, but if he were right, then who should not be restrained.

At the same time, while I was bargaining with Boas, I told my father that Boas was trying to make me work with American Indians, already heavily contacted, instead of letting me go where things were interesting. My father, rivalrous as men often are in situations in which someone else seems to be controlling a person whom they believe they have the right—and may also have failed—to control, backed me up to the point of saying he would give me the money for a trip around the world. The trip he always wanted to take he now offered me so that I could do what I wanted to do. In the end, although he played with the idea of going to Florence to study banking practices of the Medici, he never went to Europe.

We had not then begun to discuss the ethics of manipulation of other individuals, groups, or whole societies, much less manipulation of ourselves. That same spring it appeared to me that the safest way to save the self-respect of a man who had fallen in love with me was to let him find a reason for rejecting me by letting his imagination so ready to project disappointments on others, brand me as unworthy of his love. This plan, which I hoped would protect him, gave me a sense of great virtue. Ruth Benedict did not disapprove; she only commented, "I don't know anyone for whom that would be a harder thing to do," for she knew how much I valued being understood. Later, when I seriously turned my attention to the whole question of manipulation, I began to understand that one should not use either a person's strength or his weakness against him. As I see it now, the only course that is ethically justified is an appeal to strength—not in order to throw one's opponent by means of his own strength, but on the grounds that reliance on strength will work for the good. Ruth never had this kind of trust. In many ways she expected the worst from people and steeled herself against it. In later years I had to fight for what I believed people were capable of at their best, while she acted in terms of the expected worst.

I do not advocate a philosophy of blind and naive trust. Occasionally it is clear that a person in a position of power will, if he can, block or destroy something of great value. In such circumstances it is necessary to be politic; this means, essentially, using the strengths and weaknesses of other persons or groups for one's own ends. In the same way, in wartime, a nation plays on the weaknesses—and even on the strengths—of the enemy. But there is always a price to pay later, an erosion of the capacity for trust, a kind of damage that persists after the war and makes the reestablishment of working relationships much more difficult.

But in 1925, when both Boas and my father let me have my way, I was simply gleeful. That was the year in which I wrote "Of So Great Glee," a verse in which I expressed the sense I had of being invulnerable as long as I was moving in the right direction:

She used to skip when she was small
Till all her frocks were tattered,
But Mother gently gathered up
The dishes that she shattered.
Her skipping rope got caught in trees
And shook their blossoms down,
But her step was so lighthearted
That dryads could not frown.

And when at last she tore a star
Out of the studded sky,
God only smiled at one whose glee
Could fling a rope so high.

I walked with a light step, the light step of a small, determined eleven-year old, with no weight on my shoulders, and Ruth said, "One of the reasons people criticize you is the way you walk." Years later, when Gregory Bateson read that poem, he remarked sagely that it was a mistake to confuse one's husband with God. But that poem was not about husbands, although it may have included my feeling that if I could skip as I went along, I would be able to work in a world that had not been constructed for a woman to work in. I was beginning to realize that the freedom to work as one wished was the important thing.

STUDENT: ROY WILKINS

(1901–1981)

Journalist, editor, author and civil rights leader.

TEACHERS: LULU CONVERSE
MARY E. COPLEY

When I reached the seventh grade [at Whittier Grammar School in St. Paul, Minnesota], Miss Lulu Converse, a stout woman who wore long, black dresses and button shoes, took me under her wing. Miss Converse was strict but very fair, a fine, no-nonsense sort of teacher who wore her hair parted down the middle, pulled back at the sides, and tucked into an austere bun. We sat at wooden desks arranged in orderly rows before Miss Converse's great oak desk, a bastion of authority looming up at the front of the room. Behind her was the blackboard. It looked like the wall of a firing squad to some of the slower pupils in the class. Standing before that board, Miss Converse would consult her bottomless store of simple, compound, and complex sentences. After writing out a snaking tangle of words on the board, she would turn, fix us with a dark eye, and call for volunteers to identify all nouns, adjectives, adverbs, verbs, and participles. "What's this word, and *this* and *this*?" she would bark, pointing to the words chalked on the blackboard. Heaven help the poor student who couldn't fire the right answers back. We learned spelling by rote, surviving bees and spelldowns once a week. We studied the Palmer method of writing, a style of penmanship requiring great, looping rotations of the arm and wrist. It produced elegant handwriting for the more artistic students. In me it produced a chronic writer's cramp.

Away from the blackboard, Miss Converse was one of the most popular teachers in the school. One day Miss Shaw, a martinet who served as St. Paul's music supervisor, came to Whittier on an inspection tour. "Miss Shaw is coming and she is going to test you on singing," Miss Converse warned us. "If you get a compliment from *her,* I'll buy you a box of chocolates." We thought Miss Converse was just fooling, but when our reedy voices drew praise from Miss Shaw, Miss Converse rushed right off to the sweet shop and returned with a big box of chocolates. I will always be grateful to her for attending to another vital part of my education—she taught me to dance: white schoolmarm and gawky black scholar gingerly waltzing to the thumping chords of the piano—the Ku Klux Klan would have been beside itself.

• • •

On June 13, 1915, the year Booker T. Washington died, I graduated from the eighth grade at Whittier Grammar School. The graduating class sang "The Mill in the Forest," a ballad about a sturdy blacksmith pounding his anvil deep in a lonely wood—the only words I can remember are "Clang, clang, clang." That fall I went on to the George Weitbreit Mechanical Arts High School, the best high school in the city, where I registered for a pre-engineering course: four years of math—including trigonometry and college algebra—chemistry and physics, mechanical drawing and machine shop, along with English and history. I was brash and confident in those days. I remember saying to myself, "You might as well take the toughest course and see how you do."

I don't know why I settled on engineering. Perhaps I wanted to outdo Elliott at his own game. Whatever the case, it turned out that I hadn't been born to become an engineer. The teacher who influenced me most was Miss Mary E. Copley, a tall, plump woman who wore long dresses that touched the floor. She taught English. The day I turned in my first composition she asked me to stay after class. When I arrived at her desk she had my paper lying in front of her. I wondered what disaster I had committed. For a few agonizing seconds Miss Copley studied me, then she said briskly, "You have ability, Roy. You must develop your writing skills."

With that my plans to become an engineer melted in a new lust for books and writing. Whitman once said that he was simmering,

simmering, simmering until Emerson brought him to the boil, and that is precisely what Miss Copley did for me. The high school had an excellent library, and I read everything I could lay my hands on: Chaucer, Homer, Shakespeare, Longfellow, Robert Burns, Gerard Manley, Hopkins, and Tennyson. The melodious syllables of "invictus" had me in a lather ("Out of the night that covers me, / Black as the Pit from pole to pole,/ I thank whatever gods may be / For my unconquerable soul"). I also read *Souls of Black Folk.* I knew by heart the basic axiom of Du Bois—"The problem of the twentieth century is the problem of the color line"—and his presentation of the psychological dilemma of Negroes: "One ever feels his twoness as an American, a Negro; two souls, two thoughts, two unreconciled stirrings; two warring ideals in one dark body, which dogged strength alone keeps it from being torn asunder." At the same time I was young, Jim Crow had left me mostly alone, and while I loved the beauty of Du Bois's writing, his arguments were still a little abstract to me. I was too young to go to the N.A.A.C.P. meetings that Uncle Sam attended twice a month. There was no color line at the lake house where Herman and I went boating; there were no colored seats on the trolley which we rode all over town, no colored toilet at the Ice Palace, the great, glistening castle of ice that went up each year at Winter Carnival. I was sheltered, and I went my way not knowing that Du Bois was exactly right, that a tremendous shock was waiting for me.

After that first meeting with Miss Copley, I put myself under her guidance. She believed in originality in composition and encouraged me to develop my own style. In my junior year I became the editor of *The Cogwheel,* the school's literary magazine. The English Department awarded me the job on the basis of compositions submitted during the first three years of high school. I can remember the teachers crowding around me, wringing my hand, and congratulating me. It was a wonderful day, and with it came a great surprise. When *The Crisis* [a magazine edited by W. E. B. Du Bois and published by the NAACP] reached our house that month, I found a one-paragraph news item tucked inside: "Roy Wilkins has been elected president of the Mechanical Arts High School Literary Society of St. Paul, Minnesota, over two white candidates." It would be years before I met W. E. B. Du Bois in person, but my scrivening had somehow attracted his attention. After that paragraph it no longer occurred to me to be an engineer.

STUDENT: MARIAN ANDERSON

(1902–   )

Contralto.

TEACHER: GIUSEPPE BOGHETTI

Shortly before I left high school I was introduced to Giuseppe Boghetti, who remained my teacher for many years, with breaks here and there, until he died. Dr. Lucy Wilson, my high school principal, had arranged to have me sing for David Bispham, an outstanding American baritone. Mr. Bispham said kind things, but nothing more happened. Then Lisa Roma, a young musician and a friend of my principal, offered to take me to Mr. Boghetti, her teacher.

I remember that Dr. Wilson and Miss Roma accompanied me to Mr. Boghetti's studio. Mr. Boghetti was short, stocky and dynamic. He could be pleasant, but there were times when he could be stern and forbidding. At that first meeting he was severe, even gruff. He began by declaring that he had no time, that he wanted no additional pupils, and that he was giving his precious time to listen to this person only as a favor to Miss Roma. Dr. Wilson did not look happy. I was amazed.

My song was "Deep River." I did not look at Mr. Boghetti as I sang, and my eyes were averted from him when I had finished. He came to the point quickly. "I will make room for you right away," he said firmly, "and I will need only two years with you. After that, you will be able to go anywhere and sing for anybody." Then he began to talk about his fees as if the lessons would begin at once.

They could not begin at once. There was no money for lessons. Dr. Wilson said that she would see what could be done, and I murmured something, and then we left. I might have known that my neighbors and the people at the Union Baptist Church would find a way to provide. Mrs. Ida Asbury, who lived across the street from us, and some other neighbors and friends arranged a gala concert at our church. The main presentation of the evening was "In a Persian Garden," and among the soloists was, I believe, Roland Hayes. After all expenses, about six hundred dollars were realized, and with that money Mr. Boghetti was engaged to be my teacher.

At that first audition, I should add, Mr. Boghetti had given me a scale to sing after I had finished "Deep River." Once I began to appear regularly at his studio I found out why. He had discovered unequal tones in that scale, and he set to work immediately to iron out the unevenness. It gradually dawned on me that, although I had worked with two teachers, I had not yet reached the point where I had relinquished my wholly natural and spontaneous manner of singing for a consistently controlled method.

Mr. Boghetti started by giving me exercises. First I did nothing but hum them until I could feel the vibration. Then I would attempt to place the tone exactly where I was humming. The idea was a little like Mrs. Patterson's. Looking back on all these things calmly, I can see how Mr. Boghetti's approach was more useful. In a concert hall, after all, it might be awkward to find the right kind of corner to use as a target, but if you did the focusing inside your head the chances were fair that your head would always be there with you.

The E flat was my best tone, according to Mr. Boghetti, because it was perfectly placed. He contrived vocal exercises starting from that tone, moving up and down, and he reminded me that all the other tones must be produced in the same way. His objective was to provide me with an even, unbroken vocal line from the lowest tone to the highest.

Attention was paid to breathing. Mr. Boghetti suggested holding the sides tightly and then breathing slowly to see how far I could expand the body wall. I found that I got a gratifying expansion. But when I got around to singing songs I would forget to check on ribs, body wall, and maximum expansion, and I would not pause to wonder whether or not I was breathing according to rule. So long as the breath came naturally and there was enough of it for the song I was called upon to do, I did not let it worry me.

Mr. Boghetti did not make a fetish of training any particular section of a voice. He worked with all of it—top, middle, and bottom.

When I did my exercises he got me to move up to an A, then to a B, and finally to a high C. The B and C were designed to serve as extra insurance for the A, which I used constantly on stage. We spent a good deal of time striving for agility. The exercises were done rapidly and lightly, and Mr. Boghetti saw to it that I had all sorts of embellishments to practice.

One thing I did not master in his studio was a pianissimo that pleased me. As a result I have never sung in public two songs I love most dearly, the "Ave Maria" from Verdi's *Otello,* and Handel's "Care Selve."

"Do you want to be a pianissimo contralto?" Mr. Boghetti demanded.

"No," I replied with unaccustomed boldness, "but the person who sings loudest is not always the one who sings best." He was unyielding that day. "I am the teacher and shall make the decisions," he said.

Some days later he relented and gave me exercises to develop a decent pianissimo. We worked on these exercises from time to time with occasional good results, but we did not concentrate on this problem persistently enough, and I never learned the pianissimo so as to command it securely at every tone throughout the range. The fault may have been mine. Mr. Boghetti had two sopranos as students who had beautiful pianissimi. I don't know whether these girls had these tones before they reached our teacher or whether he taught them the secret that was so elusive to me.

• • •

As it happened, there were occasions when I sang the music of Amneris in Mr. Boghetti's studio. Mr. Boghetti was a tenor, and he joined me in singing the fourth-act scene for Rhadames and Amneris. He loved to sing, and I suppose he would have preferred singing in opera to teaching. You could see his pleasure when he proposed that we do this operatic scene together rather than the usual lesson. I might have had my mind set on trying out something else, but he was the teacher, and how could one resist the gleam in his eyes as we played at being operatic figures? Once we started I enjoyed the *Aida* scenes as much as he did. I realized then that I liked doing opera tremendously, but years were to pass before I finally did so in an opera house.

With Mr. Boghetti I learned some of the songs I still sing today: Schubert and Brahms, and later Schumann and Hugo Wolf in German: songs by Rachmaninoff and other Russians, in English; Italian arias; songs in French, and songs in English by American and British composers.

Like the best teachers, Mr. Boghetti was watchful for difficulties I might encounter in the course of certain songs. I might not be able to fit a word to a tone in just the right way, and he would concentrate on that passage. He would invent exercises not to be found in any book but especially designed to overcome the problem.

It was in Mr. Boghetti's studio, too, that I became aware of the meaning of professionalism for a public performer. There I learned that the purpose of all the exercises and labors was to give you a thoroughly reliable foundation and to make sure that you could do your job under any circumstances. There is no shortcut. You must understand the how and why of what you are doing. If you do, you can give an acceptable performance even when you are indisposed. You cannot say, "Tonight I don't feel good and I won't appear." You have to be prepared to carry on even on nights when you would rather do anything else but perform.

During the years I stayed with Mr. Boghetti my tours increased. I went through all my programs for him, and he criticized and corrected. Toward the end of his life, by which time I was busy and away singing most of the time, I kept coming back to him, letting him check on what I was doing. And he was enormously helpful in this respect, too. It is easy to pick up bad habits in the stress of a heavy schedule of performances, and a teacher who is objective can notice things that have escaped your attention. Mr. Boghetti was a strict teacher. He expected you to do a lot of homework. I shudder to think what he would have said if he had known how often I failed to do mine. I was caught up in so many activities when I was young that I could not always find time for practice. Nor, for that matter, could I always find a place where I could practice without becoming a nuisance to other people. However, on days before my lessons I concentrated madly. I would take the music to bed with me and read over the words and study the notes far into the night. The next day I would take the music to school and steal glances at it when I should have been paying some mind to classwork. By the time I reached Mr. Boghetti's studio I had soaked myself in the music, and he would say with satisfaction, "I see that you have really been studying this week."

He could be terrifying, as I have said. I once saw a girl running out of his studio in tears. He minced no words; if you did not study he told you he did not want you in his studio. "I don't take society people," he would shout, "who think it would be nice to sing." When he saw that I was serious he let me stay after my lesson and listen to other pupils who were more advanced, and this was most helpful. He had a way of singing along with you during your lessons. Sometimes it disturbed you, but you did not dare ask him to stop.

The clock was always within view. When your thirty minutes were up someone else was always waiting. You watched anxiously as that clock ticked away the short time of the lesson that meant so much to you. There were times when Mr. Boghetti spent some of those treasured minutes talking, explaining things, and probably this was necessary, but you wished you could invent some way to hold back the clock or cut off conversation. Some days you felt like talking, and you had the feeling that Mr. Boghetti was watching the clock as anxiously as you did when he talked. If another pupil happened not to turn up Mr. Boghetti let you stay on, and those extra minutes you cherished and remembered.

Mr. Boghetti arranged recitals in his studio, and some of us were invited to sing for his guests. This man had an odd magnetic quality. He would sit in one of the front rows and fix his eyes squarely on yours when you were singing. Somehow he helped you to sing better than you thought you could. I noticed that he had this effect on me when I sang on more formal occasions in regular halls in Philadelphia. He was sure to be in a seat up front where I could see him. I knew he was watching me, and I just had to do what he expected of me.

There came a time when the money provided for the lessons by my friends and neighbors was exhausted, but Mr. Boghetti did not put me out of his studio. A friend of his offered to advance two hundred and fifty dollars toward my lessons in return for a promise that I appear in some concerts for him. I did not know where the concerts would be or under what auspices, and neither did Mr. Boghetti. I did not know people in the music business to whom I could turn for advice, and I was uneasy about the proposal and turned it down. Mr. Boghetti was not annoyed with me. Indeed, he carried me without payment of any kind for more than a year. During this period he went so far as to say that I need not pay and that he was wiping out the arrears. I am certain that he meant it, but in time I was fortunate to be able to repay him in full. I should add that there were times when I earned a little extra money by giving singing lessons, though I was still a student myself.

• • •

The years with Mr. Boghetti were invaluable, and as I see them in retrospect I would not wish to have been without them. I might not have spent so much time with him if a plan projected in Chicago had worked out. I happened to be in that city during a convention of the National Association of Negro Musicians, a rather strong organization with branches in some twenty-five states. For its big program the convention had a nationally famous performer and for lesser events it invited aspiring musicians. One afternoon I sang. As soon as I had finished—indeed, while I was still in the room—someone rose to make a motion that the association should help me with my musical education. The motion was seconded. People began raising their hands and pledging certain sums. Soon there were pledges of about a thousand dollars. Various music schools were suggested, and it was agreed that I should try for the Yale School of Music. I went back to Philadelphia and filled out an application, which was then forwarded to a member of the organization who had been assigned to complete the arrangements. Yale accepted the application. Unhappily, not all the pledges were redeemed, and at the start of the school term there were not enough funds in hand to pay the tuition. Whatever was raised was turned over to Mr. Boghetti. It seemed to be ordained that I should remain with him.

STUDENT: LOUIS NIZER

(1902–)

Attorney and author.

TEACHERS: MR. BISHOP THADDEUS C. TERRY

Of all the teachers before whom I sat, two left indelible impressions upon me. While all others have disappeared from memory (I hope their teachings haven't), these two are as clear in my mind as if I had spent a lifetime with them, although I took only one course of several months with each fifty-nine and forty-seven years ago.

Undoubtedly, this is due to the impact an unusual personality makes on an impressionable mind. It has nothing to do with teaching as such. Others whose names I cannot remember taught more effectively. Still others like Professor John Dewey, Professor John Erskine, Professor Thomas Gifford, Dean Harlan F. Stone of Columbia University were world-famed authorities. But they never made their subjects exciting stimuli which inflamed the mind and produced a quenchless curiosity.

I remember Mr. Bishop (the first name *does* escape me), who taught geometry and trigonometry at Boys High in Brooklyn, New York. He was about forty-five years old, and bore no mark of distinction in his thin face. He was sallow, with deep, heavily lidded eyes, a short, roundish nose, and a slightly jutting chin. His voice was unresonant and inclined to fade off in a whisper. It had a matter-of-fact quality perfectly suited to the uncompromising logic of mathematics, as if, of course, the result was Q.E.D.—quad erat demonstrandum.

All of this should have made him the most forgettable character I ever knew. But no. When he taught, the unimpassioned lucidity of demonstrations created sheer beauty in the triangles and logarithms. He was continuously voted the most popular teacher in the school. Perhaps kindness has something to do with it. A pupil who failed to understand was led tactfully onto the right path, as if it was the most natural thing to have missed originally, and how bright he was to arrive at the corrected conclusion.

The writer who later influenced me most was Emerson. His elegance and grace of diction added verve and beauty to his thought. As Judge Benjamin Cardozo once observed, style is more persuasive than the same argument prosaically phrased. Substance can titillate the mind, while style thrills it.

I refer back to Emerson, because Bishop had the same quality in explaining figures which Emerson had in explaining thoughts. We felt a fire built under us by this quiet man's expositions. We could not be certain how the fire was lit. Was it skill with which the problem was dissected so that the solution seemed to burst upon us with the excitement of a mystery unraveled? Was it the purity of mathematical logic, the beauty of which caressed the mind? Was it Bishop's own dedication and concentration which set higher ideals for us than his instructions? Or was it that supreme gift of all great teachers, a fatherly concern for their pupils which accompanies the joy of teaching? Whatever the mystery of personality, there was no doubt about Bishop's achievements. At reunions for a half-century—only one teacher was remembered affectionately. It was he. The second teacher who left his mark on a whole generation of students, including myself, was Professor Thaddeus C. Terry, who taught "Contracts" at Columbia University Law School.

Curiously enough in almost all physical respects and personality, he was the opposite of Bishop. He was about sixty-five years old. He had a clubfoot, and his limping and later use of a cane had developed powerful shoulders, which malformed him, since they jutted out horizontally. His face was so ugly that there was almost beauty in its rugged asymmetry. He was in the penultimate stage of complete baldness, only a few strands holding out. The heavy flesh over his eyes made them look slanted. His nose could not make up its mind whether to be hooked or flattened, so it was both, and looked no better from wearing an unrimmed prince-nez with a black ribbon which shivered down to his vest. Each of these features, which could have aspired for predominance, was put into shadow by his mouth. It was a thick-lipped wide permanent scowl and the red glistening inner skin, which showed when he talked, completed the ferocious face. As one would expect, no sweet voice could emanate from that face. A deep baritone sound came forth, and its resonance was constantly squeezed by sarcasm. Such sarcasm. He was a master of it. When he called your name, it sounded as if you were an illegitimate child who had adopted a false name to disguise the bastardy.

Instead of Bishop's kindliness, there was unremitting cruelty. He humiliated. He taunted. He ridiculed—but how he taught! How he made you understand the majesty of the law and its philosophical striving for justice. In his hands, the law was "a sorcerer's wand which created a new world of equity."

He used the Socratic technique, asking questions, never giving answers. You had to find your own way, but he deliberately led you into byways so that you would learn your own way back and really understand the terrain. No matter which way you answered, a barrage of questions threw doubt on your conclusion. Sometimes you were compelled to change your mind. Then the questions pushed you back to your original conclusion. At the end, you knew that the law was not a precise science, but a process of reasoning in which diverse answers might all be right depending on the perspective and social objectives which subjectively provided the greatest moral satisfaction.

So he would begin with the most elementary lesson in contract.

"Mr. Nizer, what is a contract?"

"It is meeting of the minds, sir."

"Is a meeting of the minds enough?

"I don't understand, sir."

"If you and I agree who should be President, is there a contract?"

"No, sir. There must be an offer by one party which for a consideration is accepted by the other."

"Does the contract come into existence the moment when the minds meet?"

"Yes, sir."

"Oh, it does, does it?" The snarl that accompanied this question was like the sudden appearance of dark clouds preceding a storm.

I was silent.

"Suppose A offers to sell his car for $3,000 and sends his offer in writing to B, who is in another city. Suppose that B writes his acceptance and puts it in the mail. Is that a contract?"

"Yes, sir."

"Why?"

"Because their minds have met on the deal."

"Even despite the fact that A has not yet received B's letter of acceptance?"

"Suppose that A has changed his mind and sent B a telegram withdrawing his offer and the telegram is received by B before his letter of acceptance reaches A? Is there a contract?"

"Yes, sir. Their minds had met when B mailed his acceptance."

Angrily, "Their minds had met on *what*?"

"On the offer made by A."

"How could the offer be accepted which has been withdrawn by telegram? What was there to accept?"

"But B had already mailed his acceptance." I reply with a little acerbity.

"Doesn't the meeting of the minds require communication of acceptance? How can the minds meet if A doesn't know that B had agreed?"

"I suppose that's right, sir."

"Has not the offerer the right to withdraw his offer before the contract has been consummated?"

"Yes, sir."

"Then doesn't it follow that A's offer having been withdrawn by telegram, there was nothing to accept, and that B's intention to accept was ineffectual?"

"I can see that, sir."

"So you would change your previous answer, Mr. Nizer?" The name was pronounced so as to be synonymous with dunce.

"I believe I would. Yes, sir."

"And you would now say the opposite of what you previously said, namely that there was no contract under the circumstances."

"Yes, sir," spoken with resignation of one who permits his shoulders to be pinned to the mat.

Professor Terry stared at me for a long time. Then he called on another student.

"Mr. Thomas, do you agree with Mr. Nizer's last answer?"

"Yes, Professor Terry."

"Why?" The challenge was flung at him as if nothing had happened in the past several minutes.

"For the reason you gave, sir."

"I gave no reason. I asked questions. Stand on your feet! I have asked you why?"

"Well, the offer being withdrawn by telegram there was nothing to accept."

"But hadn't B already accepted when he wrote that he did?"

"But his writing had not been received by A."

"Why is that necessary?"

"Well, until received, there was no meeting of the minds."

"Where do you get that idea from? If I hold out a proposal to you and you agree, even without mailing such agreement to me, haven't our minds met at the instant you accepted?"

"Sir, I might agree one moment and then change my mind the next."

"In the hypothetical case I gave, B's acceptance was not a mere mental concept. He wrote it out and placed it in a mailbox, beyond his power to control. Would that make a difference?"

"Yes, sir, perhaps it would."

"Perhaps? It would, wouldn't it?" The booming voice sounded like an explosion of a cannon shot, reverberating around the room.

The mental and physical assault was intimidating.

"Yes, sir, it would."

"Furthermore, if each party must learn that the other has agreed, wouldn't A's receipt of B's acceptance have to be communicated to B? And then would A have to learn that B got it? Wouldn't it be an endless chain which would prevent a contract from ever being consummated?"

"Yes, sir," almost inaudibly.

"So you would say that the withdrawal of the offer was too late, because the minds had already met as evidenced by the overt act of mailing the acceptance, is that right?"

"Yes, sir."

"And you would go back to Mr. Nizer's original answer, which he changed after questioning?"

"Yes, I would."

A long stare. "Mr. McGraw, who do you agree with—Mr. Nizer's *final* answer or Mr. Thomas' *final* answer?"

The word "final" put the spotlight back on Thomas and me, just when we were recovering in the darkness of inattention.

"I think there is a contract when B mails his letter of acceptance. Nothing thereafter can change that fact."

McGraw's jaw jutted out. His voice was angry as if in anticipation of the harassment he was about to endure. Having seen the fate of his predecessors, he was determined to take a position and stick to it. If he had to go down, he was going to do so with flags flying, not in a surrendering whimper. We could sense the impending battle.

"Nothing can change that?" asked Professor Terry, his voice slow and ominously sweet. He smiled at McGraw for what seemed hours. We could see McGraw quiver, as Terry finally turned angry and the red glistened from his inner lower lip.

"Suppose two minutes after B has mailed his letter of acceptance, he calls up A and says, 'I've decided not to buy your car. By the way, I mailed a letter of acceptance to you a short while ago—just ignore it when you get it.' Is there still a contract?"

McGraw was defiant and definite.

"Yes, sir. When B mailed his acceptance, A's offer ripened into a contract. The fact that B called later can't change that."

Professor Terry's face lit up, announcing to one and all that the trap had been sprung.

"Suppose then that A, having received the telephone call from B, sells his car to C—Can B sue A for breach of contract?"

"Well—"

"Well—what?"

"I don't think he can. After all, he told A he was not buying. So A had a right to sell to someone else."

"But if the offer had 'ripened into a contract'—nice phrase Mr. McGraw [the compliment could assuage the distress on the recipient's face]—then no call thereafter could wipe it out—wouldn't you agree?"

"No."

"Didn't you say a few moments ago that when a contract comes into being nothing can change that?"

"Yes, sir."

"Well, if nothing can change it, isn't B entitled to sue A for having breached his contract by selling the car to someone else?"

"I suppose so."

Terry turned away in disgust.

"Mr. Harrison, do you agree with that?"

It didn't matter which position Mr. Harrison took. He was run down just as mercilessly. And this was only the first and most elementary lesson. What fireworks awaited us, as the really involved problems of contract law were exploded.

It eventuated that all our answers were right. Some states follow one rule, and some the other. What would be held to be a contract in Massachusetts would not be in New York. That was why one of the courses still to be taken was called "Conflict of Laws." Which of the conflicting rules applied under varying circumstances? For example, does the rule of the forum where the case is tried prevail, or the rule where the contract was consummated? So, even in the very first session, we learned that the law was not an exact science. It was a philosophical pursuit of moral precepts, and the logic used in the quest was not irrefutable. We were to become sculptors molding the law to desirable ends, and we would thus be engaged in an art not a science.

Entering Professor Terry's classroom was an adventure, and a frightening one. We studied with particular care the cases he had assigned the previous day. Yet we knew that if called upon we would be stripped mentally and compelled to stand nude and foolish in the presence of witnesses. We dared not laugh at our neighbor's discomfort because we knew our turns would come, and the exposure would be as inexorably embarrassing.

Despite our fear (which we did not experience in any other course), we were thrilled by the intellectual exercise Terry put us through. If we had more such teachers, students wouldn't want to turn to pot and LSD for excitement. We literally trembled as we entered his class. And later, for hours, we would talk among ourselves about the brilliance of the technique which made us turn somersaults, as if we were animals being put through our paces by the trainer. Only then could we afford to laugh at ourselves.

Strangely enough, Professor Terry's uncompromising pressure, which often seemed tinged with viciousness, did not make us bitter toward him. A deep affection set in for the man. We understood that he was dedicated to us; that he was determined to equip us for our profession, not by drumming some rules of law into our heads (for anyone can go to the library and find them), but by developing our reasoning powers, so that we would rule the law, not its reciters; so that we would be historians of the law who would divine its future;

in short, so that we could achieve the highest standard of the profession to be wise enough to be *advisers.*

Professor Terry encouraged discussion with him after the lecture, as if he recognized that a runner who had run a hard race could not stop suddenly, but must taper off. So we crowded around him continuing the discussion. Then for the first time, we knew he was our friend, and that the punishment he had meted out was for our own good. And when in the course of that more informal exchange at the podium he put his hand on our shoulders, we felt as if we had been knighted. Finally, he would limp off while we stood around in small groups too stimulated to leave.

Professor Terry became a legend at Columbia Law School. Thousands of students who passed through his classroom over the years remembered him above all other teachers.

STUDENT: ALGER HISS

(1904–)

Attorney, General Counsel of the Agricultural Adjustment Administration, State Department officer and President Carnegie Endowment for International Peace.

TEACHER: FELIX FRANKFURTER

When I was a student at the Harvard Law School, from September 1926 until June 1929, Felix Frankfurter was far and away the most colorful and controversial member of the faculty. Brilliant and irrepressible, he was much more than a campus figure. His innumerable close friendships with leaders all over the country and abroad had already made him a man of national prominence by the time I was his student.

He was always conspicuous, despite his small structure, as he moved about the campus. This was because as he bounced along—short, dynamic, articulate—he was invariably surrounded by a cluster of students. Frankfurter was always teaching, in class and out. His didactic style was challenging, even confrontational. He invited discussion and he reveled in sharp exchanges. These continued after class had ended.

But Frankfurter was not popular with the majority of his students or his fellow faculty members. In both cases the reasons, I believe, were the same.

Frankfurter was cocky, abrasive, and outspoken. His style was simply not theirs. In addition, Frankfurter was the leader of the liberal wing of the faculty. Most of his older colleagues were politically conservative, as were most of the students.

The great legal scholar Dean John H. Wigmore of the Chicago Law School was among Frankfurter's opponents in the dispute over the Sacco and Vanzetti case, calling Frankfurter with distaste a "plausible pundit"—fighting words in the mannerly decorum of academia in those days. A stout civil libertarian, Frankfurter was a vigorous champion of the innocence of Sacco and Vanzetti, right up to their execution in the summer of 1927 and afterward. He participated actively in groups formed to aid them, and he spoke and wrote tirelessly in their behalf. Frankfurter and those who shared his views were shocked at what they considered glaring errors in the conduct of the trial by the prosecutor—errors uncorrected, and indeed compounded, by the judge. Prejudice had run high against the defendants as Italians and as anarchists, and Frankfurter was outraged by instances where prejudice affected the conduct of the case. It raised questions about the fairness of Massachusetts justice, polarized opinions in that state, and aroused strong feeling throughout the nation and the western world.

Frankfurter's prominence in the Sacco-Vanzetti case made him a marked man in Boston, an object of bitter hostility on the part of the conservatives. It brought him into sharp conflict with the president of his own university, A. Lawrence Lowell, who served on the Massachusetts commission that recommended against clemency. The executions did not put a stop to Frankfurter's charges of a gross miscarriage of justice, or the rancor aroused by the case. Wherever Frankfurter went, he attracted attention. During intermissions at Symphony Hall, where Boston's prominent citizens gathered, he was both glared at and beamed upon as he bounded and bobbed through the crowded lobbies. He seemed to enjoy the notoriety.

At the same time that Frankfurter's fearless championing of Sacco and Vanzetti made him a target of conservatives, it won him national acclaim from liberals as a defender of civil liberties. His stand was thoroughly consistent with his political views in general. He tended to speak with almost ribald disapproval of those he considered the reactionaries in our society, including Judge Webster Thayer, who had presided at the trial of Sacco and Vanzetti and had expressed his prejudices against them to a golfing companion. Such people, Frankfurt would say impishly, regarded themselves as men of importance but were really closer to being "the scum of society." He would utter such comments only at home with friends, but he never attempted to disguise his views in class, either.

Harvard Law School's traditional method of teaching involves sharp, incisive, even sarcastic questioning. While the technique often causes embarrassment or humiliation for the students, the practice, at least in my day, was generally accepted as a helpful means of sharpening their wits, teaching them to think and speak precisely when challenged. Frankfurter's obvious enjoyment of this form of verbal fencing made many of his students feel that he was displaying personal hostility, engaging in unfair ridicule. I didn't take any of his large lecture courses, so I can't personally assess those complaints. But I can well imagine Frankfurter being carried away by his showman's gifts and a large audience.

Frankfurter was a dedicated teacher, generous with his time, sympathetic to the aspirations of youth. I think his unpopularity with many students was based less on his teaching style than on his political views.

We students in his small seminars had full opportunity to benefit from his remarkable personality. His energy, his vitality electrified the room from the moment he came in. Yet his manner with us was gentle. Usually in high good spirits, he would from time to time explode into laughter or into an outburst of friendly remonstrance if one of us said something he found ludicrously or perversely incorrect. He was so demanding of us for accuracy, as he was reputed to be of the men in his large classes, but with us there was no hint of ridicule.

In two seminars I took with him, our subjects were the federal courts and administrative tribunals. They were fields he had made his special domain. In another's hands, the material might have been dustily technical. Felix, as we students spoke of him to one another, had the love of his subject, and the ability to impart it, that marks the true teacher. He venerated "the rule of law" and passionately strove for its evenhanded administration. He knew personally, or knew all about, the judges and commissioners whose rulings we examined. He was understanding of the pressures they faced, but when they failed to exemplify the high standards he set, he was stern in disapproval. His emphasis on practical realities, including the human factors, made the courses seem like internships.

Frankfurter's enthusiasm for high-principled federal service was infectious. Many of us who were his students at Harvard later responded to the New Deal's need for lawyers, and he presided proudly over our recruitment into federal service.

I had come to Cambridge with a letter of introduction to Frankfurter from William Marbury, a Baltimore lawyer who was a mutual friend. As a result, I got invited to the Sunday teas. It was there, in his rambling, comfortable Cambridge house on Brattle Street, a brisk walk from the law school, that Frankfurter was at his most winning.

The house itself was undistinguished, made of dark-stained wood. One entered almost directly into a large, high-ceilinged, awkwardly shaped living room. There were overstuffed chairs and sofas, tables piled with magazines, newspapers, and books. Along the wall were shoulder-high bookcases.

That room was the soul of the house. Its scholarly clutter and disarray were inviting. One felt immediately that it was designed for reading and talk. Frankfurter, a restless man, moved quickly about the room while carrying on a rapid-fire conversation. He flew from book to book, magazine to magazine, like an adult Peter Pan. Those books and journals were the props of his great performance as a conversationalist.

Sprightly intellectual discourse was an art form in those days. Many of Frankfurter's close friends—men like Judge Learned Hand, Walter Lippman, Harold J. Laski, Dr. Alfred E. Cohn of the Rockefeller Institute, and Thomas Reed Powell, the law school's flamboyant, witty professor of constitutional law—had mastered the skill. Frankfurter's idols, Supreme Court Justices Holmes and Brandeis, were renowned conversationalists and welcomed Frankfurter for the brilliant, spontaneous flow of his ideas. He, in turn, was the idol of those few lucky students who were invited to Sunday teas at the Brattle Street house.

There would be ten or a dozen in the room. Frankfurter was a generous host and frequently had weekend guests. Some of his special faculty friends—Powell, James Landis, Roger Foster, Calvert Magruder—would be there. His wife, Marion, intelligent and beautiful, was always a gracious presence, and she too spoke well and readily.

Frankfurter himself was at once the impresario and the catalyst. He directed the flow of talk, calling on this one or that as if conducting an orchestra. The topics ranged from politics and law to literature and history, but practically nothing was barred, and the inspiration could come from anywhere. For example, Frankfurter traveled widely, and if he was just back from a trip to Washington or Albany, he would be full of his meetings with the great and the near-great, recounted with wit and brio. These tales could take the discussion far beyond the confines of Cambridge. The spirit of informality at Felix's house was a special treat for us favored students. Here we were in the presence of a revered, nationally prominent professor and his august friends, free to express our personal views and join in the discussion. One of the risks of participating, of course, was that if we spoke without adequate logic or supporting detail, Felix would expose our shortcomings.

After our host and his illustrious guests had expressed their views on whatever topic was under discussion, Frankfurter often would turn to one of us students and say, "And what do you think?" The query always left me momentarily speechless. One time he asked for my comments on Lord Acton's famous dictum that all power tends to corrupt, and absolute power to corrupt absolutely. I had never heard the dictum before and could only come up with a lame observation, something to the effect that great ends call for great power. But there was, on this occasion as on all others I remember from the Brattle Street teas, a saving grace in the friendly manner with which Frankfurter put his question and challenged the answer.

Felix was extraordinarily well informed in many fields and gifted at extracting personal experience, knowledge, or opinion as he moved from guest to guest. It was, however, his own scintillating talk that made these gatherings most memorable.

Organizing his thoughts cogently, possessed of an astounding memory, fluent and brimming with energy, Frankfurter was an arresting speaker on any occasion. At home on Brattle Street, making use of the books and articles that lay at hand, his discourse became a great performance. Citing a passage from a book or a legal opinion, he would dart from his chair to a bookcase or a crowded table and seize a volume or a journal. Quickly and unerringly, he would turn to the page he wanted and read the supporting passage. He was credited with reading a page at a glance, with a photographic memory that enabled him to recall the exact page whose contents he was citing. Analytical, quick-witted, and eloquent, he possessed a histrionic ability that made his converstional powers unique.

Yet the performance was but his way of conveying the content. We students were meant to, and did, enjoy the afternoon, but what we came away with was what we had learned—what Brandeis had said about a recent Supreme Court decision, what Holmes had said about some point of philosophy, what Governor Franklin Roosevelt had done for conservation in New York. Frankfurter's zest and skill as a performer were at the service of his interest in ideas.

Frankfurter maintained friendships with many of his students during and long after their law school years. He cared about the personal life and intellectual opinions of each of us as though this large group were a small circle of his intimates. I always felt that Felix was available, and a note from him or an invitation to see him never seemed to me unusual. I recall being asked to join him and Dr. Cohn for dinner at the Ritz in Boston while I was in law practice there. Instead of regarding this as a special gesture in my direction by an incredibly busy man, I took it as a normal friendly meal with FF (as his friends spoke of him), not really out of the ordinary at all.

I continued to see Frankfurter often after I graduated from the law school, particularly during the years 1930 and 1931, when I was practicing in Boston. During that period, he became an adviser to Franklin D. Roosevelt, then governor of New York, a relationship that led to Frankfurter's important offstage participation in the New Deal and eventually to his appointment as a Supreme Court justice.

Our friendship was such that when I became the defendant in a sensational trial for perjury, he did not hesitate in responding affirmatively to my lawyer's wish to call him as a witness to testify to my good character. This he did even though it was predictable that he would be attacked for thus supposedly impairing the dignity of his office. Indeed he was attacked, and it is a measure of how controversial his reputation still was that, so far as I am aware, his more conservative colleague, Justice Stanley Reed, who also appeared as one of my character witnesses, was not so attacked.

These attacks on Felix led me to spare him and also Justice Reed, the risk of embarrassment by appearing in my second trial. And on my release from prison, I avoided direct contact with Felix in order to spare him further hostile criticism. I kept in touch indirectly through friends and through my brother Donald, who, while a student at the law school, had become as close to Felix as I was—indeed, Frankfurter had chosen Donald as one of Holmes's secretaries as he had earlier selected me. Donald maintained constant warm relations with Frankfurter and was the executor of his estate. But, after my first trial, I never saw Felix again. There was no change in my regard for him, and I knew from Donald that there was no change in his regard for me. His coming to my aid was in keeping with his earlier acts of moral courage, and I am happy to express here my gratitude for his testimony in my behalf.

STUDENT: MacKINLAY KANTOR
(1904–1977)
Author.

TEACHER: GRACE BIDLACK

My own private American squirrel-stew was cooked to pungency by a school-teacher who built a hot fire under the pot. She was an enormous woman, unwomanly in every movement and gesture, lumbering through middle life as if her feet hurt her. And probably they did.

For she had the size and proportions of a heavyweight wrestler. Her black hair, coarse and kinky, was turning slightly gray. Her tiny, red-rimmed black eyes lived deep within a perpetual squint. A faint mustache curled on her upper lip; and those few portions of her flesh not covered by her ample gowns showed the swarthiness of a Moor. Her walk was something between a fat lady's waddle and a plowman's stride.

And, God love her memory, her name was Grace.

I stared in amazement, the first time I ever saw her. When she had quaked up into our school building, I asked another child, "Who on earth is *that?*"

"That's Old Lady Bed-slats."

The boys called her that—Bed-slats—a far-fetched jest upon her name, which was Bidlack. She was the most impressive visitation the boys of Webster City [Iowa] ever experienced; and without doubt she will be remembered worshipfully by them when their grandsons trot to school beneath elms serene and elderly.

I don't know where our superintendent of schools found her. Mr. Kelly's intuition was as long as a prairie furrow. . . . He had found Miss Bidlack somewhere, and brought her to us. She began to set her brand in our skins and souls; the proud marks she made will be there until we die.

When we entered her room as a student, she had already become an institution. Bidlack, Bed-slats, history books, the merry-go-round, parliamentary drill: all these were now regular departments in the life of Webster City boys.

Miss Bidlack would not teach girls. If she did not completely despise the dulcet feminine whisper in all nature, at least she chose to ignore it. The female eighth graders had been relegated to the stewardship of a truly feminine woman; and Grace Bidlack, that disgruntled blacksmith masquerading in petticoats, built a high wall around her boys and barred the gate.

The gods had visited her cradle in the village where she was born, and had wafted their endowments to her even while her homely infant face was wrinkled in sleep. They had given her the power to teach young boys, to teach them well if strangely. She spent her natural life doing just that. I never met a human being with more single-minded purpose.

To begin with, she worked fifteen hours a day. She had demanded a key to the school building, and she toiled up the street from Mrs. Letts' rooming-house each morning long before the school janitor arrived.

Lunch, to Grace Bidlack, was a midday annoyance to be disposed of hastily with an apple and a mouldy sandwich or some such equally disgraceful weapons. Supper was something that you gobbled hastily at Mrs. Letts' table so that you might lose no time in assaulting the mound of papers waiting to be corrected, and probably those papers would occupy you until ten in the evening. And then came sleep. (I wonder if she ever dreamed, and what her dreams were.) Then came seven o'clock, and the schoolhouse.

Usually, however, she didn't sit alone during those early morning hours. There were boys with her much of the time, and for a considerable period I was one of them.

Old Lady Bed-slats had exclaimed to me, in her hoarse but nasal voice, one winter day a few months after I came to her:

"I can't make anything out of your arithmetic paper. It doesn't make sense. No arithmetic paper should be this bad."

I sulked.

"I don't understand it," she persisted, coming down the aisle with her quick, massive tread. "Some of these examples are things you must have done in the sixth grade. Your long division is no good. And you can't multiply a simple decimal."

She got the truth at last, and so did I. It was a horrid thing to face, there in the eighth grade. Never adept at numbers, I had been passed through several grades with only a meager knowledge—not even a working knowledge—of the simplest mathematical procedure. My former teachers seemed to have been charitable but utterly incompetent.

"There's only one thing to do," said Miss Bidlack. "You've reached the eighth grade somehow. Here you are. Your papers were terrible all fall, but I thought maybe you'd improve. Well, you haven't. You're getting more fuddled as the work advances. One thing to do: you'll have to stay after school every night."

"I can't," I wailed. "I've got to carry my paper route." She was utterly impassive. "All right. Come mornings, then. Come tomorrow morning; every morning. Be here at seven o'clock."

. . . Sometimes there was snow beating through the darkness as I ran to school. Sometimes the snow had already fallen, and lay trodden into ice beneath my overshoes. No matter how I hurried, Grace Bidlack was always there before me. Once I very nearly beat her to the schoolhouse door . . . a massive squaw wrapped in an old plush coat, trailing stubbornly through the drifts.

The heat wouldn't be turned on yet. It could be very cold, at seven o'clock in the morning up on the third floor of that rickety building. We would sit, she in her coat, I in my mackinaw, and the staunch columns of decimals would march before us. Later I would go to the blackboard and do "examples," with the cold chalk squeaking like a banshee under my thumb.

An hour or an hour and a half of this then we would have breakfast, and historical discussion along with it. I, munching the sandwiches and fruit which my grandmother had prepared; Miss Bidlack, chewing a slab of dry bread or coffee-cake brought in a little paper sack from Mrs. Letts' rooming-house.

I grew to know Mrs. Letts later—a shrewd and salty old woman who enjoyed good food. Certainly she did not prepare those clammy morsels with which Grace Bidlack fed her great body. Probably Miss Bidlack had a private bread-board in her room. Through motives of economy, I think, since she was paid something like eighty or eighty-five dollars a month, and had an old mother to support in her home town.

But if she did not feed herself on succulent fare, she fed me with arithmetical sustenance. I was never betrayed by a fraction or a decimal from that year forth. I am no mathematician, but I can manipulate complicated sums if I need to; and income-tax holds no horror for me, except the natural dread of having to pay it.

However, arithmetic was a side-line with Miss Bidlack—something to be tossed off in the dark watches of a winter morning, perhaps, but nothing to sustain interest and emotion. She had one almighty interest and emotion, and she gave that to us with violence and purpose.

It was America: the benefits, trials, excitement and beauty which had come to the people living here.

Miss Bidlack's America was not a matter of railroad subsidies and corporate indolence and legislative dawdling. Doubtless she knew that these fat vices had flourished in the past and might bog our nation down in the future. But she disregarded completely any evils of which her historical sophistication may have made her aware.

The America she gave her boys was a heritage of sweat, bullets, tattered flags, war-whoops, red footprints in the snow. To children who previously had found stimulation in the exploits of the Harry Castlemon heroes, she suddenly discovered the thrill and significance of our national past.

We galloped with Nathaniel Bacon. We snaked through the swamps with King Philip. We ate horse-meat with Benjamin Church. We paced the chilly streets of Philadelphia with Robert Morris, ringing doorbells, demanding money for the ragged Continentals. We struck and fled through the live oaks with General Francis Marion. With Lawrence and Decatur we tussled against African pirates, and at last we flung ourselves, dying, with Bowie and Crockett in the Alamo. We wrenched a cane from the maddened statesman who attacked the delicate Sumner, and we shivered beneath the oratory of Clay and Calhoun.

A guidon snapped in the wind, the minnie-balls squealed around us. Historical slogans. Catch-words. Gigantic and appropriate (and God knows, oftentimes fictitious) utterances beat against our ears. Don't fire till you see the whites of their eyes. There are the British; we must beat them today or Molly Stark is a widow. Open, in the name of the great Jehovah and the Continental Congress!

Tippecanoe and Tyler too . . . Remember the Alamo . . . Fifty-four-forty or fight . . . Go west, young man, and grow up with the country . . . That's Stonewall Jackson's way . . . Find out what kind of whiskey General Grant drinks, so that I may send a barrel of it to each of my other generals . . . Now he belongs to the ages . . . Remember the Maine . . . You may fire when ready, Gridley.

They came shouting at me, shouting at me now, dream voices of the American past: the dreamer's America, the child's America, the patriot's America. And, most certainly, Grace Bidlack's America.

I am by no means tricked into falsehood along with my sentimental recollection. I have not lost touch with my youth. I see others of Miss Bidlack's boys every now and then, and we always talk of her.

Every boy had a history book. Not a text-book, although we had those too, but a blank paper notebook in which to paint and inscribe his own version of national heroics with red and green ink, with every shade of wax crayon. We embalmed history within those books and within our memories. We made maps showing the penetration of European explorers upon this continent, and the areas where their possessions lay. All these maps were colored alike, after the rhymed key the great Grace taught us:

"Englishmen red, for the blood which they shed."

"Frenchmen blue, for their dealings true."

"Yellow we'll use for the Spaniard bold, who spent his time in search of gold."

"Purple for Italy's sons so grand, who won much fame but kept no land."

"Brown for the Dutch, whose native soil is wrest from the waves through years of toil."

"Green for the Swedes, who fought with the Dutch. Through trials they had, they didn't keep much."

Throughout the school year we maintained a contest. There were five rows of seats, and each row was named after a motor car. A chart, crowded against the wall among flags and battle scenes and pictures of Washington and Lincoln, showed the progress of each car along the rocky road to good citizenship and decent scholarship. Ford, Mercedes, Chalmers, Chandler and Lexington: they were speeded on their way by good deportment, willingness to learn, activity in programs and speaking contests, and by model behavior of the occupants when they moved outside the school house walls.

There were a lot of tabus; if you violated one, it could put your car in the ditch for days and arouse the fanatical wrath of your car mates. Did Merlin Clark cut across the courthouse grounds where the new grass was trying to grow? The Mercedes went into the ditch and stayed there awhile. Did Buster Fassett carelessly throw a scrap of paper into a schoolyard flower bed, and was it found by the janitor, with Buster's name upon it? The Ford went into the garage for repairs.

How she kept this excitement and interest alive in our hearts for nine mortal months is something I do not yet understand. But Grace Bidlack did it. It seems to me now that there was something symbolic in the fact that she was the dominating presence for a nine-month period at the termination of our childhood. We were fastened to her by an invisible umbilical cord. On June we came forth from the womb of her teaching, hearty and lusty, excited beyond measure by the valiant masculine experiences awaiting us.

And meanwhile, as we grew and strengthened, Bed-slats had been dosing herself with the tinctures and tonics which her unholy habits of eating made necessary to her peace of mind and body. I found out all about this in after years, from a teacher who was intimately associated with her.

Miss Bidlack visited a drugstore each week, and bought practically every kind of worm elixir, emulsion, vegetable prescription, golden medical discovery, antacid, vermifuge, chill tonic, alterative compound and blackberry balm known to the imagination of quack manufacturers. With this repulsive array of bottles she felt equipped for existence, and she sampled the dosages continuously throughout the school year. At the end of the year, it was her habit to have a grand cleaning-up—and probably a grand cleaning-out—as well. It is literal fact, sworn by those who knew her habits, that, annually, in one week, she made away with the leavings in her entire dresser-ful of bottles. On occasion, her colleagues were compelled to fear for her life. But after a period of agony, she arose ready to wrestle with demons again. Master of every patent-medicine in the decalogue, she had the stomach of a goat.

Possibly due to a secret anguish which she never mentioned, no one of us ever saw her affectionate or tender. Often we did see her with temper flown wild, with brows knit and breath coming angrily. Often we felt her huge paws upon us. Often we tasted the chalk dust of the schoolroom floor.

She would no more brook insolence from a boy than she would interference with her manner of teaching. When she felt impelled toward castigation it was a fearsome experience for all concerned, not excepting the spectators. She didn't exactly beat boys. She whirled them around. . . . I have always thought of "trouncing" as a fit term for this ceremony, though perhaps that implies more in the manner of blows that she was accustomed to give. She cuffed and wrestled, she flung the boys into the air. The brawniest dullard, man-grown but still boy-minded enough to be a student in the eighth grade, could become a quivering pulp within Bed-slats' clutch. The whirling frenzy to which she treated the recalcitrant was called in schoolyard legend, "the merry-go-round." No boy ever wished to ride upon it, but only a few escaped.

A shocked parent whose family dignity had been torn to as many rags as his son's shirt waited upon Superintendent Kelly in apoplectic ire. He poured out his tale. He cried that corporal punishment should be a thing of the past, that no two-hundred-pound woman should "pick on" a thirteen-year-old boy. With all of which Mr. Kelly agreed in theory, but his final shrug and retort left the angry father silenced.

"That's all true, Mr. Sanderson! But she makes the boys *learn*. And they *like her.*"

Her grab was as masculine as the law and ordinary custom of that day and place would allow. I think that she wore no more than four costumes throughout that entire nine months; probably four were all she had. A gray woolen dress, piped with red; a red woolen dress, piped with black; a black dress with the plainest and ugliest embroidery imaginable; and, for warm weather in fall and spring, a shirtwaist and skirt. And all of these were high-collared, long-cuffed, worn solely to conceal the powerful body which she hated cordially because it had been made according to the wrong pattern.

She shook us, she wiped up the floor with us. And somehow in the process she communicated a portion of her forthright eagerness for America. We had never known what it was to Address the Chair, to Rise to a Point of Order, to make a senate of our classroom and senators of ourselves; but we performed even that miracle a generation ago. By these means, and in other manners as well, Miss Bidlack was equipping us to live in the nation of which we were a part and of which she was so proud.

In her we learned trial by ordeal and trial by gooseflesh as well. Sometimes it seemed that reincarnation was occurring before our eyes: thirty-three pairs of eyes that never left Grace Bidlack's face as her man's mouth rolled out the words of Daniel Webster.

"When mine eyes shall be turned for the last time to behold the sun in heaven, may I not see him shining on the broken and disordered fragments of a once glorious nation. . . . "

It seems that this should read "my eyes," and not "mine." Perhaps it was a faithful transcription of Webster's reply to Hayne—I know that oration only as she gave it to me. Or it may have been an archaic fancy of her own. But that was it, always: the hoarse voice, throaty and yet somehow coming through the nose; the fury and fire behind it. The glinting gaze, seeing the United States Senate chamber which in fact she had never seen.

"When mine eyes shall be turned. . . . "

We left her at last. We left her eagerly, for most of us were to enter high school in the fall. Yet high school and all the novelty it entailed seemed flat and futile the next autumn, when we walked the halls of an unfamiliar building and knew that last year's seventh graders had succeeded to the history books, the parliamentary drills, the chilly morning sessions and winter twilight tutorings which had been a part of our especial existence.

We struggled on through high school, and to the America awaiting us, and to the other lands where some of us went. Grace Bidlack stayed and taught in Webster City. It was something she had said that she would never do. She said it frankly that a three-year stint was enough for any school-ma'rm in any town, and that she would leave at the end of her third year; she had always done so.

But Mr. Kelly and the school board prevailed upon her to reconsider. They raised her salary; another year or two went by, and then more years and another raise. All the time she was growing old. A long time afterward, when I was in the East, I learned that she was dead, and I experienced a physical shock at the news. It was as if the illusion of Lincoln were dead too; as if the Declaration of Independence had mildewed into vanishment.

Miss Bidlack gave us the America of which so many children dream; we were able to keep that shiny, chevroned notion of a bold America longer and more ardently than those who were never taught by her. She would not have countenanced a slogan like, "Tell Woodrow the Yanks aren't coming," if such heresy had been published abroad in those days.

Some of her boys went out to support personally the legend she implanted in their hearts. Some of them died in muddy ravines where the machine-guns were pounding, or in barracks where the flu walked thick. I can't get over the notion that they witnessed a wild, bugling, American marvel when their eyes were turned (like the eyes of Grace Bidlack and Daniel Webster) for the last time to behold the sun in heaven.

STUDENT: B. F. SKINNER

(1904–1990)

Psychologist, professor, inventor and author.

TEACHER: MARY GRAVES

Miss Graves taught reading, and that meant *A Tale of Two Cities, Macbeth, Ivanhoe, Silas Marner, The Idylls of the King,* and *The Last of the Mohicans.* The high-school library had a set of the Harvard classics—not the full five-foot shelf, rather more like three and a half feet—in which I read Darwin's *Voyage of the Beagle.* (In the town library I found a battered copy of Darwin's *Expression of Emotion in Man and Animals,* and I spent a great deal of time trying to imitate that French actor who could put horizontal, vertical, and diagonal wrinkles in his forehead at the same time.) I also read the *Autobiography of Benvenuto Cellini,* and I was impressed by Cellini's zeal as he threw his best plate into the melting pot to get enough metal to finish a statue, as well as his good luck in getting a fever which, with its natural version of diathermy, cured him of a venereal disease. I did not read Adam Smith's *Wealth of Nations* or a volume by Edmund Burke bearing on the spine the surprising title of *On the Sublime and Beautiful French Revolution.*

• • •

Mary Graves and I were, so to speak, promoted through grade and high school at about the same rate, so that she taught me a bit of drawing through all twelve years and reading through the last six. Her father, James Graves, had begun life as a teacher, interested in astronomy and botany. He taught briefly in the "Little Red School House" made famous by the popular naturalist John Burroughs, who was one of his pupils. Later he became a stonecutter, working in marble, and came to Susquehanna [Pennsylvania] as such, but he continued his intellectual interests. He was a member of the Asa Gray Memorial Association, published articles in various journals, and corresponded widely with botanists. He championed unpopular views. He was a staunch defender of Darwin and evolution, and with the same fervor he debated lesser issues. He had insisted, for example, that the year 1900 was the last year of the nineteenth century, and that the town should wait a year to celebrate the birth of the twentieth. He was also the village atheist, a fact which the editor of the *Transcript* tactfully concealed in reporting his death:

> All his life he was a seeker of truth. His mind was ever concerned with the great question of Being and his views were based on his interpretation of nature. It is typical of his whole mental makeup that in the days of his early manhood, his interest inclined to astronomy and the vaster fields of human thought. In his prime he directed his attention to the concrete earth he saw around him; and in the evening of life he turned again to his Universe and reached out to the Infinite.

He never lost his interest in teaching. If he came across a boy or two on his way home from work, he would stop to point out features of the night sky while his wife and children waited supper. He also impressed his views on his family. His wife, ten years younger than he, is said to have resented his didactic measures, but at least one of his children accepted them and gained from them.

An early photograph of Mary Graves shows an attractive young woman with dark, penetrating eyes and full lips, hair gracefully waved before being drawn back and held with a clip at the back of her head. I remember her much later, when her eyes were still bright but her lips had grown thin and were easily pursed. She was then what was called a homely old maid. She could have sat for the portrait in the Prado of "*La Venerable Madre Jeronima de la Fuente*" by Velasquez. She usually wore patterned shirtwaists and dark skirts reaching to the ankles of her black buttoned shoes, and her graying hair was drawn back in a tight bun.

As a young woman she kept a notebook, in which she would devote a whole page to an exact description of a caterpillar and another to an account of how it constructed a cocoon, using a leaf but only after anchoring it securely to the branch of the tree. Other pages of her notebook listed the birds and flowers she saw.

The family enjoyed an intellectual life far beyond anything else in Susquehanna. On those evenings when my father and mother were rehearsing their roles in *Esmeralda,* the Graves family was reading aloud from the Waverley novels, Shakespeare, Emerson, Goldsmith, or Thoreau. Even so, her father and mother were not college graduates, and Miss Graves seems to have been aware of shortcomings. As a teacher she attended annual enrichment conferences in Montrose and kept careful notes of the lectures she heard, recording the punctuation of foreign words and names and the definitions of unusual terms.

She began teaching in primary schools, and at the end of the first year she wrote in her diary:

> A year's teaching past. A very pleasant and profitable year. Teaching grows more beautiful to me—*teaching!*—who am I that I can *teach*? I feel more and more after the year's work how responsible I am for what I teach. I commenced the work last September with a very blind feeling but the work has opened to me more and more and I have been blessed with some success, enough to make me wish to strive harder and harder for more. . . . In June the School Board re-elected me primary teacher at an increase of salary—$37.00 per month instead of $32.00. I am very glad of course. I want to spend it wisely and well. Much for the family needs, some for necessaries of my own, and a little for luxuries—a long-wished-for book perhaps; and *save* some.

That was to be essentially her program with a meager salary throughout her life. Her father was often out of work and died when she was young; her brothers went off to New York, and she was left as the main support of her mother. They lived in a house at the corner of Broad and Oak streets. (The kitchen door opened directly on Oak Street; perhaps the house was built before the street was formally laid out.) On the Broad Street side there was a large yard which needed more care than Miss Graves could give it, and in which strange trees and bushes collected by her father grew almost wild—a "leather" tree with a flexible but very tough bark, and an "iron" tree the wood of which I could not cut with my knife.

The living room had been closed off, and I doubt whether the rotting front porch which ran alongside it would have borne a heavy man's weight. I always entered by the kitchen door and almost never did so without finding Mr. Graves there at work.

The only other room in use on the first floor was probably built as a dining room, but it now held a long table, a golden-oak secretary, a bookcase with a glass front, and a few chairs. Here I spent an occasional Sunday afternoon talking with Miss Graves—her mother, very small and gray sitting silently at the window at the far end of the room. There were treasures in the house, and I suppose I eventually saw them all, but they were husbanded carefully, and no more than one was ever shown to me on a single Sunday. I recall an illustrated *Sinbad,* various shells and pieces of rock, and—treasure of treasures—a letter from the Prince of Monaco to Miss Graves' father offering to exchange botanical specimens. There was also an unfired clay head modeled by a brother who had gone off years before to become an artist. His wife had left him and come back to Susquehanna, to keep house for the aging photographer Delly Harding, and to serve as librarian, but Miss Graves always spoke of him with pride when she spoke of him at all. She told me once that he was a specialist in perspective and that other artists often came to him for help in laying out tile floors on their canvases. She once gave me a broken clay figure he had left behind, and I softened the clay and made a plaque of Venus rising from the sea.

On a Sunday afternoon Miss Graves sometimes took her Sunday-school class for a walk in the pasture and woods back of the Laurel Hill Academy. There was a spring in the pasture, a real spring with clear, cold, drinkable water. She taught us to spot birds and flowers, and showed us how to find sassafras (we chewed the bark and dug up bits of the root to take home) and how to identify the birch with the bark that tasted like birch beer. The world she showed us was fascinating, and she was often embarrassed by our excitement.

It more than made up for the embarrassment we all felt when we exchanged gifts in the Presbyterian church on Christmas eve. She and her mother could not afford substantial gifts for five or six boys. One year we did get small, nicely bound copies of Charles Kingsley's *Greek Heroes* (possibly she managed to pick up half a dozen copies at a special price), but in general her presents were mere tokens, and she would wince as we opened them and simulated our delight.

She had a way of passing on curious bits of information. She told me that Sarah Bernhardt painted her ears so that they looked translucent, that a Hindu could steal a blanket from underneath a sleeping man by using a feather to get him to roll from side to side, that Robert Louis Stevenson spent as much as twenty minutes on a single sentence, and that a pianist, whose performance before a king had been interrupted when dinner was announced, remained so uneasy at the table that the king asked him what was wrong, and he begged permission to go back and play the last chords of the composition. She also told me that when a monk finished copying a long manuscript, he would add the Latin for "Finished, thank God," and I have often wondered whether she interpreted the significance of that expression correctly.

Miss Graves, spinster, loved small children. She wrote stories for her nephew and niece, and, like a fond parent, relayed the bright sayings of a neighbor's child whose older sister used to bring him to see her. Until I reread *Silas Marner,* the only bit I remembered was Silas's ineffectual discipline—the child's comment, "Effie in de toalhole," and Silas's refusal to continue punishment—and I suspect I remembered it only because of the warmth and affection with which Miss Graves must have discussed it.

With older students she found teaching difficult. The books we read were evidently chosen to sample life over a period of many centuries and, I think, had that effect, though I was to reread most of them years later with greater understanding and enjoyment. They were not relevant to life in Susquehanna (we were not yet "ready" for them) and the tougher boys paid little or no attention. One or two were even more refractory, and the principal would have to be called in.

Her influence was felt outside the school. In that small Pennsylvania town she stood for culture. She kept up with things. She once confided to me in a conspiratorial tone, as if it were something disreputable, that she was reading "the strangest book—it is called *Lord Jim.*" She organized and ran the Monday Club, an afternoon literary society to which my mother belonged. Miss Graves carefully prepared for its meetings, looking up the pronunciation or meaning of difficult words in the things they were reading. (They spent much of one winter on *A Doll's House.*) In the town library she selected most of the new books the town could afford, and for a while on

Saturday morning she read to groups of children—from *Uncle Remus* and Kipling.

She subscribed to serious magazines like the *Outlook* and brought her copies to school. I have good reason for not forgetting that fact. Once a week the whole school assembled in the high-school auditorium, which could be enlarged by opening two great doors into a side room. One morning someone who was scheduled to perform was ill, and Miss Graves and Mr. Bowles called me aside and showed me a copy of the *Outlook*. It contained a short article about an island in the Pacific which had come under the jurisdiction of the United States at the end of the war, and they asked me to read it to the assembled company. I had no time to go through the article but took it out onto the stage. I glanced at it, looked out over the audience, and in a loud voice announced its title: ''Yap.'' Harold Craft was the first to laugh.

As early as 1903 Miss Graves had gone to a nursing home in the Adirondacks in New York State to recover from tuberculosis. There were other attempts at a cure, one of them paid for by grateful members of the Monday Club, but by my junior year it was evident she was quite ill. She began to take a short-cut through a back lot to school rather than walk around by way of Myrtle Street and Jackson Avenue. She brought milk and snacks to be eaten between meals, and she was embarrassed when I once came upon her as she was drinking milk on the far side of the chemistry table in the science room.

By the end of my senior year she was forced to resign. Summer came and I heard very little about her, though I knew she was dying. Near the end of June I called on her for the last time. It was a quiet evening, and in the kitchen I found her mother, then eighty-four and tinier than ever. She understood at once why I had come, asked me to sit down, and disappeared upstairs. I waited for a long time, and eventually she came down to tell me I might go up.

I have said that Miss Graves would have been called a homely old maid. I was always glad to see her but almost not as a person. She was someone who listened to me, answered my questions, and almost always had something interesting to say or a suggestion of something interesting to do. Perhaps it was not until I went into her bedroom that summer evening that I really saw her as a human being.

There was no light in the room, and it was beginning to grow dark. She was sitting in a rocking chair by a window where I could see her in profile. She had on a kimono of some figured material which seemed almost festive. There was a rug across her lap, and her hands lay on it, white but very graceful. She motioned me to a chair which had been placed at the far side of the room. She may have been afraid of contagion or she may not have wanted me to see the ravages of her illness. She had, however, and possibly for the first time in her life, given some thought to her appearance. She had made herself attractive. Fever had rouged her cheeks, and her eyes shown brightly. Perhaps she knew this. Had her mother held a mirror for her? In any case she could have read the truth in my eyes: for once in my life, for a brief moment, I thought she was beautiful.

Teaching is sometimes represented as a kind of infection. We say that the teacher infects the student with an interest in art or a love of Shakespeare. As a teacher I have been required to have a skin test for tuberculosis, and I have always given a positive reaction, though my lung X-rays are clear. Did Miss Graves indeed infect me with more than a love of literature and art, with more than a sense of the Bible as literature? Somehow I rather hope she did. But where is the test that will show the other infections?

And how important to Miss Graves was her effect on me? She lived not only for others but for herself. In her notebook she copied this from Thoreau: "In proportion as one's inward life fails, we go more constantly and desperately to the Post Office. You may depend on it, that the poor fellow who walks away with the greatest number of letters, proud of his extensive corespondence, has not heard from himself this long while."

But she was proud of the role she strove so hard to play in the lives of her friends and acquaintances, and she marked this passage in her copy of *Walden*:

> An elderly dame, too, dwells in my neighborhood, invisible to most persons, in whose odorous herb garden I love to stroll sometimes, gathering samples and listening to her fables; for she has a genius of unequalled fertility, and her memory runs back farther than mythology, and she can tell me the original of every fable, and on what fact every one is founded, for the incidents occurred when she was young.

But my guess is that the best clue to what was important to her is to be found in a quotation from Emily Dickinson which she copied into her notebook:

They might not need me—yet they might.
I'll let my heart be just in sight;
A smile so small as mine might be
Precisely their necessity.

STUDENT: JESSE STUART

(1907–1984)

Teacher, poet and author.

TEACHER: MRS. ROBERT HATTON

This was the year that I began to try writing poetry. It was because of the wind I heard in the dead leaves and the loneliness of sounds at night. This was my first year to study literature. I had the course under a southern woman, Mrs. Robert Hatton. She was one of the finest teachers I ever had. I knew more grammar when I entered Greenup High School than many pupils who leave high school today, even though I'd had approximately twenty-two months of elementary education in one-room Plum Grove rural school. Grammar came easy to me. I also had the urge to write themes when I entered Greenup High School.

My getting a teacher like Mrs. Hatton was one of the finest things that could have ever happened to me in my youth. Mrs. Hatton was born Hattie McFarland somewhere in Missouri. She was a graduate of the University of Missouri, and she was one of the best-qualified teachers for that day to step inside a high school. She had a major in English, and in music and journalism as well. And she had something else as important as her educational qualifications. She had a deep love for all the pupils she taught. To her, they were her sons and daughters. She was an inspirational teacher.

Mrs. Hatton was tall and slender and she walked slowly. Her voice was soft, and she talked very gently. Her husband, Dr. R. E. Hatton, who was superintendent of the Greenup city schools, walked fast, talked fast, and did everything on the run. They had one son, Robert, six-feet-four, who finished Marshall University at seventeen and in his last two years played college football. I was very fond of the Hatton family.

Where I came to know and love Mrs. Hatton was in the English classroom. Here learning was love, and we never finished a class assignment on time because we discussed so many things. And we accumulated so much work ahead that we held a few extra sessions to complete these assignments. Mrs. Hatton had an English schedule like this: Two days of the week were for grammar; one day for written work; a day for assignments from our literature books; then, one day was given to memory work. There were no more schooldays in the week, but she added more work. We had Literary Current Events, for Mrs. Hatton said there were two kinds of English, written and spoken; and since we spoke more than we wrote, we should be able to stand on our feet and address a group. Since she required us to speak before the class, she said we should give the best current events of the day from the best magazines and papers. In addition to this, we had to read twelve novels each semester and make book reports on these. We had to learn how to outline a novel and a short story. I received under Mrs. Hatton the best English courses I have ever had in my life.

The part of my English class assignments I liked best was "Theme Day." Mrs. Hatton called this period "Creative Writing." She had her ideas about this, too. We were given freedom in this class to write about any subject we chose. She said the things we knew the most about we could write about with the most enthusiasm, and therefore, she concluded, we could do our best writing about these subjects.

Quickly I learned by experience that this was true. And she let us choose our favorite medium of creative expression—poem, short story, one-act play, and had one of us been ambitious enough, a novel. She never gave us topics unless one of our class asked her for a subject.

I didn't know about as many things then as high-school youth know about today. But I knew another kind of world, all about snakes, terrapins, and toads, lizards, possums, minks, foxes, rabbits, groundhogs. I knew the flora and fauna that covered the landscape. There was hardly a tree in the forest I couldn't identify. I knew and could identify most birds. I knew the predatory birds and animals and those they preyed upon. I knew the habits of wild animals, birds, and reptiles—how they nested or lived in the ground or in hollow trees and whether they gave birth to living species. For instance, the blacksnake, lizards, turtles, and terrapins laid eggs. The poisonous copperheads gave birth to their young. I grew up observing wildlife and living with it. Then, I knew about our domestic animals, for I worked horses and mules, and I fed cattle and milked cows. I wrote about these things.

One of the themes I wrote was about finding a hen's nest in a papaw grove with twenty-two eggs in it. When my mother requested that I remove the eggs from the nest, I left one. The hen went to setting on this one egg and hatched a young rooster. She took him to the hills, scratched for his food, and raised him. He grew up a fighting rooster. He killed our roosters, then went to our neighbors' homes and killed their roosters. Their hens followed him to our home, and we had trouble with people who accused us of stealing their chickens. And I closed this theme with the tragic fate of my rooster. One night a cowardly little screech owl flew into the white oak tree where he roosted with a number of hens. While my rooster, Nest Egg, was asleep, the owl pecked him to death. Mrs. Hatton gave me an A for this one. She laughed until she wiped tears from her eyes. "It's the best theme that has ever been written in one of my classes," she said. I titled this theme "Nest Egg."

When I went to college, I took "Nest Egg" and other themes I'd written for Mrs. Hatton. Since I entered college with $29.30 in my pocket, I worked a half-day and went to school a half-day but carried a full schedule. Although I never stopped writing themes and poems, I also submitted in my college English classes themes I had written for Mrs. Hatton in high school. I submitted "Nest Egg" first, always to the different English teachers I had in college. After graduating from Lincoln Memorial, I went to two more schools. And I submitted "Nest Egg." This theme made twenty-seven A's in all. Twenty years after I had finished high school, I submitted "Nest Egg" to the *Atlantic Monthly.* "Nest Egg" was accepted. Then I knew twenty-seven schoolteachers had been right. "Nest Egg" has since been reprinted in a college textbook and high-school literary anthologies. This was written when I was sixteen and a sophomore in Greenup High School.

We had a few pupils who claimed they couldn't write a theme. Mrs. Hatton asked these to write her a letter and tell her why they couldn't write a theme. And several of these letters were read in class, for they were excellent themes. She never had to ask me to write her a letter and tell her why I couldn't write a theme. Since there was no division for the eight grades in Plum Grove, where I had done my first writing, every pupil listened when I read a theme. And many a time, I had everybody in school laughing. I had already learned that I could create myself an audience by putting words into sentences, sentences into paragraphs, and paragraphs into a theme or story. Now, in Greenup High School, under Mrs. Hatton, I had a different kind of audience, a more critical and a more appreciative one. I found only one fault with "Theme Day." I didn't get to read enough. To say I took only one piece of writing each day to Mrs. Hatton's class, as my classmates will remember, would be an understatement. I have taken as many as twenty-four pieces of creative writing, theses, articles, and poems at one time. If my classmates didn't have their written work, I'd read for all who didn't have, if Mrs. Hatton would permit me. I wasn't exactly bashful.

Mrs. Hatton gave me a volume of Robert Burns's poetry. She read poetry well. She stressed Robert Burns because she loved his verse. I would read his poetry every spare minute I had. I carried his poems wherever I went. I thought I had never heard words more beautiful than those in "Flow Gently, Sweet Afton." It was sung in school once or twice each week. The sentiment of that song choked me, for I loved it deeply. And there was "Highland Mary," "John Anderson My Jo," and "The Cotter's Saturday Night." I feasted on the poetry of Robert Burns. It seemed as if something big in life had taken hold of me. I wanted to write poetry like Robert Burns. He was a Scottish plowboy. I read all that in his life. Now I knew it didn't always take the boys that wore sweaters like Burl Mavis to do things. And my prayer then was to write poetry that would endure like the poetry of Robert Burns.

STUDENT: HARRISON E. SALISBURY

(1908–)

Journalist, editor and author.

TEACHER: ANNA VON HELMHOLTZ PHELAN OSCAR W. FIRKINS

Dr. Anna [Von Helmholtz Phelan] . . . was a phenomenon, immensely tall, tall as a Grenadier Guard, six feet four, a Brunhild come to earth, in pince-nez, dark blue professional-cut serge suit and white shirtwaist, only letting her small girl's wonderment run riot in hats of magnificent diameter and plumage. She took each of us with total seriousness, total assumption that we were *writers* and that writing was the only thing in existence, and by that assumption confirmed us in the profession. She inspired us to perform miracles. Most of all, each week, she encouraged us, sitting around the oblong table, to devour each other, to read and criticize each other's work with a ferocity that sent young women to tears and young men to the verge of blows. It was jungle war. We learned to survive. We had to if we were to remain in the seminar. I spent two years in that golden circle and anything I ever acquired of style or taste was born there. Imitation was always present, but toward the end some of us began to work our way through Hemingway, through Fitzgerald, through Dreiser, Lardner, Van Vechten, O'Neill, Dorothy Parker and that miraculous, long-faded Algonquin crowd, into something closer to the reality of our lives.

I began to write of Oak Lake. I wrote about the Sixth Avenue rooming house and its black boarder. I was very proud of this absurdity and included it in a collection that five of us published privately, called *Broken Mirrors*; there were eighty-two copies, some in purple velour, some in gold-and-black wrapping paper, set and printed at the Fairbault School for the Deaf, where the parents of one of us, Gordon Roth, taught. *Broken Mirrors* reeked of Dostoyevsky, incest, murder, lust, insanity, delirium tremens, miscegenation, suicide, hangings. It would be many, many years before I turned back seriously to creative writing.

Anna Von Helmholtz Phelan. In appearance, accent, bearing, breeding, education, she was a caricature of the "Good German," the German who could be depended upon not to make a revolution because the sign said: "Don't Walk on the Grass." You could see her silver helmet and her breastplate and almost hear the doom tones of Wagner. One young man took the girl he hoped to marry to meet Dr. Anna. Years later, the girl remembered the cats—a row of them, each named for a medieval poet, crouched on a railing above eye level, looking down at her with cruel green eyes. Another young man asked Dr. Anna after his first daughter was born: "How long will it be before I feel any love for her?" How could this woman inspire a room of anarchistic young men and women, leavened by a few perfumed, eye-shadowed Sapphos and Beardsleys who drank wine and formed a society which met by cloistered candlelight? I do not know now nor did I then. We Hemingways used to debate the question over our mugs of home brew. I expect the wine drinkers did the same. I do not think Anna Phelan ever had a student who did not leave her seminar with a deep debt of gratitude. The University of Minnesota rewarded this remarkable woman in exemplary academic style. When she retired in 1949 at the age of sixty-nine, after forty years of teaching, she still held the lowly title of assistant professor.

If one thing could be said for Minnesota, at least it provided a seat for Oscar W. Firkins. (He was never called Oscar Wilde Firkins, even in his obituary.) The presence of Firkins, I thought justified the existence of the university. He was sui generis. He lived in an 1860s clapboard house, built by an early St. Anthony farmer, a few blocks from the university. He was, in the opinion of many playwrights, actors and directors, the best serious critic of the American theater in his day. He did not possess the savagery of Nathan nor the joie de vivre of Woollcott nor the authority of Percy Hammond.

What he had was taste, knowledge, love, style, humor, analysis and devotion to the theater—the whole theater from the Greeks to Broadway. He was a bachelor and lived with his three sisters, Ina, Orra and Frances, all unmarried. Ina was librarian of the university. Frances helped her brother in research and reading. Orra kept house. Oscar Firkins's vision was so poor he could not see beyond the first row of his classes. How he managed to see performances in the theater I do not know. He went to New York twice a year, at Christmas and in the spring. He saw all the plays. Then he returned and delivered his lecture on the current theater. There were sixty students in each of his classes (he offered two), the capacity of the classroom. For the twice-yearly theater talks there might be twice that number, including faculty and people from outside. I do not know whether, with his poor vision, he realized the tremendous crowds he attracted.

A visit to his house, a rare privilege for a student, was like stepping into a New England play by O'Neill (whom Firkins regarded as the playwright of our day). Firkins in black worsted wool suit with starched wing collar, his three sisters equally prim and severe, the housekeeping Orra a little less so, a neat coal fire in the grate, tea, quite a high English tea, the tea poured from a fine silver pot into very thin cups, very tasty scones—all this in a small parlor of black walnut and mahogany, very mannered, I sitting on the edge of my chair, hoping that I would not make a gaffe, certain that I would, dependent on Firkins's charity not to mention it.

Conversation was no problem. Oscar Firkins liked to talk and uttered, in a rather nasal Yankee tone, periodic sentences as though he had memorized his lines. Perhaps he had. His memory was phenomenal and he could quote whole plays by Shakespeare or Sophocles. He spoke in epigrams about events in the morning paper, prefacing his lectures each day with a few minutes of commentary, invariably sardonic, about a political event that had caught his eye or a campus oddity. He was in many respects a radical, with a sharp nose for the underdog and no tolerance for the frailties of his fellow academics, which was why the university had created a department for him of which he was the sole member, not even a clerk or secretary. Would that he had been alive during the Vietnam war; I do not believe Lyndon Johnson could have survived his merciless tongue.

Firkins knew all the gossip of the New York theater and actresses like Florence Reed, Blanche Yurka, Ina Claire were dedicated to him. He watched over them carefully, even tenderly, giving advice on roles, on the plays they should choose, the playwrights whose work best suited them, the most interesting directors. He was for many, many years the inside critic of the American theater, known within the theater but unknown to the public, a secret man, almost a mysterious man, offering his advice cryptically as Pasternak offered his to Stalin.

Oscar Firkins had no use for most of the formalities of academia. Once, it was said, he gave every one of his students an A without reading their papers because his colleagues had criticized his grading methods. He dictated to his students an outline of his lectures because, as he said, he could give them better notes than they would take. Then they could sit back and enjoy the lecture. He didn't care a whit if students brought their books and notes to class for use in examinations, but one hot day when many students removed their jackets and loosened their ties, he announced: "I am not accustomed to giving lectures to stableboys." It was his view that students came to the university to obtain an education. They were adults. If they were too stupid to make use of their opportunity, if they did not study or attend class, that was their loss. He was not a policeman or a guardian of morals. Students rushed to sign up for his classes. Being in Firkins's classes was like being admitted to a secret society.

What did I learn from Oscar Firkins? The virtue of independence: the virtue of using my mind, of not taking anyone's word, of going back to the source, of trying to work out a philosophy of existence; he taught me the wonders of the classics, the eternal and absolute wonder of the Greeks. No one taught me more. And to rebel. Never to accept banality. That was the main thing.

For whatever reason, possibly because, being a rebel, Oscar Firkins sensed a fellow spirit, I was privileged to share his friendship, talking with him in his office, visiting at his house and on two occasions being invited for very formal Sunday dinners.

There were occasions when efforts were made to persuade Oscar Firkins to move to New York and become a resident critic. Twice he took leaves of absence to serve as critic for New York literary reviews and he contributed over the years to *The Nation,* the *Atlantic Monthly,* the *Yale Review* and the *Saturday Review of Literature* (then a literary journal of some merit), criticism, essays, reviews written in that finest of tongues, the English language. Firkins was flattered by and enjoyed the attention that was paid to him in New York, but he always returned to Minnesota. I think he was right. He carried a furled umbrella every day of his life and he never entered an automobile. He rode streetcars. I do not believe he could have existed outside the circle of his three sisters and their New England house in southeast Minneapolis. He died in 1932, and soon the three sisters died too, one after the other.

STUDENT: GEORGE W. BALL
(1909–)

Attorney, investment banker and Undersecretary of State.

TEACHERS: GEORGE WHIPPLE BERNARD DE VOTO

Evanston Township High School had quite a different quality from the schools I had known in Des Moines and, for a boy of eleven, the transition presented more than the usual problems of adjustment. Although the school now has the shape and appearance of a large, bureaucratized institution, it was then still small, with a curriculum heavy in Latin and Greek. Standards were high, and I had to work far harder than before; but the academic fare was solid, and I found it exhilarating. The physical embodiment of the school's meaning, as it appeared to me, was an impressive Mr. Chips named George Whipple. He had total confidence in his own culture and standard of values. Latin, as he taught it, was far more vivid than any modern tongue, while the ringing plains of Troy became as familiar as our school playing fields. I suppose that in many ways he was the first truly civilized man I had known—a gallant specimen of a rapidly vanishing species. Like the passenger pigeon, his kind will not be seen again, and so much the worse for all of us.

While I could adapt to Professor Whipple with easy gratification because I was not expected to deal with him on a level of equality, relations with my classmates were difficult. Evanston was still a small town dominated by a group of rich families, far more worldly and experienced than those I had known in my innocent years in Des

Moines ("sophisticated" was the word I used to myself without being very sure what it meant). In the summer, the established families went off to Europe or to smart resorts or to vacation houses in the country. During the school years, there were parties and dances accessible only to those in the local social register. But what increasingly set the elite apart was their constant chatter of the future. Those whom I most envied and admired talked in vibrant anticipation of Eastern colleges, where their names had been inscribed from childhood. I made few friends. By nature gregarious, I was forced in on myself more than I would have wished. But within a few days of entering Northwestern University, I met the first (after my father) of a small number of individuals who critically affected the course of my thought and, indeed, the pattern of my life.

Bernard De Voto ("Benny" as we all called him) was not in any sense an overpowering personality, but, pursued by devils of self-doubt and insecurity, he instinctively understood my adolescent awkwardness and could teach me the defenses by which he sustained his own vulnerable ego. Since my brother Stuart, who preceded me at Northwestern, had already worked with Benny, I was overjoyed when—within a fortnight after the opening of school—I was assigned to an experimental English class over which De Voto presided. We were a specially anointed group of eighteen or twenty students and we revelled in that knowledge, exhibiting a cockiness that De Voto first sought to demolish and then to direct toward targets. Though he was then only twenty-nine years old and had been a mere four years at Northwestern, Benny was already widely known not merely as an outrageously irreverent young instructor but also—it was grudgingly admitted—as a writer of promise.

More than a writer, he was also a gifted teacher—at least for those who were charmed by his provocative manner and were eager to read and talk. The studied unorthodoxy of his teaching methods first shocked us to attention; then as the rich resources of his reading and perception became evident, we developed mounting respect. De Voto's classroom manner—when he held formal classes at all—was light-hearted and taunting. Perched on the edge of his desk, he began by insulting his students. Most of us would not, he said, be interested in what he would teach and were incapable of learning it; if anyone wanted to avoid his sessions, so much the better. Then he would walk up and down the room, conducting colloquies with individual students, teasing the girls—particularly the prettiest ones—

berating the Rotarian spirit that then afflicted the university, and denouncing contemporary tastes and mores.

Yet Benny took a warm interest in the private problems of students who responded to him. The fact that he once or twice adjourned class so that he and I could play tennis, or that I could talk with him at almost any time during the day, gave me the sense that I was, after all, thought worthy of interest by the most interesting man in the university. Too young and preoccupied with my own small problems, I did not suspect that my new mentor had even more agonizing doubts and fears of his own. What I acquired from Benny is hard to assess even after all this time. It was, I suppose, what General de Gaulle referred to as an *idee certaine* of myself and my relation to the rest of the world. As to the immediate scene, he confirmed my belief that Northwestern, at that moment in history, was something less than my romanticized view of what a great university should be—a comforting excuse for my involuntary aloofness. Benny turned my personal awkwardness and lack of public acceptance into virtues, transforming me in the process into an obnoxious little intellectual snob. Then, at the end of my first year, he departed, refusing the assistant professorship he had been offered and opting for a life in New England untrammeled by institutional obligations. Yet he did not abandon me entirely but arranged before leaving to pass me on to his closest friend on the faculty, Garrett Mattingly, a man of intellect and sensitivity who later made a distinguished reputation as a historian with his books *Renaissance Diplomacy, Catherine of Aragon,* and *The Armada.* Mattingly was at all times sympathetic and generous with his time.

STUDENT: BURL IVES

(1909–)

Actor, singer and author.

TEACHERS: CLARA LYON
ELLA TOËDT

The teacher was one Madam Clara Lyon. I went to her home for my first singing lesson. I was very much struck by the simplicity and sincerity of my new teacher. She had a foreign accent as she explained what we would attempt to do with my very ordinary voice. It was from her that I first heard the songs of Schumann, Schubert, Robert Franz, and many songs of old Italian masters. I thought them very beautiful. She would sit at the piano and sing whole programs of the great song literature while I and a few other students sat around and absorbed as much as we could.

Madam Lyon had been born in France. Her father had been a friend of Paderewski and at an early age she had learned to play the piano and had been associated with great players and singers. She had studied with Schumann-Heink, had spent several years at Yvette Gilbert's school in Paris, spoke a number of languages, and was a cultured woman in the true sense of the word.

Madam Lyon and I became good friends and she told me that some day I might be a singer. As time went on she started asking me questions about some of my doings, and goings about, in the town of Terre Haute. I was a little reluctant to tell her of some of my escapades and of the people I knew. She assured me that all people were more or less alike and that the people in the bootlegging joints were probably better people than some of the respectable citizens of Terre

Haute. I saw that she was a person with a broad understanding of life and I told her several stories of what went on around town.

A few days later I had a lesson. At the end of the lesson the Madam said to me, "Would you take me to hear Big Ion?"

Now Big Ion was a Negro woman who weighed about three hundred and fifty pounds. She would sit on a piano stool and hang down like a bag all the way around. And she would sing dirty songs. I do not mean clever or clean dirty songs, such as some of the folklore songs which happen to be about very natural functions with no smuttiness. But Big Ion's songs were just downright filthy. When the Madam asked me to take her to hear Big Ion, I tried to discourage her. She laughed loudly and said, "I have been in the cabarets of Paris and I am sure heard much worse."

So I said, "Okay, I'll take you."

At the appointed time, ten o'clock one night, I arrived with my motorcycle and sidecar and knocked on the door. The Madam came down dressed very elegantly and I took hold of her hand and gently placed her in the sidecar of my gallant Harley-Davidson. We roared off down the street. In a very short time we arrived at Chumpy Markum's which was some distance outside of town. I led the Madam up to the door and gave the signal; we walked in. I introduced the Madam and Chumpy whispered to me, "Who the hell is that?"

I said, "Madam Lyon."

He said, "Jesus Christ, boy, you shouldn't have brought her here."

I said, "Don't worry about her. She's been in all the cabarets in Paris."

We were given a table in a very advantageous position to see the show. As the Madam looked around she was surprised to see certain husbands of her friends with younger ladies at their tables. She was surprised but they were flabbergasted and embarrassed. One of them came over to the table and said hello, another one back in the corner took a powder.

Big Ion was announced, she came out and sat down on the piano stool, and started a song which I shall not give you the words of. The audience was much more interested in Madam Lyon's reaction to this number than in Big Ion's performance. It was they who were embarrassed as they watched the Madam who didn't change her expression one iota. When the song was over the Madam gave a polite hand and said to me, "There's nothing like this in the French cabarets. The French are just slightly naughty compared with this gross thing, but it's interesting in itself. From where would such a woman come? What are her real thoughts? What are her real ambitions? In her face you can see that she is not a bad person. This is probably the only way she can make a living."

Before long, tongues were wagging and Terre Haute gossipers, of which there were many, had a subject that they could really get their teeth into. "Did you hear about Madam Lyon riding down the middle of town in the sidecar of a motorcycle and then brazenly going to Chumpy Markum's bootlegging joint?" One of the Madam's friends asked her about it and the Madam replied it was one of the most exciting evenings she had spent in Terre Haute. "Reminded me a little of Paris. Mr. Ives was a very charming escort."

Well, that took care of that, but not the tongues. They did wag and wag as such tongues will always do.

Soon after that, Madam Lyon asked me, "Do you like to read?" I said, "No, I couldn't even manage to read my book reviews in school."

She said, "Would you like to come tonight? I am going to read a book to some students."

I said, "No, I don't think so. Books bore me to death."

"Well, come anyway once and then if you don't like it you won't have to come again."

I agreed and she read a book on Paris, the life of the artists and the salons and cabarets and the people, and I had never heard anything so wonderful. So I went again and again. I never missed one of those sessions.

One day she brought me a book. She said, "Here is a present for you. You see I have written in it 'For Burl from the Madam.' Read it," she said.

I said, "All right, I will. Thank you so very much." And I read the *Autobiography of Benvenuto Cellini*.

The next book she gave me was the *Memoirs of Casanova*. After that she gave me *Beethoven, the Creator*, by Roland, and many other books. Finally she handed me *Jean Christophe* and said, "Here is a great book which a boy of your age should read."

By this time I was no longer spending my evenings in bootlegging joints. I was reading, learning classical songs, listening to symphonies on the radio. "Barbara Allen" seemed a long way off.

Finally the time came when the Madam said, "You should get out of Terre Haute. This is no place for you. Study with me this summer and in the fall you must go to New York. There you can learn many things.'' Her husband was ill and had to go back to his home town, Elkhart Lake, Wisconsin, and the Madam left Terre Haute. In order that I might continue studying for the rest of that summer I went there and took a job in a jazz orchestra. I was the guitarist and singer for Howard Cramer and his Vikings.

Hour after hour, night after night I beat out rhythm on a guitar to the dullest music ever written. I hated every minute of it, but I saved enough money to travel to New York the following fall.

• • •

I had been writing to my old teacher, Madam Lyon, of my difficulties. She finally answered, ''Go to Mrs. Ella Toëdt. She is the only teacher who has ever adequately explained voice placement to me. She is a great teacher. Perhaps she will take you.'' I called for an appointment.

On a rainy afternoon I boarded the subway and rode down to Columbus Circle. I walked over to Fifty-eighth Street near Seventh Avenue to an apartment building. I arrived soaking wet at Ella Toëdt's studio door and rang the bell. I heard the piano. It stopped playing and a clear voice rang out, ''Come in.'' I walked into a small hallway attractively lacking the usual autographed pictures of great artists. There was one single picture of Brahms at the piano adorning the hallway.

I entered a large room where stood a fragile old lady with gray hair and sparkling eyes which squinted and looked me over from head to foot. I was sized up completely in the fraction of a second. ''How do you do,'' said she. ''Mrs. Lyon has written me of you. I want to hear your voice. Let's not waste time.'' She sat down at the piano, hit a note and said, ''Sing Ah.'' In the next fifteen minutes she put me through an examination vocally and musically. She levied no judgment. ''Have you brought a song to sing for me?'' ''Yes.'' ''What is it?'' I didn't know, I had several. She said, ''Make up your mind, let's not waste time.'' I chose two songs from the *Dichterliebe* of Schumann, *Wenn ich im deine Augen Seh'* and *Im wunderschonen Monat Mai*. She played the piano beautifully for me. I sang the songs tenderly. As we started the second song her head began to move to the music and I saw that she was enjoying it.

She played the last chord. Her head did not turn but her two half-closed eyes rolled to me, and for a moment she looked straight into my eyes. She said, "So! You have something to say. You have warmth, and real feeling for song. But your voice is not good: your resonators are filled with some kind of pithy, soft substance. It will have to be removed before you can ever get a clear tone." I said, "Yes. I have sinus trouble, the doctor wants to operate and remove a bone." She looked at me again, again she sized me up. "Don't let any doctor cut on you yet awhile," she said. "I'm willing to work with you, if you are willing to work. We'll see what can be done. Let us try."

And try we did. She was patient, and I worked hard. For six months I sang nothing but falsetto exercises. During this period I felt things moving in my head in the region of my eyes. I began to feel vibrations and could breathe through my nose. At the end of a year my voice had improved tremendously and my sinus was nearly cured, my nasal passages were free and I felt light and happy. I ran out of money and told Madam Toëdt I would have to stop for a while. She said, "Keep coming. When I am dead and gone I am sure you will give a hand to someone who needs it. I believe in you, you are going to sing."

I believed it too. The day she said those words I left her studio and walked out into the street. It was cold and damp, people hurried, their necks huddled into their coats but to me the sun shone and wild flowers sprang from the curbs along Fifty-eighth Street.

Soon I was able to pay Madam Toëdt again. Then at her suggestion I registered at New York University Music School to learn some of the theoretical subjects of music. I took dictation, harmony, sight reading and theory. I rose early each morning and went to classes, studied all afternoon, taking time out only for the job, picking up dishes in the cafeteria, that supplied me with my food.

• • •

Were there no persons in this representative conglomerate of peoples from all over the world and all parts of the United States who would understand my songs? There were weekly musicales at I.H. I had done one successfully, a program of *lieder,* and was asked to give another. This time I decided to give them my beautiful ballads and folk songs. A good crowd came to hear me sing that Sunday afternoon, and cheered when I came on with my guitar. I had not finished the first song before reactions from the audience were evident to me. People were restless. Some talked, the Juilliard students gave each other knowing smiles. Juanita looked out of the window most of the time. They did not like the songs. I finished the whole program in spite of decreasing interest. Applause for the last song, the beautiful old ballad "Barbara Allen," was very light indeed. As I left the stage I knew that my songs were pearls, the audience was wrong.

There was one man, a student of poetry and English literature who, as I left the hall, came to me, his face shining with enthusiasm. "Do you know any more of these beautiful old English ballads?" He was eager to hear more. We adjourned to a room and I sang to him for two hours.

We discussed the negative reaction I had received. I had figured it out, I thought. The greater part of the students at the House during this period were Americans from the hinterlands, studying at Teachers College. Coming from small towns and rural districts, these songs represented a life they were trying to get away from. Thinking themselves sophisticated, or intellectuals at least, they resented the simplicity of the songs and refused to hear them. Like my university professor, they were afraid to identify themselves with the cultural expression of the common man. Both represented a group of musical and intellectual snobs who had no taste of their own and desired to belong to the elite circle that worshiped only the classic symphonies and operas.

The afternoon after my failure I had a lesson with Mrs. Toëdt. I had been working on the ballads for two months but had not said anything about them to her for fear she would not approve. I brought my guitar to the lesson but left it in the hall before greeting her. We went through the technical exercises as usual. When we had finished she said, "You are beginning to sing. I am very pleased." She had a nice twinkle in her eye as she gave me the old quizzical look. "What songs are we going to work on today?" We always sang and worked on repertoire to finish off the lesson. I hesitated a moment, thought "here goes" and said, "I play the guitar, Mrs. Toëdt, I don't think I've ever told you, and I sing American ballads and folk songs and accompany myself. They are very beautiful. Would you like to hear one?"

She smiled, "Did you bring your guitar?"

"Yes, I left it out in the hall."

"Go get it," she said. "Isn't this nice. I will have a concert."

She sat in a straight-backed chair and folded her hands in her lap.

I tuned my guitar. I was a bit nervous and began to apologize, "They're very old songs. . . . "

"Come on. Let's not waste time. Your audience is waiting."

First I sang "Lord Thomas and Fair Eleanor." I watched her face. What a joy to sing these songs for her! I sang and sang and sang. Her next student arrived and became part of my audience. Before I knew it I had sung a full hour. She said when I finished, "The minstrels of old must have sung that way." No man ever received greater praise.

STUDENT: EUDORA WELTY

(1909–)

Author.

TEACHER: LORENA DULING

From the first I was clamorous to learn—I wanted to know and begged to be told not so much what, or how, or why, or where, as when. How soon?

Pear tree by the garden gate,
How much longer must I wait?

This rhyme from one of my nursery books was the one that spoke for me. But I lived not at all unhappily in this craving, for my wild curiosity was in large part suspense, which carries its own secret pleasure. And so one of the godmothers of fiction was already bending over me.

When I was five years old, I knew the alphabet, I'd been vaccinated (for smallpox), and I could read. So my mother walked across the street to Jefferson Davis Grammar School and asked the principal if she would allow me to enter the first grade after Christmas.

"Oh, all right," said Miss Duling. "Probably the best thing you could do with her."

Miss Duling, a lifelong subscriber to perfection, was a figure of authority, the most whole-souled I have ever come to know. She was a dedicated schoolteacher who denied herself all she might have done or whatever other way she might have lived (this possibility was the last that could have occurred to us, her subjects in school). I believe she came of well-off people, well-educated, in Kentucky, and certainly old photographs show she was a beautiful, high-spirited-looking young lady—and came down to Jackson to its new grammar school that was going begging for a principal. She must have earned next to nothing; Mississippi then as now was the nation's lowest-ranking state economically, and our legislature has always shown a painfully loud reluctance to give money to public education. That challenge *brought* her.

In the long run she came into touch, as teacher or principal, with three generations of Jacksonians. My parents had not, but everybody else's parents had gone to school to her. She'd taught most of our leaders somewhere along the line. When she wanted something done—some civic oversight corrected, some injustice made right, or even a tree spared that the fool telephone people were about to cut down—she telephoned the mayor, or the chief of police, or the president of the power company, or the head doctor at the hospital, or the judge in charge of a case, or whoever, and calling them by their first names, *told* them. It is impossible to imagine her meeting with anything less than compliance. The ringing of her brass bell from their days at Davis School would still be in their ears. She also proposed a spelling match between the fourth grade at Davis School and the Mississippi Legislature, who went through with it and that told the Legislature.

Her standards were very high and of course inflexible, her authority was total; why *wouldn't* this carry with it a brass bell that could be heard ringing for a block in all directions? That bell belonged to the figure of Miss Duling as though it grew directly out of her right arm, as wings grew out of an angel or a tail out of the devil. When we entered, marching, into her school, by strictest teaching, surveillance, and order we learned grammar, arithmetic, spelling, reading, writing, and geography; and she, not the teachers, I believe, wrote out the examinations: need I tell you, they were "hard."

She's not the only teacher who has influenced me, but Miss Duling, in some fictional shape or form, has stridden into a larger part of my work than I'd realized until now. She emerges in my perhaps inordinate number of schoolteacher characters. I loved those characters in the writing. But I did not, in life, love Miss Duling. I was afraid of her high-arched bony nose, her eyebrows lifted in half-circles above her hooded, brilliant eyes, and the Kentucky R's in her speech, and the long steps she took in her hightop shoes. I did nothing but fear her bearing-down authority, and did not connect this (as of course we were meant to) with our own need or desire to learn, perhaps because I already had this wish, and did not need to be driven.

She was impervious to lies or foolish excuses or the insufferable plea of not knowing any better. She wasn't going to have any frills, either, at Davis School. When a new governor moved into the mansion, he sent his daughter to Davis School; her name was Lady Rachel Conner. Miss Duling at once called the governor to the telephone and told him, "She'll be plain Rachel here."

Miss Duling dressed as plainly as a Pilgrim on a Thanksgiving poster we made in the schoolroom, in a longish black-and-white checked gingham dress, a bright thick wool sweater the red of a railroad lantern—she'd knitted it herself—black stockings and her narrow elegant feet in black hightop shoes with heels you could hear coming, rhythmical as a parade drum down the hall. Her silky black curly hair was drawn back out of curl, fastened by high combs, and knotted behind. She carried her spectacles on a gold chain hung around her neck. Her gaze was in general sweeping, then suddenly at the point of concentration upon you. With the swing of her bell that took her whole right arm and shoulder, she rang it, militant and impartial, from the head of the front steps of Davis School when it was time for us all to line up, girls on one side, boys on the other. We were to march past her into the school building, while the fourth-grader she nabbed played time on the piano, mostly to a tune we could have skipped to, but we didn't skip into Davis School.

STUDENT: EARL SCHENCK MIERS

(1910–1972)

Author and editor.

TEACHER: EARL REED SILVERS

On one of Nana's [grandmother's] visits the Great School Crisis occurred. It seems incredible that in a metropolis as large as Brooklyn I should never have encountered another cerebral-palsied child. By modern medical statistics, they were there, but where were they kept? They were not on the city's streets or in its parks. They were not in the public schools.

Mother did nothing; she possessed a nervous child who under the law had rights she intended to obtain. I was to go to school. I cannot recall the name of the principal of P.S. 72 who interviewed us, but I can see her round, florid face covered with perspiration. The principal was an enormous woman with a bosom that spread like lava on the table when she was seated. She spoke like an army sergeant.

"Mrs. Miers, what do you expect me to do with this child?"

"I expect you to teach him."

"A—a—child like this?"

"A child like what?"

"Now, really, you can see for yourself. This child belongs in an institution. Now, tell me—"

My mother also claimed a good-sized bosom and suddenly these two women were standing mountain to mountain with storm clouds gathering over the peaks.

"Tell you what?" Mother repeated. "That you don't understand? That this child is going to receive the education which is his just due?"

It was a breathless moment. The mountains heaved. Across both peaks, lightning flashed.

"Mrs. Miers, I will enroll this child but he won't last a week."

"He'll last or I'll know why."

And so I was entered in P.S. 72 and Mother marched home in triumph. But her confidence had been pricked and she confided her misgivings to Nana. "Maybe I am asking for a miracle."

"Why not?" Nana demanded. "Why do the blowhard Catholics have to claim all the miracles?"

• • •

From my first day in school until I was graduated from college, I never experienced any exceptional difficulty in obtaining an education. The spirit of the age may have helped me: teachers then were as dedicated as clergymen. Quickly I learned to read and I became almost at once a proficient student of history as though all of Nana's ancestors whispered to me how they had reacted to events gone by. I behaved well in school, being too frightened to act otherwise.

The great historian of the college [Rutgers] then was a one-time president, William Henry Steele Demarest, Class of 1883, who, since he could not control his false teeth, was known to the students as "Whistling Willie"; yet there was a breathless majesty when he described how S-S-Simeon DeWitt, Class-s-s of 1776, had been the geographer who had charted the route by which Wash-sh-sh-ington had cornered Cornwallis-s-s at Yorktown. Dr. Demarest's hand swept from portrait to portrait as the stories spilled out in an endless flow and the wooden pews blistered our wriggling behinds. Still, the warmth and dignity of this old man made us love the college for his sake; we stopped calling him "Whistling Willie" and told ourselves it was a most unusual man who could pronounce benediction and whistle taps at the same time.

The week ended with the hazing of the freshmen by a group of idiots called sophomores. We were required to crawl along College Avenue with one knee on the curb and the other on the pavement while a fire hose, spraying the road, added to our misery. The inane theory behind this common torment was that we were being welded together as a class. The fags among the sophomores cheered on the masochists who held the fire hose for, as we quickly divined, only perverts had been admitted to the Class of 1932. I had crawled about half the length of a block when a hand touched my shoulder and a gentle voice commanded:

"Get up, son—this isn't for you."

I flushed with resentment. Damn it, here I was once more being set apart—the unwanted fraternity pledge who could not even be soaked to the skin with dignity.

Smiling down at me was a short man with graying hair. His name was Earl Reed Silvers and he wore a hearing aid which, I later learned, he switched off so that he could sleep through faculty meetings. Dozens of books for boys had streamed from his old Oliver typewriter. They were stories about boys who played fairly, shed shameless tears when the old school lost a football game, acted like sexless nitwits in the presence of girls, joined the right fraternities, and thereby became a credit to God and country. I had read many of his books, and captured by the dream of going to school like one of his heroes had saved $1,800 from my newspaper work to realize this ambition, but the little man who now clutched my arm and pulled me back from the shouting and knee-bruising and hose-spraying along College Avenue so heightened my tension that I trembled all over.

"You let me go," I blubbered. Hot tears of anger rolled down my cheeks.

"No," he said stubbornly. "You come with me."

Stormily I obeyed, walking into one of the finest friendships of my lifetime.

• • •

Almost unconsciously, we grew up in college. The hell-raising tapered off. As we matured, in our own slow, giddy, stumbling way, we learned that the essence of wisdom was compassion, a willingness to yield to others a margin for error. Perhaps we learned to laugh at ourselves. I hope so, for acquiring this gift is in itself worth a baccalaureate degree.

No man taught me this truth quite so quickly, or so well, as Earl Reed Silvers. Friends who loved him called him Reed, and those who feared his power called him Sil—he knew, I knew, everyone knew that those who said Sil were deeply jealous of the gifts that he possessed. For he inspired love, loyalty, obedience by the simplest of formulas: he gave love, loyalty, and obedience in return.

To those who were "his boys"—all those undergraduates who, in composite, became that son in a lonely grave—his door was always open. They could talk to him about anything: troubles at home, troubles in college, troubles within themselves. Although his title was Director of Alumni and Public Relations, he was really a father-teacher, now a rare character on the American campus.

He could not be sure at what hour of what day a boy was going to awaken intellectually, for boys were not alike, but he had the patience to wait. He gave nicknames to all of his boys and mine was Flash, because of a compulsive temper that took off like a Roman candle and fizzled out almost as quickly. Never once, when high tension overwhelmed me, did he command me to relax, for he understood—as so very few people do—that if I could relax I would not be handicapped.

Our relationship, though beginning awkwardly when Reed jerked me away from the hose-sprayers during Freshman Week, soon settled into a spirit of unusual camaraderie. His office was on the ground floor of Old Queen's, probably the finest example of Georgian architecture in America. This building, in use since 1811, possessed a gentleness, a mellowness that fitted Reed's personality. He was a wonderful listener. Within a term he knew more about me than my parents. He had a laugh—rather, a high-pitched giggle—that was infectious. He giggled at my derby and spats, at my sassiness toward the instructor over the ink blots, at my revolt against fraternities. As the depression deepened and the neutrals grew in power and prestige so that we were a political force to be reckoned with, he giggled most at those colleagues in the administration who, as fraternity boys, had grown older rather than up.

"Hop Brill thinks you'll blow up the D.U. house one night," Reed chuckled. I was not pleased by this comment for Hop, as the university's purchasing agent, had a strong voice in choosing the editor of the campus newspaper, a position no nonfraternity man had held within living memory. "To hell with Hop," Reed said breezily; at heart he was an inveterate manipulator. Again, when I wrote somewhat risque stories for the college magazine about Mattie and Emory and other Negroes I had known during my newspaper-selling days in Hackensack, Reed laughed at the Dean of Men's concern for my loose morals. "To hell with him, too," Reed said. "You've got talent and style."

In that shaky junior year, when Sam loaned me his last $300, I moved from Hegeman to the attic of a rooming house on Bartlett Street, cramped quarters that I shared with Archie Milligan, a good-humored Irish classmate. To eke out our rent Archie and I made baskets of sandwiches that we sold in the dormitories late at night.

Reed came through handsomely, securing for me the job as campus correspondent for the *Newark Evening News*, the best paying job of its kind. He taught me how to write short stories for the Sunday School weeklies and once or twice a month I would receive a check for twenty-five dollars. The sandwich route was forsaken and I planned in my senior year to move to a two-room suite in Ford Hall, then the Rutgers equivalent of a Gold Coast.

I was determined to become the editor-in-chief of *Targum*, the campus newspaper, without question the most influential undergraduate office in the college. The position not only paid a share of the profits earned by the paper (approximately $400 a year), but also automatically placed the recipient on Student Council and into Cap and Skull, the senior honorary society. My heart was set on becoming editor-in-chief, and Reed encouraged this ambition, but he knew that I was bucking tough opposition: the fraternities, Hop, tradition.

The *Targum* occupied a ramshackle frame building on College Avenue; to me it was a castle. In lieu of any cash remuneration, the managing editor lived in a room on the second floor and apparently never washed for the bathtub was littered with old newspapers and gin bottles (gin sold for two dollars a fifth if you knew on which door to knock on Holy Hill, where the theologians lived). Never had I labored harder than in this old building. Our standards, self-imposed, were far above the quality of anything we were taught in the School of Journalism; and the editor was a czar, a tyrant, who treated freshmen and sophomores like Mexican peons—his was a majestic office, dazzling and lovely for his ego.

Without Reed, I never would have broken the tradition and become editor-in-chief. . . .

• • •

In 1944 Reed Silvers finally escaped as a myth maker and became dean of men, permitting him to indulge all the fatherly impulses that were so basic to his nature. To the students he was never a stiff-necked disciplinarian but an indulgent friend and adviser talking about the ancient virtues that had filled his twenty-seven books for youngsters. In a magnificent tribute Dr. Clothier once said: ''He has been called Rutgers' Mr. Chips. He was far more than that. He was Rutgers' Reed Silvers.''

Reed moved from Rahway to the dean's house on College Avenue. His study was like a model in a magazine, but for Reed's creative spirit the place seemed sterile. He talked bravely of the books he still cared to write, but his words were strangely unconvincing. He needed the clutter of the old attic room in Rahway, the stutter of the antiquated Oliver typewriter, if he wished to go on recapturing youthful dreams.

From year to year, toward the end from month to month, I could see him aging. A hard siege of pneumonia weakened him frightfully and he went to Sarasota, Florida, hoping to recover. How long he had suffered with an ailing heart no one can say—perhaps from as long ago as those days when as a skinny youngster he had run the longer distances on the college track team—and on a night in late March of 1948 a heart attack killed him. He was only fifty-seven.

We devoted an entire issue of the *Alumni Monthly* as his memorial.

STUDENT: MAY SARTON

(1912–)

Poet and author.

TEACHER: AGNES BOYLE O'REILLY HOCKING

Mrs. Hocking was the wife of the philosopher, William Ernest Hocking, and the daughter of the poet, John Boyle O'Reilly; revolutionary blood flowed in her veins. The school was born of this marriage of poetry and philosophy, and though philosophy was worshiped, poetry ruled. Mrs. Hocking never referred to her husband otherwise than as ''Ernest Hocking,'' and always with the same intonation, which suggested that she considered him a deity. Once, discovering in the subway station at Harvard Square that she had forgotten her purse, she walked right past the collector, uttering the magic words ''Ernest Hocking will give you five cents tomorrow'' and sailed through the wicket.

As children in her school, we were caught up in a spiritual climate as bracing, as rich and unpredictable, as that of New England itself. We were not subjected to a theory of education. We were set down in the center of a primal force at work. We never knew what would happen next, but what did happen was always immensely interesting. We might, for instance, suddenly be punished—all sent to Coventry because one small person had fallen down and sprained an ankle. There was no logic in this meting out of judgment, but we thrived on it as did the Greeks on the changeable moods of Pallas Athene. It made us both stoical and imaginative. Mrs. Hocking was poetry incarnate. Her very person, glorious in red velvet on a special occasion, but more often resembling the old woman who lived in a shoe, was exhilarating. Soft wings of hair covered her brow; under them deep-set eyes twinkled, wept, or burned. She had small, quick hands, full of sudden caresses. I believe that she flew rather than walked.

She did not administer, she created, and part of the creation was, of course, to find teachers who would go their own way, unadministered. The word "co-operative" in the school's early name was as literal as the word "open-air." Shady Hill was founded to give the children of professors an ideal school, which the parents would invent and run themselves, and which would be within their limited means. There was not money to speak of; there were many scholarships. The excellent staff was made possible by the parents' pooling their skills, as helpers of all kinds, just as Henry Copley Greene became the official lighter of school plays, and Mr. Helburn, the official trainer in rock-climbing, who took groups of us off on Saturday afternoons to explore the rock-cliffs in the neighborhood of Cambridge. My mother taught applied design at Shady Hill for years, as she did later at the Winsor School. She believed that children, like primitive peoples, would enjoy making variations on simple geometric themes and applying these designs to useful and beautiful objects. What brilliant results emerged in this way from a design painted on a round ice-cream carton or wooden chopping bowl! The results had style and form, two elements that modern theories of "free painting" have apparently ceased to consider important. But I believe that children long for form just as grownups do, and that it releases rather than cramps creative energy. I was interested to rediscover the other day the original brochure advertising the school and to note that its aims were defined as: "To keep childhood alive to open-mindedness and a love of learning; to provide life with all possible richness and fullness; to secure freedom *with* self-control." *With* is underlined in the printed text, and one of the strengths of Shady Hill through the years, and long after Mrs. Hocking's retirement, was that that significant preposition was not forgotten. As I look back over the years that I spent in the school, I am very much aware that the emphasis on creativity and spontaneous expression was always balanced by a sense of the responsibility of each child toward the community, and above all respect not only for talent in each other, but for the ethical qualities summed up in the word "citizenship."

• • •

This was all very well, and in fact magnificent teaching, but it was not the very core of the school under Agnes Hocking. For the core of the school and its unique strength lay in the one fact that here poetry was made centrally alive. Agnes Hocking taught this subject—if what she did can be called by any such formal name as teaching—to the whole school. She did it all day long, by bursting into spontaneous prayer when the spirit moved her, by those sudden noble angers, and, more formally, by meeting with each class for a scheduled hour. No doubt there was method, but to us it was heavenly madness, was delight—the opening of a door into a land where everything on earth seemed gathered together and harmonized. It was, on the whole, a noisy school. But I have seen Agnes Hocking, sitting on a low chair before the open fire in the Big Room, create such stillness in a hundred or more boys and girls of all ages that they themselves quite clearly heard the silence above the noise of a passing trolley and the crackle of the fire. She did not tell us about poetry; she made us live its life. This creation of stillness, for instance, was the introduction to a little poem by Edward Rowland Sill called "Peace." One or another of us might be called on to say it, or we might say it together, or she might say it. But no one spoke until there was perfect silence, until all of us together had sat with our eyes shut for perhaps two minutes, and when the final line was spoken, "Peace is here," no one moved for ages and ages; peace *was* there. This was a fairly complex delight for small children. She also gave us simpler ones. Sometimes we all became seals, a thing rather easy to do if you are already sitting in a gray woolen bag. We simply lay down on our backs on the floor, while the Big Room became an ocean, and murmured:

> "Where billow meets billow, there soft be thy pillow;
> Ah, weary wee flipperling, curl at thy ease!
> The storm shall not wake thee, nor shark overtake thee,
> Asleep in the arms of the slow-swinging seas."

The floor swayed slightly below us and we rolled over. Mrs. Hocking, also in a gray bag on the floor, was the Seal of Seals.

Even purely technical matters became magic. Once she turned on me in apparent fury and shouted "You goose!" and then, before I had time to burst into tears, added in an explanatory tone, ''That's a metaphor.'' I never had to be told in so many words that metaphor explodes and simile is pale beside it. ''You goose! That's a metaphor'' had made it abundantly clear.

We were not given a poem to read or study; we learned each one through hearing it repeated by Mrs. Hocking until we knew it by heart. Knew it by heart? We had become whatever it was long before we guessed we were learning it. We learned poems by osmosis—the only good way, I am convinced. Our memory of the words was a reflex action that accompanied certain gestures—for instance, making the long ears of a hare when we repeated Walter de la Mare's ''Witch Hare.'' Even now I find it embarrassing to recite this poem because I can't keep my hands at my sides; they wish to become ears. Alain, the philosopher, speaks somewhere of poetry as ''a kind of music which is physiologically right.'' Therein lay its excitement for us. It was not something told, it was something happening to us all the time. On warm spring days, we moved outside to sit on benches under a large red maple. There, one day, we discovered that Sir William Watson's poem about April, for all its sentimental diction, was absolutely real. In the very middle of our reciting:

> ''April, April,
> Laugh thy girlish laughter;
> Then, the moment after,
> Weep thy girlish tears!''

a shower fell upon us and drove us in, suffused with laughter—in this case, the laughter of recognition. Did Agnes Hocking summon that cloud herself, I wonder. It would not have surprised us at all if she had.

• • •

Almost all of this is ancient history. The school is no longer ''open-air.'' It has moved into larger grounds and new buildings at the other end of Cambridge. But until very recently Miss Edgett was still making huge decimal points on the blackboard; Miss Putnam was helping generations of boys and girls to be not only knowledgeable but humble and wise. Shady Hill is no doubt still to many a child the best school in the world. But we, the prehistoric ones, who remember Mrs. Hocking and the genius who succeeded her, will, I trust, be forgiven for secretly thinking, "I knew a phoenix in my youth, so let them have their day."

STUDENT: RICHARD M. NIXON

(1913–)

Attorney, Member of Congress, United States Senator, Vice President and 37th President of the United States and author.

TEACHERS: DR. PAUL SMITH
ALBERT UPTON
DR. J. HERSCHEL COFFIN

In college, as in high school, I continued to plug away at my studies. For the first time I met students who were able to get good grades without working very hard for them, but I needed the steady discipline of nightly study to keep up with all the courses and reading.

Each of my teachers made a great impression on me, but a few in particular touched my mind and changed my life.

Dr. Paul Smith was probably the greatest intellectual inspiration of my early years. I took his courses in British and American civilization, the American constitution, and international relations and law. He was a brilliant lecturer, who always spoke without notes. His doctorate was from the University of Wisconsin, where he had studied under the great Progressive historian Glenn Frank. Dr. Smith's approach to history and politics was strongly influenced by the Progressive outlook, and it came as a revelation to me that history could be more than a chronicle of past events—that it could be a tool of analysis and criticism.

Albert Upton, who taught English and was the director of the drama club, was an iconoclast. Nothing was sacred to him, and he stimulated us by his outspoken unorthodoxy.

At the end of my junior year he told me that my education would not be complete until I read Tolstoy and the other great Russian novelists. That summer I read little else. My favorite was *Ressurrection,* Tolstoy's last major novel. I was even more deeply affected by the philosophical works of his later years. His program for a peaceful revolution for the downtrodden Russian masses, his passionate opposition to war, and his emphasis on the spiritual elements in all aspects of life left a more lasting impression on me than his novels. At that time in my life I became a Tolstoyan.

Dr. Herschel Coffin influenced me in a different way. He taught a course called "The Philosophy of Christian Reconstruction," which I took in my senior year. This course was better known by its subtitle, "What Can I Believe?" It involved a weekly written self-analysis based on questions raised in class. We studied the theory of evolution, the literal authenticity of the Bible, and the nature of democracy, and at the beginning, middle, and end of the course, we had to write an essay answering the question, "What Can I Believe?"

• • •

Thanks to my teachers I studied hard and received a first-rate education at Whittier.

STUDENT: THEODORE H. WHITE

(1915–1986)

Journalist, editor and author.

TEACHERS: MISS FULLER JOHN KING FAIRBANK

. . . I first became aware of the word "history" in the sixth grade at the Christopher Gibson School [in Boston]—and my teacher was Miss Fuller.

How can I say what a ten-year-old boy remembers of a schoolteacher lost in time? She was stout, gray-haired, dimpled, schoolmarmish, almost never angry. She was probably the first Protestant I ever met; she taught history vigorously; and she was special, the first person who made me think I might make something of myself. She was the kind of teacher who could set fire to the imaginations of the ordinary children who sat in lumps before her, and to do so was probably the chief reward she sought.

Her course in American history began, of course, at a much later date than the history we were taught in Hebrew school. In Boston, history began in 1630—when the Puritans came. It then worked back and forth, but every date had to be impeccably remembered; Columbus was 1492, Cabot was 1497. Cortes was 1519, as was Magellan; and so on, moving through Jamestown, 1607; New York, 1614; Plymouth Colony, 1620; then other dates that led up to the settlement of Boston—1630! 1630! 1630! We also had to know the names in the tests: William Penn, Sir George Carteret, King James (which had to be written King James I, or else you were marked wrong).

Miss Fuller did not stop with names and dates. First you had to get them right, but then they became the pegs on which connections between events were to be hung. In this she was far ahead of most of the teachers of her day. For example: Thanksgiving. How did it come about? What would you have thought that first winter in Plymouth, if you had come from England, and survived? How would you invite the Indians to your feast? She decided we would have a play the day before Thanksgiving, a free-form play in the classroom, in which we would all together explore the meeting of Puritans and Indians, and the meaning of Thanksgiving. She divided the class, entirely Jewish, into those children who were American-born and spoke true English, and those who were recent arrivals and spoke only broken English or Yiddish. I was Elder Bradford, because I spoke English well. "Itchie" Rachlin, whose father was an unemployed trumpet player recently arrived from Russia, and who spoke vivid Yiddish, was Squanto, our Indian friend. Miss Fuller hoped that those who could not speak English would squawk strange Indian sounds while I, translating their sounds to the rest of the Puritans, all of us in black cardboard cone hats, would offer good will and brotherhood. "Itchie" and the other recently arrived immigrant children played the game of being "Indian" for a few minutes, then fell into Yiddish, pretending it was Indian talk. Miss Fuller could not, of course, understand them, but I tried nevertheless to clean up their Yiddish vulgarities in my translation to the other little Puritans, who could not help but giggle. (*Vos is dos vor traef?* said Itchie, meaning: "You want us to eat pig food?" and I would translate in English: "What kind of strange food is this before us?") Miss Fuller became furious as we laughed our way through the play; and when I tried to explain, she was hurt and upset. Thanksgiving was sacred to her. But she was a marvelous teacher. Once we had learned the names and dates from 1630 to the Civil War, she let us talk and speculate, driving home the point that history connected to "now," to "us." America for her was all about freedom, and all the famous phrases from "Give me liberty or give me death" to the Gettysburg Address had to be memorized by her classes—and understood.

She was also a very earnest, upward-striving teacher. I realize now that she must have been working for an advanced degree, for she went to night school at Boston University to take education courses. This, too, reached from outside to me. One day she told my mother about a project her night-school seminar was conducting in how much independent research a youngster of ten or eleven could do on his own—one of those projects now so commonplace in progressive schools. Would my mother mind, she asked, if I was given such an assignment, and then reported on it to her seminar? My mother said yes after Miss Fuller promised to bring me home herself afterwards.

My assignment was to study immigration, and then to speak to the seminar about whether immigrants were good or bad for America. Her seminar mates would question me to find out how well I had mastered the subject. The Immigration Act of 1924—the "Closing of the Gates"— had just been passed; there was much to read in both papers and magazines about the controversy, but my guide was my father. He put it both ways: the country had been built by immigrants, so immigrants were not bad. He had been an immigrant himself. On the other hand, as a strong labor man, he followed the A. F. of L. line of those days. The National Association of Manufacturers (the capitalists) wanted to continue unrestricted immigration so they could sweat cheap labor. But the American Federation of Labor wanted immigration restricted to keep the wages of American workingmen from being undercut by foreigners. This was a conundrum for my father: he was against the capitalists and for the A. F. of L.; but he was an immigrant himself, as were all of our friends and neighbors. He helped me get all the facts, and I made a speech on the platform of a classroom at Boston University Teachers College at nine one night, explaining both sides of the story and taking no position. I enjoyed it all, especially when the teachers began asking me questions; I had all the dates and facts, and an attentive audience, but no answers then just as I have none now. I must have done well, for Miss Fuller kissed me and bought me candy to eat on the streetcar. It became clear to me, as we talked on the way home, that immigrants were history, too. History was happening now, all about us, and the gossip of Erie Street and the problem of whether someone's cousin could get a visa back in the old country and come here were really connected to the past, and to Abraham Lincoln, Henry Clay, Sam Adams, Patrick Henry and the elder William Bradford.

If I went on to the Boston Public Latin School, I think it was because of Miss Fuller and my mother; it was Miss Fuller who persuaded my mother that there was something more than a lump in the boy, and pointed me in the direction of the Latin School.

• • •

At Harvard, thus, I made the third round in American history: Miss Fuller had guided me the first time around, the Latin School the second, and at Harvard a large covey of professors gave me the final tour. But [Arthur] Schlesinger [Sr.] and [Paul] Buck had set the tone: proud and patriotic as Miss Fuller had been, they saw American history as a struggle from which the good usually emerged triumphant. I was thus early bent to this patriotic view, and confirmed in it by higher learning, before I went out to see the story myself.

• • •

Yet the teacher who, more than any other, spun me off into history as a life calling was a young man who arrived at Harvard only at the beginning of my junior year: John King Fairbank, later to become the greatest historian of America's relations with China. Fairbank was then only twenty-nine—tall, burly, sandy-haired, a prairie boy from South Dakota; soft-spoken, with an unsettling conversational gift of delayed-action humor; and a painstaking drillmaster. He had himself graduated from Harvard in 1929, but on his way back to the Yard had made a circuitous route via Oxford and Peking to become a specialist in modern Chinese history. He had a freshly minted Ph. D. and was on trial at Harvard both as a tutor and Orientalist; since I was the only undergraduate majoring in Chinese history and studies, I was assigned to him as tutee. No two young people could have come of more different backgrounds. The tutorial system at Harvard was then in its early years, exploring the idea that each young mind needs an older mind to guide it. Tutors at Harvard now are usually embittered graduate students, rarely, if ever, emotionally committed to the undergraduates they guide. But Fairbank approached me as if he were an apprentice Pygmalion, assigned a raw piece of ghetto stone to carve, sculpt, shape and polish. He yearned that I do well.

It was not only that I was invited to my first tea party at his home, learning how to balance a teacup properly; nor that, by observation, I learned proper table manners at a properly set breakfast table in the little yellow cottage where he lived with his beautiful young wife, Wilma. It was his absolute devotion to forcing my mind to think that speeded the change in me. We would talk about China and he would tell me tales of life in Peking as chatter—but only after our work was done. He was insistent that I read. I spent six weeks plowing through St. Thomas Aquinas, which, he agreed, was useless, yet necessary for a professional historian's understanding. He would make the hardest work a joy, and his monthly assignments were written with a skill and personal attention that no tutor at Harvard, or anywhere else, today gives to his students. One of his assignment memos, which I still treasure, shows how a great teacher goes about his calling.

WHEREAS [read his communication] it is not possible to live (long) without thinking, and not possible to live well without thinking well; and

It is not possible to think well without making distinctions between this and that, or heredity and environment, or cause and effect, or the group and the individual, or the law and the facts, or tactics and strategy, or rights and duties, or man and woman, or nominalism and realism, or communism and fascism, or collectivism and individualism, to say nothing of up and down, or backwards or forwards; and whereas

It is not possible to go very far in making distinctions without making use of categories of thought, such as a category of laws and a category of events, or a category of noumena and a category of phenomena, or a category of spirit and a category of matter; and whereas

It is not possible to think with critical power without being critical of the categories with which one is thinking; and

It is not possible to avoid receiving certain categories at an early age from the contemporary intellectual environment;—

THEREFORE—

Philosophy is a most necessary and admirable subject, and

You are cordially invited to be present at a meeting on Friday, January 8, 1937, at which there will be a discussion of Whitehead's volume Science and the Modern World (entire) conducted by none other than Mr. Theodore H. White.

Thus I was introduced to Whitehead's philosophy as to myriad other ideas by Fairbank's loving and disciplined tutelage.

Yet, though he molded me, he was pursuing his own cause, too—which was understanding the revolution in Asia in our time. The fossil Sinologists of Harvard's Oriental Department felt that all Oriental history ended with the end of the Ch'ien-lung dynasty, in 1799.

Professor Elisaeff, the department chief, insisted that everything after that date was journalism. Fairbank held otherwise—that history was happening now. He was probably the only man in all Cambridge who recognized that the Long March of Mao Tse-tung, the year before he himself joined Harvard's faculty, was epoch-making. Thus, then, in my senior year, young John Fairbank was allowed to teach a course—History 83b—on China from the death of Ch'ien-lung down to our times. It was a magnificent series of lectures, ground-breaking in intellectual patterns, and those few students who attended it caught the swell of what was happening in China and Asia from his wry, caustic, surgical stripping of myth from fact, noumena from phenomena, his separating Dr. Fu Manchu and *The Bitter Tea of General Yen* from what was really going on in China. His course reinforced what my father had told me of China and what I felt by instinct. It inflamed my itch to be off, away and out—to China, where the story lay.

We differed, Fairbank and I, in an affectionate quarrel, over my senior thesis. I was shooting for fellowships and highest honors and I wanted to write about the delicate interaction of force and order. I wanted to take as my thesis subject the war lords of modern China and their brutalities over the thirty-year span of collapse of China's civil order. Fairbank insisted it was too broad a matter for a college senior to write about. I had become obsessed with force as the engine of history: who gathers the guns together at what point to hammer at the state or the enemy. Fairbank wrote back to my remonstrance a long letter on the causes of human action in man, saying that "force forces them at times, fear of force more often—and ideals still more often." He insisted that I display my knowledge of Chinese historiography by writing about the Twenty-One Demands of Japan on China in 1915 from Chinese bibliographical sources. This kind of scholarly paper, he pointed out, might get me a fellowship in the Harvard-Yenching Institute as a candidate for a doctorate. I set out to pursue this thesis in my senior year; and did so. This study of Japanese imperialism may have been, in a tiny way, useful to scholarship. But already, in my senior year, after two years with Fairbank, I knew I was leaving home.

STUDENT: ISAAC ASIMOV

(1920–   )

Author and professor.

TEACHER: MISS MARTIN

On February 1929, I entered 5B1, and my teacher was a Miss Martin. She was the best teacher I had had since the first grade—and for many years afterward—and I loved her more than any other. She was unfailingly good-natured and never scolded shrewishly. She read to us from books and, in fact, introduced me to Hugh Lofting's books about Dr. Doolittle which, for some years to come, were nectar and ambrosia to me.

Furthermore, she was clearly fond of me and didn't mind that I was my usual disruptive self in her class. Her liking wasn't reflected in the marks I got. For two months running, I remember, I brought back my report card with an A in schoolwork and a D (in *red,* for failure) in deportment. Fortunately, my parents knew what deportment meant now, and merely lectured me.

But despite my deportmental villainy, Miss Martin liked me. For one thing, she gave me the chance to recover from a particularly painful setback I had had in 5A1.

Not long after I had joined PS 202, the school's semi-annual spelling bee came up. Every class within a certain range would send out its representative, and the bee would be held in the auditorium. The students all loved it because it was exciting. After all, you could root for your own class and laugh and hoot like fiends if anyone missed. (The old hand-on-the-shoulder, "Well played, old man," was totally foreign to us.)

Naturally, I was sent into the fray by 5A1. I hadn't been there long, but I had already proved that I was death on spelling. I could spell any word I had ever seen.

So there I was on the stage.

It wasn't as though I had never been on the stage before. Every schoolchild gets his chance, whether he wants to or not, because every class is bound to have a class play, and every youngster in the class is somehow involved. If he misses in one term, he gets it in another.

I, too, had been in plays. I had once played a Russian soldier in a play that was set in Russia. As I recall, the little heroine, a poor girl, was so unhappy with her lot that her fairy godmother told her she could change places with anyone, just by shaking hands with them. The little girl then met a series of other people, all of whom seemed to be better off than she was, but she always found something about them that made her shrink away. The princess who enters is frightened of thieves, so the little girl thinks that if she were only a soldier she wouldn't be afraid of anyone.

That was my cue to enter (age seven, I think, at the time), with my woolen hat's earflaps coming down and buttoning under my chin to represent a soldier's helmet, and my arms crossed over my chest to indicate resolution and valor. I had but to appear and the entire audience did what they always seemed to do when I appeared—they burst into loud laughter. Fortunately I was used to it, and I delivered my lines with *sang-froid*. By the time I had detailed the hardships of a soldier's life, the heroine wouldn't shake hands with me. But that was a play—in a familiar school before familiar fellow pupils.

Now, two years later, I was in a contest, facing strangers in a strange school. And it was a competition that was particularly unfair. Victory was only what I expected and would give me no great pleasure. Defeat, however, would be an unthinkable humiliation. I had nothing particularly to win; everything to lose; and there was no fun in it.

My teeth chattered, my body shook—not so much out of fear as out of tension. When it was my turn, I was asked to spell "weigh." I stood up and said, "Weigh, W-I-E-G-H, Weigh," and knew I was wrong the minute I transversed the two vowels.

I went down and walked back to my seat, with hoots and catcalls ringing in my ear. I had missed the first word.

Even if everyone at school had not made it their mission to remind me of this now and again, I would not have forgotten.

When the time came for the next term's spelling bee, I was in 5B1 and Miss Martin said, "Is there anyone in the class who would like to represent us in the spelling bee?"

Two or three hands went up; mine stayed firmly down. Once was enough for one lifetime.

Miss Martin looked at me. "Aren't you volunteering, Isaac?"

The class looked at me. I said, "I missed last term, Miss Martin. I don't think the class wants me."

Miss Martin said to the class, "Isaac has the best marks for spelling this term, and I think he can win. How many in the class want him?" Once she expressed her preference, of course, all the little sycophants raised a cry on my behalf, and I was forced to be the 5B1 representative in a bee that included all the classes in the fourth, fifth, and sixth grades.

I was nervous again, but this time, at least, I had the comforting knowledge that I could not do worse than the term before. As soon as I had spelled the first word correctly, I was ahead of the game. And once I was ahead, I calmed down and was certain I would win.

It wasn't quite that easy. By the time the period ended, another boy (from one of the sixth-grade classes) and myself were still on our feet. We had to fight it out in a tie-breaking session a few days later in the principal's office.

We were both shaking with tension and barely able to enunciate, and the principal kindly tried to ease the situation by telling us that we would have two tries at every word. When I spelled "customer" C-O-S-T-O-M-E-R, my face went into a spasm of unhappiness.

The principal said, "Try it again, Isaac," and I got it right the next time.

After a few more words, the other boy spelled "disappointment" D-I-S-S-A-P-O-I-N-T-M-E-N-T. I tried to keep my face frozen. The principal gave him another chance and, after some hesitation, he spelled it *the same way.* I was astonished.

The principal said, "Can you spell the word, Isaac?" Of course I could and did, and I won. I didn't really enjoy the victory, however, because I had been the first to miss, and if it had not been for the relaxation of the rules, the other boy would have won. I have never forgotten this.

I got a fountain pen as my prize, the first one I had ever owned.

Till then the only pens I had were those with steel points that you fitted into a wooden holder and dipped into an inkwell. Every desk had an inkwell, which the teacher filled out of a tall ink bottle when necessary and which, sooner or later, got all over the clothes of every pupil in the class (sometimes accidentally, sometimes maliciously).

I don't recall that we had any spelling bees after that. I don't know why they were stopped, but I was tremendously relieved. I would certainly have been class representative if they had continued, and I didn't want to be. The second time out I had a failure to make up, but afterward I would merely have been defending champion with nothing to gain and everything to lose.

One final gift of Miss Martin's came when the class was over and the summer vacation had begun. In the final days of the class, she announced that she would take a few selected members of the class, those who had done very well in both work and deportment, on a visit to the Statue of Liberty.

It was clear I wouldn't make it, for the pair of D's in deportment placed me out of the running under even the most liberal interpretation of what "good marks" might be.

That bothered me for several reasons.

First, I had never gone *anywhere* without my parents, except to the local library, and it would be thrilling to do so. Second, I wanted to see the Statue of Liberty. Third, when my parents found out (and somehow they would, I was sure) that selected members of the class had been chosen for this outing and that I hadn't qualified, I would be in for a sticky half hour.

So I sat there, looking disappointed, and Miss Martin, ever an Isaac enthusiast, said to the pupils, "Class, shall we make an exception for the brightest pupil in the class even if his deportment is bad?" Once again all the little sycophants cheered, and I got to go.

She was *such* a softhearted teacher. I saw her once or twice during the next year, but then I left PS 202 and I never saw her or heard from her again. Still—thank you, Miss Martin, wherever you are.

STUDENT: GEORGE MCGOVERN

(1922–)

Professor, Member of Congress, United States Senator and author.

TEACHERS: GRACE COOLEY
ROSE HOPFNER
BOB PEARSON

When I was small, my most serious handicap was a painful bashfulness in the presence of strangers. My first year in school was a nightmare. Although I had learned to read prior to the first grade, I refused to participate in the oral reading exercises. The teacher promptly placed me in the circle of the poorest readers. I remained with that group for the balance of the year, sitting red-faced and silent when it came my turn to read. Nor did I recite in class, or volunteer answers, or ever raise a hand for recognition. I desperately wanted to go unnoticed and to remain silent.

Somehow my teacher sensed, perhaps from my written work, that I was not totally stupid and she passed me "on condition" to the second grade. There I encountered a determined young instructor who first started the process of loosening my tongue. She did it by a rather direct implication that I would either recite in class or be bounced out of school. But this message was given to me in private after school and she kept me with her in these after-school sessions for several days, forcing me to read and recite to her. She was firm and, indeed, insistent, but the slightest stammering response on my part brought words of strong assurance. The shyness continued, but I did begin to participate, however reluctantly, in class recitations. And I was impressed with that concerned, youthful teacher.

Then, in the third grade, I came under the influence of Grace Cooley—a self-confident, witty, dedicated woman who enlivened her courses with stories of her experience in international travel. I desperately wanted to please her, and I believe she detected a few possible indications of intelligence in me.

There were setbacks from time to time in the struggle against shyness. One embarrassing experience occurred in the second grade when I had been postponing a visit to the rest room rather than raise my hand and ask to be excused. After a painful hour of repressing the forces of nature, a trickle appeared on the floor below my desk. This brought an excited shriek from Dorothy Nash, a girl with a high-pitched voice who sat next to me: ''Oh, look what he's doing!'' I have never been closer to total heart failure.

Looking back to the committed teachers of the Mitchell [South Dakota] public-school system, I am convinced that good teachers may be as important in the development of a child as good parents. It was two high school teachers who steered me onto a course that explains much of my subsequent development.

As a high school sophomore I took a course in English composition from Miss Rose Hopfner. She was the first teacher to single me out for high praise combined with specific advice. She told me one day that I had a sensitivity and clarity of expression that was rare for a sophomore. Then she urged me to talk with Bob Pearson, the history teacher and debating coach, about participation in the extracurricular debate program. A few days later I stood up at an evening meeting of the debate program squad to refute the proposition ''Resolved that the several States should adopt a unicameral legislature.'' The speech was a disaster. It was supposed to take ten minutes. I spoke for two minutes in barely coherent terms and then sat down humiliated and filled with a sense of failure. But Bob Pearson was soon on his feet giving a serious critique of what I had said and assuring me that it was an adequate first effort. No other person did more to strengthen my confidence and draw out my latent powers of expression than Bob Pearson.

Competitive high school debate literally transformed my personality and my approach to life. I learned to organize my thoughts, to buttress my ideas with evidence and to speak extemporaneously. The practice of debating both the affirmative and negative side of each year's debate proposition forced me into the complexities of major public questions.

• • •

One day during my junior year at Mitchell High, Bob Pearson had departed from an American History lesson long enough to give us a brief outline of his philosophy of life. I was ready by then to follow his advice on anything—but especially on the meaning of life. The most important goal, he said, is "the service of others." And, he added, the most vital ingredient in a useful and satisfying career is "imagination." It did not require much further stimulus on my part to decide that I wanted to follow Bob Pearson's career of teaching history.

STUDENT: JIMMY CARTER

(1924–)

Farmer, businessman, Georgia State Senator and 76th Governor, 39th President of the United States and humanitarian.

TEACHER: JULIA COLEMAN

Within my memory, whenever anyone has ever asked me what I wanted for Christmas or my birthday present, I always replied, "Books." When I was four years old my godmother, also a nurse like my mother—though apparently not a great reader—gave me a set of the complete works of Guy de Maupassant. It was, of course, years later before I read through this set of volumes.

My life was heavily influenced by our school superintendent, Miss Julia Coleman, who encouraged me to learn about music, art, and especially literature.

Miss Julia was a spinster, who died recently, and she encouraged all of her students to seek cultural knowledge beyond the requirements of a normal rural school classroom. We were highly competitive in debating, an essay contest called "Ready Writing," music appreciation, one-act play productions, spelling bees, and other cultural activities.

Every student in the classroom was required to debate, to memorize and recite long poems and chapters from the Bible, and to participate in spelling contests. Each of us had to learn the rudiments of music and play some musical instrument—if it were only a ukulele, harmonica, or even a small piccolo.

Miss Julia had poor eyesight, and the discipline of her classrooms evaporated during her later years of supervising school work. However, this was certainly not the case when I was her student.

As a school boy who lived in an isolated farm community, my exposure to classical literature, art, and music was insured by this superlative teacher. She prescribed my reading list and gave me a silver star for every five books and a gold star for ten book reports.

Miss Julia remains alive in my memory. She was short and somewhat crippled, yet she was quite graceful as she moved along. Her face was expressive, particularly when she was reading one of the poems she loved, or presenting to a class the paintings of Millet, Gainesborough, Whistler, or Sir Joshua Reynolds.

When I was about twelve years old she called me in and stated that she was ready for me to read *War and Peace*. I was happy with the title because I thought that finally Miss Julia had chosen for me a book about cowboys and Indians. I was appalled when I checked the book out of the library because it was about 1,400 pages long, written by the Russian novelist Tolstoy, and of course not about cowboys at all. It turned out to be one of my favorite books, and I have read it two or three times since then.

STUDENT: SHIRLEY CHISHOLM
(1924–)

Teacher and Member of Congress.

TEACHER: LOUIS WARSOFF

When I graduated from Girls High in 1942 I drew several scholarship offers. I wanted to accept either one from Vassar or one from Oberlin. But my parents argued that they could not afford my room and board at an out-of-town school. I had to admit they were right, and in the fall I went to Brooklyn College.

If I had gone to Vassar, the rest of my life might have been different. Would I have become one of the pseudo-white upper-middle-class black women professionals, or a doctor's wife with furs, limousines, clubs, and airs? I can't believe that would have happened, but one never knows. At any rate, Brooklyn College changed my life. I was still naive about most things when I entered college, not quite eighteen. My fiercely protective parents had given me a sheltered upbringing that was incredible, considering the time and place in which I grew up. In school, my intelligence had put me in a special category. In college, I began to bump up against more of the world.

One needed an 89 percent average to enter Brooklyn College then, so there were only about sixty black students in the day school. Brooklyn was the largest of the five city-run colleges, and its campus was supposed to be especially for bright lower-class, poorer students. Tuition was free; it was a "subway campus," and one would have expected more black students. The trouble was, of course, that the grade and high schools they attended—then as now—did not do enough to overcome the handicaps of their background. So 98 percent of the students at the city colleges were white.

Brooklyn College was alive with activity. Bulletin boards and walls were full of posters for meetings, clubs, and programs. There were more organizations and extracurricular activities than anyone could count. Many of them were politically oriented and most of these were ultraprogressive. Brooklyn's president, Dr. Harry Gideonse, was always under attack from some office seeker who claimed that the faculty was riddled with Reds. It wasn't of course, but for those days it was radical.

I had already decided to become a teacher. There was no other road open to a young black woman. Law, medicine, even nursing were too expensive, and few schools would admit black men, much less a woman. Social work was not yet open to blacks in the early 1940s. If I had other ideas about what I might do, I dismissed them. My youth may have been sheltered from boys and some other realities, but I was black, and nobody needed to draw me a diagram. No matter how well I prepared myself, society wasn't going to give me a chance to do much of anything else. (My sister Muriel, who entered Brooklyn College a few years later, majored in physics and graduated magna cum laude. She was unable to find a job, even as a laboratory technician.) I knew it would have to be teaching for me; but I took no education courses, for some reason. I majored in sociology and minored in Spanish.

There was one all-black student group, the Harriet Tubman Society. Some upperclassmen had started it, about a year before I joined it in my sophomore year. There I first heard people other than my father talk about white oppression, black racial consciousness, and black pride. The black students kept to their own tables in the cafeteria. We talked. No one said ''rap'' then, but that's what we did. I had some things to contribute, more out of my reading than my experience. I knew about Harriet Tubman and Frederick Douglass, W. E. B. Du Bois and George W. Carver, and I had managed to find some books in the public library about our African heritage that few people then studied or talked about; I knew about the Ashanti kingdoms, for instance. Some of the Tubman Society speakers warned of the future: ''The day is going to come when blacks and whites will be at each other's throats in their own communities.'' We found that hard to believe then, although the 1943 Detroit riots had happened to serve as a portent.

Other experiences sharpened my feeling for how racism was woven through American life. I belonged to the Political Science Society, which naturally thought itself progressive. Some of its speakers, I became aware, looked at my people as another breed, less human than they. Politicians came to talk and gave us such liberal sentiments as, "We've got to help the Negro because the Negro is limited," or, "Of course, the Negro people have always been the laborers and will continue to be. So we've got to make it more comfortable for them." Few white speakers would dare to say such things even to all-white audiences now. They were innocent about prejudice twenty years ago.

For a long time I watched such white people closely, listened to them, and observed silently the treatment blacks were given in social and political situations. It grew on me that we, black men especially, were expected to be subservient even in groups where ostensibly everyone was equal. Blacks played by those rules; if a white man walked in, they came subtly to attention. But I could see their fear, helplessness, and discomfort.

When I looked at the white people who were doing this, consciously or not, it made me angry because so many of them were baser, less intelligent, less talented than the people they were lording it over. But the whites were in control. We could do nothing about it. We had no power. That was the way society was. I perceived that this was the way it was meant to be: things were organized to keep those who were on the top up there. The country was racist all the way through.

More and more people, white and black, began to tell me things like, "Shirley, you have potential. You should do something with your life." I felt they were right. There must be a role for me to play, but what? As a teacher, perhaps I could use the talents people were telling me about and which I felt were there to do something that would be of service to society—especially to children. I volunteered to work in an Urban League settlement house, teaching art classes and sewing, and writing and producing skits and plays, which I loved. I decided to devote my life to children. But the resolve was also there (I did not realize yet how fierce it had grown) to do something about the way whites treated my people. Political action was hardly even a fantasy for me at that time. But I decided that if I ever had a chance, somehow I would tell the world how things were as I saw them.

A blind political science professor, Louis Warsoff, became interested in me, and we had long talks. I called him ''Proffy,'' affectionately. He was one of the first white men whom I ever really knew and trusted. Our white neighbors and my father's co-workers had never been friends; they did not visit us and we did not visit them, and our interrelations were always a little strained even when they were at their best. From Professor Warsoff I learned that white people were not really different from me. I loved formal debating particularly, and once after I starred in a match he told me, ''You ought to go into politics.'' I was astonished at his naivete.

''Proffy,'' I said, ''you forget two things. I'm black—and I'm a woman.''

STUDENT: DANIEL K. INOUYE

(1924–)

Attorney, state legislator and United States Senator.

TEACHER: RUTH KING

It was my sophomore year in high school that I first came under the warm and rewarding spell of Mrs. Ruth King, a teacher whose influence in my young life ranked just behind that of my mother and father. She certainly didn't look inspiring, a short, plump lady in her middle forties with graying hair and eyes that seemed to look vaguely out from behind a pair of rimless glasses and to see practically nothing. But the truth was that she saw practically everything, surely nothing of any real importance that happened in her classroom escaped her notice.

Hers was the top tenth grade class at McKinley High. I don't know how I got into it and, from the very first day, I wanted out. In place of all my live-and-let-live buddies from Moiliili and McCully, I found myself rubbing shoulders with a breed of kids who kept trying to pretend that their skin was white and their eyes were blue. And there in the midst of this pretense, surrounded by all those starched white shirts and shined shoes, was rough-and-tumble Dan Inouye, to whom a necktie was a garrote on the spirit, and shoes an encumbrance to be suffered through at funerals and in church.

In those days, McKinley High School was jokingly referred to as Tokyo High. Thanks to an ingenious system of segregation, nearly all of us there were of Japanese ancestry, and from the least affluent *nisei* families, at that. It worked through a device known as the English Standard School and neatly sidestepped the law that, theoretically, opened all the public schools to everyone regardless of race, color or creed. To be admitted to an English Standard School—which by invariable coincidence had better facilities and better faculties—one had to pass an examination. The written part was fair enough since everyone had an equal chance. But the oral test served as an automatic weeding-out factor, for rare indeed was the student of Asian parentage who could properly pronounce the "th" sound, the "r" and the "l." The obvious result was that the English Standard Schools became almost the exclusive province of Caucasian youngsters, and that handful of Japanese and Chinese whose parents could afford to give them private tutoring. Not until 1955 was the last of this subtle segregation eliminated from Hawaii's public school system.

I was too young and unknowing then to be troubled by the concept of "Tokyo High." Only my stiff-necked classmates bothered me and sometimes it seemed that the only person who ever talked to me in that grade was Mrs. King. "Your grammar leaves something to be desired, Dan," she would say to me privately. "Why don't you stay after school today and we'll work on it?" And I would, happily, because to be in her presence was suddenly to glimpse something beyond the narrow horizons of the life I'd known, to sense that being a clerk, or even a beach boy, was not the ultimate and only hope for a kid like me. She took me seriously, which is something that no one, not even I myself, had ever done.

All at once literature was exciting and history was real. Washington and Jefferson and Lincoln suddenly stepped out of some mythical haze and became men of flesh and blood, men with great problems and the great courage to face them. I felt the bitter cold and despair of that winter at Valley Forge. I felt a sharp sense of personal loss at the death of Lincoln, the lost opportunity to bind up the nation's wounds. Whereas Japanese history had always sounded like some great impersonal pageant, the story of America had the ring of an adventure in human progress, troubles and setbacks and the inexorable march down to the present.

But most important of all, I came to believe that the giants who made American history were *my* forefathers. Always before, I had been a little embarrassed singing about the "land where my fathers died," and I always spoke of the *the* fathers of *the* country. It was Mrs. King who, in some wonderfully subtle way convinced me of the essential relationship between America's founding fathers and all of America's people.

In mid-year, Mrs. King recommended me for membership in McKinley's two junior honor societies, the Torch Society and the McKinley Citizenship Club. My mother and father glowed with pride although I tried to pretend that it didn't matter to me one way or the other, the truth is that I was really excited by the prospect. On the appointed afternoon, beaming with good fellowship, I strode before the Student Council for my interview. They sat behind a long table, four seniors trying to look as stern as bankers. They didn't ask me to sit down.

"Why do you think you belong in an honor society?" one of them asked.

I shrugged. "It was Mrs. King's idea. I . . . "

"Why don't you wear shoes?" another suddenly shot at me, a Japanese kid I'd known for at least five years.

"Because I only have one pair," I said to him. "They have to last." It was a silly question, he knew I only had one pair. He probably even knew that they'd been bought two years ago, and bought two sizes too large so I wouldn't grow out of them, and that until only recently I'd had to stuff the toes with paper to keep the darned things on.

But the silly questions were only beginning. "Why don't you wear a white shirt?" they asked. "Why don't you wear a tie?"

I didn't know what to say. I looked from one to the other, a gathering fear inside me, like dirty fingers squeezing my stomach. What was this all about? I thought they were going to interview me about my interests and ideas, about my schoolwork maybe. Why did they care what I wore?

"Are you going to answer the question?"

"I don't know," I said. "My shirt is for church . . . "

"Don't you care how you look in school?"

Not wanting to, I looked down at my sports shirt and my denim pants and bare feet. "My clothes are clean," I mumbled. "I don't know what's wrong."

"What about your friends?" one of them barked, and rattled off a list of kids from my neighborhood. "Are *they* your friends?"

"Yes," I said, and all at once I knew that they were going to turn me down. "What's the matter with them?"

"Delinquents!"

"Because they don't wear shoes?" I said, and it was not a question. "Because they're poor? They're no more delinquents than I am Or you are." All the disappointment, all the fear had suddenly boiled up in anger, and when they tried to interrupt me I shouted them down: "Hey, listen, I thought this was an honor society—honor, scholarship. But if all you're looking for is guys who wear white shirts and shoes, you don't want me and I for sure don't want you. I wouldn't trade one of my friends for . . . for both your honor societies and all four of you, so just forget the whole thing!"

For a long, long time afterward I would stiffen with an inner fury every time I remembered those moments of humiliation, and I remembered them often. Nor was that the end of it. Somehow I had to explain to my parents that I had not been accepted into the honor societies without telling them the real reasons, for they would then have blamed themselves. So I stammered and stuttered through some lame explanation that fooled them not a bit, and their eyes grew sad and there was no more for any of us to say. As for Mrs. King, who seemed to know everything there was to know about my unhappy encounter with the Council without my saying a word, she was so deeply hurt by their behavior that not once in my next year at McKinley High did she recommend another candidate for the Torch Society or the McKinley Citizenship Club.

STUDENT: NAT HENTOFF

(1925–)

Journalist, jazz critic and author.

TEACHER: MISS FITZGERALD

Boston Latin School from eight in the morning until three in the afternoon. Among the alumni: Cotton Mather, Sam Adams, Charles Sumner, Ralph Waldo Emerson, Francis Child (the collector of the Child Ballads), George Santayana, John F. (''Honey Fitz'') Fitzgerald (grandfather of Jack Kennedy), Joseph P. Kennedy (father of Jack Kennedy), Bernard Berenson. And way up high, carved into the walls of the assembly hall, were other resounding names of those who had preceded me from 1635 on. What would the herring man have made of all this? In the extreme improbability of his ever going so far from Blue Hill Avenue as to come through these formidable doors across town on Avenue Louis Pasteur, the masters and the students would have laughed at him. Up their sleeves, of course, since they were gentlemen. And would I have gone up to him, and welcomed him, and reminded him of the free pickles he used to give me when I had never even heard of the Boston Latin School? Fortunately the herring man never left his place beside his barrel.

I would not have been at Latin School to speculate on such matters had it not been for Miss Fitzgerald, my sixth-grade teacher at the William Lloyd Garrison School, where nearly all the students were Jewish and nearly all the teachers were Irish. Miss Fitzgerald expected everyone to learn exactly what had to be learned in her classes, and without excuses. Oh, she might have taken a heart attack into account, but children did not have heart attacks. She allowed no nonsense in the classroom—and everything not directly pertaining to the subject at hand was manifestly nonsense. She thought the most useful way to deal with the tender sensibilities of the young was to toughen those sensibilities. She snapped, she roared, she pounded her desk, and she froze miscreants of all sorts and sizes with the coldest eye I have ever seen. (Years later, musicians would describe, and I sometimes myself saw, Benny Goodman directing his Medusa eye—"The Ray"—at a fumbling sideman. There was nothing else like it in all of jazz. But in a faceoff, Miss Fitzgerald, without the slightest exertion, would have instantly turned Benny into stone.)

One afternoon Miss Fitzgerald marched from the William Lloyd Garrison School, all the long way down Elm Hill Avenue, turned into Howland Street, and proceeded to knock firmly on the door of our apartment. Accepting a glass of the usual scalding tea, which she polished off without a blink, Miss Fitzgerald told—actually, commanded—my mother to allow me to take the entrance examinations for Boston Latin School. If I applied myself, Miss Fitzgerald glared at me, I could do the work. And unlike the local high school, or, for that matter, all the other secondary schools in the city, Boston Latin School led to sure success in later life. Success for those—she glared at me again—who had the stick-to-it-iveness to stay the course.

Abruptly, she thanked my mother for the tea and commended her for letting me try to get into Boston Latin School. My mother had not said any such thing specifically, but her somewhat bewildered nod had been enough, for Miss Fitzgerald could not imagine any immigrant parent holding a child back from so bounding a head start on the ladder that might one day reach to the names carved high on the walls of the assembly hall on Avenue Louis Pasteur. That night, my father, of course, agreed. No one had asked *me,* but I would never have thought of crossing Miss Fitzgerald. Besides, as I knew quite well, even at ten, this was the way to penetrate the great mystery of my life. I would be going to *their* school, in *their* part of town, and so I would be not only learning Latin and Greek but learning about *them.*

STUDENT: DAN RATHER

(1931–)

Journalist and author.

TEACHER: HUGH CUNNINGHAM

The dream begins, most of the time, with a teacher who believes in you, who tugs and pushes and leads you on to the next plateau, sometimes poking you with a sharp stick called truth.

Mine was named Hugh Cunningham and he taught journalism in 1950 at Sam Houston State Teachers College. With an enrollment sometimes as low as 700 and no pretensions, Sam Houston blended quietly into the red clay and piney woods of East Texas. Traces of the Old South still existed in that part of the state, where cotton, though never king, was about all anyone had. Cotton, lumber and a few scraggly cattle.

With a population of five thousand, Huntsville had grown up around the school, a lean, scenic town with a colorful history. General Sam Houston had built a cabin there and came back to it to die. So the school was named after the liberator of Texas, the hero of San Jacinto and the first elected president of the Lone Star Republic.

For whatever interest it may hold for historians, until the 1920's the official name of the college was the Sam Houston Institute of Teaching. When freshmen started wearing sweatshirts with the school's initials the state legislature hastily passed an act and renamed it.

How Hugh Cunningham happened to wind up there, with a master's degree from the Missouri School of Journalism, young, with a mind that could light up a room, I do not know. But it was a break for me. Otherwise I would not have lasted in college longer than three weeks and most likely would not have gone on to whatever career I have had. That may be putting too much on one man's conscience, but I owe a debt to Hugh Cunningham.

Actually, my ticket to college was to have been football. Based on my size (I weighed one-fifty), and my talent, which was marginal, there was no reason, other than for my own ignorance, for me to think that the gridiron would become my salvation. But I had started at end in my senior year at Reagan High School in Houston and I had shown I could catch a pass. There was nothing to indicate I was a gifted athlete, nothing to feed the hope that it would pay my way through college, except that it was the only hope I had.

So near the end of my last high school year I dropped by the gymnasium to see the coach, a man named Lamar Camp. Football coaches tend to be a major influence on a young man's life. Coach Camp had kept me in school when I wanted to drop out and get a job, the choice people in my neighborhood often faced around the tenth grade.

"I want to start looking for a college," I told him.

"That's fine," he said. Coach Camp was a taciturn man.

"It occurs to me that it might help if I had a letter from you," I replied.

He stared at me for several moments. I thought he hadn't understood what I meant. Finally he just said, "Look, you're not going to play college football. You're not big enough. You're not fast enough. You're not good enough."

There was no misunderstanding what *he* meant and I was absolutely crushed by it. I went home, in a daze, to decide if college was so important after all. Neither of my parents had finished high school. My father, Irvin Rather—known to his friends as Rags—had worked as a pipeliner for twenty years, which meant that he dug ditches for a fair amount of his lifetime. He met my mother, Byrl, at the Travelers' Hotel in Victoria, where she worked as a waitress, fresh off the farm, sending money back home every week to help her family through the Depression.

Mother later passed a high school equivalency test and took a few night classes at a junior college. But, basically, they were not people who understood what a college education represented, other than as something a lucky few people strived for, a goal. Their immediate concern was to feed and clothe three kids. I was the oldest, born on the last day of October, 1931, at Wharton. Then came Don and Patricia, six and eight years younger.

I don't intend for this to sound like another version of Up from Poor. We were not poverty-stricken, but money was always tight. My father felt that if I finished high school that would be achievement enough, as indeed in the 1940's it was. As far back as our heirloom Bibles recorded, no one on either side of our family had ever attended college.

Yet, in a curious way, I developed my passion to become a reporter through my father. That was all I could ever remember wanting to do, to work for a newspaper. I never thought of broadcasting as a career until I was nearly out of college. But radio did intrigue me. As a boy in Houston I listened to the broadcasts of the roller derby at the City Coliseum. Sometimes as I walked to school I would reconstruct in my mind my own roller derby play-by-play. I was, vicariously, the greatest roller derby describer who ever lived.

At home I was surrounded by newspapers. My father was an impulse subscriber, a voracious reader, and a man of sudden angers who would leap from his chair and cancel whichever paper had offended him. We went through every newspaper in town, the *Post,* the *Chronicle* and the *Press,* which was part of the Scripps-Howard chain and known locally for its muckraking policies. There was a constant harangue about newspapers in our house. My father would read something in the *Press* that riled him and he would shout, "Mother, cancel the *Press.* We're through with that paper forever. I don't want to ever see it in here again."

At one point we were down to the *Christian Science Monitor* and the St. Louis *Post-Dispatch,* which arrived in the mail, usually a week late.

Out of that cycle, somehow, grew my interest in the news, how it was gathered and reported and in what form it reached our home. I had always written for the school papers, usually on sports, and in the summer of 1948 had worked at the *Press* as a *gofer.* That, of course, was just below a copyboy. I'd go for coffee or cigars or egg rolls, or whatever the reporters needed.

I was still determined to get to college and my mother, bless her, was adamant that I should make the attempt. I considered myself fairly street-smart. I had been to sea briefly one summer, at sixteen, worked on an oil rig, and dug pipeline ditches. But no money had been set aside for my schooling. It was that way with most families. So I picked out the nearest small school with a full, four-year enrollment, and that happened to be Sam Houston State, seventy-five miles northeast of Houston.

• • •

Later, when I signed up for classes, I paid my first visit to the young journalism professor, Hugh Cunningham. He had started the department and only had five or six students enrolled. That suited him fine. His idea was to work with a small number of young people and turn out a handcrafted product.

Where journalism was concerned he had a jealous nature. "Why are you here?" he demanded. "Do you know why you want to major in journalism?"

I said, "It's the only thing I've ever wanted to do."

He said, "What makes you think you can do it?"

I kind of bristled. "Well, I *know* I can."

With that reply, he barked out a half dozen facts and he had me sit down and write a news story for him. Now that I think about it, I was in the odd position of having to try out for the journalism department even before the football team.

From that moment Cunningham took me under his wing. When he heard about my football plans he threw up his hands.

"That's crazy," he said. "You don't want to be a football player. You'll get killed."

"There's no other way I can stay in school," I said. "This way I'll get a scholarship."

He laughed out loud. But he didn't push me about it. Possibly he knew it would do no good. Sometimes we ought not to be talked out of our mistakes. But I had to survive the next three weeks before the football practices started, and during that time Cunningham literally fed me out of his own pocket.

I struggled through that spring and, in spite of everything, the odd jobs and the strange meal arrangements, Hugh Cunningham managed to capture and hold my attention. He was about five nine, slight, with dark hair combed straight back. An intensity poured out of him like water from a fire hose.

His idea of teaching journalism was to get you away from the classroom. He didn't believe the reporter's craft could be taught in school, and when he did, it was only because the state required it. The college had to have a curriculum. There had to be a Journalism 101. But Hugh Cunningham didn't really give a damn about any of that. He wanted us out in the field. "Write stories," he kept hammering at us. "Go interview the college horticulturist. Go downtown. Hang around the courthouse. Ride with the police. I don't want to see you the rest of the afternoon."

I learned long ago that the term *a good teacher* is redundant. While the phrase *a bad teacher* is a contradiction in terms. Rare is the teacher who fully understands what a tremendous difference he or she can make, but Cunningham was one of them. He picked the courses his students needed to get a degree, and he set their standards. Often he lectured me: "Coming out of a school this size, with no reputation at all, your only chance is to make virtually straight A's."

That admonition I took to heart. I studied as hard as I could without actually feeling pain. Before breakfast, in the afternoons and at night I worked at money-paying jobs. Classes were crammed into the morning hours. Homework was done in snatches of time during the day and after midnight. In between and all about was the school paper. With Cunningham and Cecil Tuck, we put out the *Houstonian* twice a week. Tuck was another of Cunningham's prize students. He eventually went to Hollywood and has done well writing for television. He helped to discover and promote Glen Campbell, among others. Cecil was in much the same financial shape as I was, maybe worse. He stayed in school that semester by writing bad checks and then scrambling to cover them. Truth to tell, we often covered for one another with criss-crossing hot checks. We always paid our bills, but some semesters it took longer than others.

Meanwhile, Cunningham kept preaching experience to us, that you learned to write by writing. Cecil and I would compose stories and mail them to the Houston *Post*. Heaven knows, most of the time no response came and none was really expected. We would just send them off into this great vacuum. We'd do a feature story on a football player, or a teacher, or some campus character. Once, we sent out a piece on the lady who maintained Sam Houston's home. That was the big bone. The story was published and we were very proud. (You could get that feature printed almost every year. Even today. There is something about Sam Houston still having a housekeeper that seems to impress big city editors.)

Cecil was a major presence at the college. He was sloppy and fun and we hit it off from the beginning. He came from a sawmill town near Jasper and for that place, and for those times, he was an authentic free spirit. I believe he still holds the Lone Star Conference record for gin consumed by a third-string linebacker. He would occasionally show up for football practice under the influence, as they say, and he did not take many things seriously, including Cunningham.

Hugh was always torn. He knew he was a gifted teacher, knew how much of himself he was putting into us. But at the same time he wanted to be on the cutting edge of journalism. He was always taking summer jobs at newspapers like the Atlanta *Constitution*. He saw things in us and tried to express them in the way a father would, but he finally gave up trying to convince Cecil.

He couldn't talk to Tuck the way he could to me. Cecil would fall asleep or say, "Aw, come off that shit." So Cunningham would say to me, with a wrenching earnestness, "You can do it, Dan. You can go all the way." Keep in mind that for Hugh Cunningham, getting a job with the Houston *Post* was going all the way. A byline in the Houston *Chronicle* would have given him raptures. That was going all the way.

• • •

My survival was due to Cunningham, and he would not sit still for a thank-you. He was like a man cleaning out an attic so he could see what was there. He wanted you to get on with your future, go to class, make your grades and, when you had the time, read the Chicago Great Books Series. Hugh wouldn't classify himself as an intellectual, not then and I suppose not now. He probably would have laughed at the idea. But he had a restless mind and a decency impossible to overstate.

He was also a very tough editor. He would keep kicking material back to his students. It was not uncommon to have to rewrite a story as many as a dozen times before it suited him. And when it came to the student paper he was a lion defending the cubs. Once, an executive whose company published a house organ walked through the journalism offices. Cunningham instantly indexed this outlet as a job resource, a place where one of his graduates might break in, writing for the company publication.

The visitor was politically conservative and he questioned Hugh about a couple of items in that week's student paper. Looking back, it was ridiculous, but he wondered if these stories didn't smack of Left-wing socialism. Now, communism might have been big in the eastern academic circles, but it hadn't reached Huntsville yet. Socialism was still our big threat.

Cunningham simply threw him out. No fuss, no ceremony. And Hugh himself was by no stretch of the imagination a liberal. But this was ground where strangers were not welcome. He cared so much about news gathering, and the integrity of it, that he would tolerate no compromises. Later Hugh's principles would lead him into difficulty with the college.

Cunningham's practices might strike someone at Columbia University, or Northwestern, as quaint, but each semester when we returned to school he required us, in class, to repeat out loud the journalist's creed: "A public journal is a public trust . . . "It was like the Boy Scout oath and he took it seriously. In a way it was beautiful. Not very sophisticated, perhaps, but then he was not dealing with sophisticated minds.

Without my being aware, I had the best of two worlds. On the one hand, I had Cunningham drilling into me the fundamentals—who, what, when, where, why and how. Get it, get it right, get it fast. Over and over again. "I want to know *exactly* what was said," he told us. "Treat it fairly. Write it fast." He often emphasized the need for quality writing, but he knew that reality was a city desk clamoring to meet a deadline, caring less if you made the language pretty.

That approach, I would learn in time, was tailor-made for broadcasting. Meanwhile I was working at a radio station where nothing was closed to me. I could do anything I was big enough to try. This led to some comic crises, but it was the richest kind of training.

• • •

Between us [Cecil Tuck and me], I regret to say, we were responsible, at least indirectly, for Cunningham's leaving Sam Houston State. By 1953 the McCarthy era was in full swing, and the Korean War almost devastated the campus of able-bodied males. The administration hurriedly arranged for the formation of an ROTC unit, which provided a shelter of sorts for those students who needed, or wanted, to avoid the draft. They drilled in makeshift uniforms, in shirts that didn't match their pants. Cecil and I wrote pieces in the student paper poking fun at the ROTC's ragtag army. I must say that Cecil's stories were much funnier than mine. He was always much better when a story called for a light touch. This was a comical subject, in some ways, but the humor was lost on the school's officials, who had gone to considerable lengths to bring in the ROTC and, really, for good reasons.

Now here was the school newspaper making fun of what the college had done. So Cunningham was called on the carpet, a form of bullying that he took badly. He was told to exercise more control over his department. He said it was a matter of principle with him to teach his people independence. "I give them guidance," Hugh said, "and help them with their writing and editing, but they decide what goes into the paper. I don't decide that for them."

This may have been very small potatoes in the context of where we were and the times we were in. But Cunningham did not take the scolding lightly. Not long afterward he left. He wasn't around when I graduated, but he had given Sam Houston State a journalism school, against what odds only Cecil Tuck and I could fully appreciate. He had said to us several times, almost in despair, "You know, I feel guilty because I really should be encouraging you to go to Texas. It's the only university in the state with a journalism department worthy of the name, and you are good enough to make it there."

I never felt that I suffered for having attended Sam Houston. Among other reasons, I had opportunities that would not have been available at a larger school. One of them was the closeness that could develop with a professor like Hugh Cunningham. He stayed in teaching—it was and is his life—and has taught for years at the University of Florida. He encouraged us to think, and read, and form opinions. On our own time he had us reading the work of people such as Elmer Davis. Then he would grill us with questions in that Gatling-gun style of his. "For the working reporter," he demanded, "what's the most important thing Elmer Davis said?"

There was silence in the room. None of us knew.

"Don't let the bastards scare you," he said.

STUDENT: FLOYD PATTERSON

(1935–)

Boxer.

TEACHER: VIVIAN COSTEN

Then, of course, there was Miss Vivian Costen. I've waited a bit to bring her into this story, because what she did for me is a story all by itself. She was an old-maid school teacher and somehow she took a liking to me and I took to her. I'd go to her every time I had a problem. She was like a mother to me. She left the school soon after I did. She died a little less than a year before I won the title. It was a great loss to me.

Miss Costen gave me confidence in myself. She made me feel I was important. She could tell that I was impressionable and a great sufferer. She knew that I was hurt by a raised voice. She wouldn't accept my protests that I couldn't learn to read or write. She was so kind and considerate and understanding that I wanted more than anything else in the world to please her. She bought me clothes and gave me little gifts. I had to return that to her in some way, and the only way I knew—or was able to—was to be what she wanted me to be.

The big thing, I guess, was the individual attention she gave me without my realizing I was getting it. Back in Brooklyn there were thirty or thirty-five kids in a class, and the teachers had no time to work with those who didn't get everything right away. The teachers would write something on the blackboard once and that was it. You got it or you didn't. There was no going back to check if you understood. At Wiltwyck [School for Boys in Esopus, New York] there were seven or eight of us in a classroom. At first I didn't think I'd be able to catch on, but Miss Costen would pick one boy a week to be a special monitor who stayed after class and cleaned the blackboards. She'd always have a bag of candy for him. When I got through with my work, she'd say to me:

"Floyd, I think there was a little problem you didn't get. Let me show you how it works." She'd tell me once. If I didn't seem to understand she'd tell me again, maybe three or four times. She never laughed if you didn't understand right away. She'd never seem angry. She made you want to learn.

I imagine I was a little slow, even with her patience, because in the classroom when she'd ask a question I still didn't dare raise my hand to answer. One day she asked a question of all the kids. She went around the room asking this one and that one. Everybody answered but me. I said I didn't know the answer. Then she told us the answer. Everybody in the class had been wrong, but the answer I had in my mind was correct, and I had not had the nerve enough to say it out loud.

That made me furious. I just stood up and ran right out of that room and down the hall. I could hear footsteps after me, but I didn't care. It was Miss Costen. She took me by the shoulders and lifted my head to look into my eyes. There were tears of shame and anger in them.

"I knew you knew the answer, Floyd," she said. "That's why you're crying. This should prove to you that if you have an idea, speak it out."

"I was afraid I'd sound stupid and everybody would laugh," I said.

Miss Costen put her arms around me and said, "Always remember this, Floyd Patterson. You're not stupid. You're the same as any other boy your own age. From now on I want you to answer. If you're wrong, you're wrong. Nobody's always one hundred per cent right, but you'll be right more often than you're wrong."

Well, after that I sort of woke up. I began answering questions. I wasn't right more often than I was wrong. It was the other way at first, but gradually I was right fifty per cent of the time, then sixty per cent. I got to the point where I began to grasp the thing. I felt equal to the other boys. I didn't feel any more that I had to sit there like an idiot, knowing nothing, saying nothing and caring about nothing.

After a while, in fact, I won the highest award one of the boys in my class could win, at least in my own mind. Miss Costen would invite the boy who did the best work for the week to her own home for a weekend. I was able to stay there a couple of times. It was like being in a regular house, the kind I used to dream about when I'd hide away in the movies.

After one of these weekends, Miss Costen offered me a box of candy. "You've done so well in your work," she said, "I think you deserve a special award."

There wasn't anything I wanted more than candy, but a friend in my dormitory and I had made a promise to each other. We were going to split everything fifty-fifty, which was all right with me, until Miss Costen added: "Don't let the rest of the boys eat it up on you."

The way I felt about Miss Costen, that would have meant breaking a promise to her if I let my friend share the candy with me. I turned down the candy and it wasn't until much later that Miss Costen learned why I did. "You're a good, honest boy, Floyd," she said. "You stand by a promise even if it's not to your advantage."

STUDENT: JUDY COLLINS
(1939–)
Folk singer.
TEACHER: ANTONIA BRICO

Dr. Antonia Brico taught piano in Denver and conducted the Denver Businessmen's Symphony; she was famous for being tough and demanding, and took very few new students. Her studio was in an old stone building in downtown Denver. My mother and father took me to my first appointment with her: an interview with no guarantees. The door was opened by Dr. Brico's assistant, Mrs. Page. The studio was huge and the walls were covered with photographs of men and women, singers and conductors, scribbled signatures at the bottom: "To Antonia with love, Albert" Schweitzer, "Wonderful concert, love, Jean Sibelius," "To my beloved Antonia, Queen Juliana of the Netherlands." There were photos of people I had seen in *Time* and *Look* magazine—Toscanini, Casals, Rubinstein, musicians from all over the world, as well as royalty. The room had a polished wood floor covered by a carpet that stretched underneath two mammoth Steinway pianos. There were full-sized bronze busts of Sibelius and Beethoven, of Mozart. It was an awesome room, the habitat of someone important whose life possessed dimensions of which I could only dream. Dr. Brico's face matched the monumental look of the building she lived in and the room where she taught.

I scuffed into the room in my oxfords, gripping my grubby music in my hands. Dr. Brico had large features, and she looked to me like the busts of Schumann and Beethoven. I remember a scent of citrus in the room. She nodded at my parents, indicating the chairs where they could sit, and motioned me over to the piano bench, taking a seat beside me.

"All right, little Judy, what do you have to play for me?" I put my music on the piano rack and began a Debussy piece, "Snow Is Dancing" from *The Children's Corner.* I played very fast, stumbling over the eighty-eight keys. My fingers were jelly and I couldn't find the pedals under my feet. My father and mother sat a long way away, back at the other end of the room. They sat with their hands in their laps, and my father had a smile on his face. He always thought I was wonderful no matter what I did. My mother had a worried look on her face. She could see the room's heavy, imposing decor, whereas my father could only hear his little girl playing the piano, and he loved her and thought she was great, and he knew that this doctor woman would think she was great too. His face said, "She's my little girl, and isn't she wonderful?" My mother wasn't so sure.

When I finished playing, Dr. Brico sat still, looked at my hands, and then turned to my parents.

"Little Judy has great hands, but her technique is not all that wonderful." A frown came over her face like clouds in an already dark sky. "This is going to be a lot of work," she said. She seemed enormous and angry, then her face was suddenly smiling and tender.

"I am going to take you as a student. We will have to work very hard, little Judy. The way the fingers scramble around, flying in the air, we will change all that. You have the feel, that is the most important thing, you understand Debussy. Now we will teach you to express what you feel, and you have the hands! Your hands are of the best quality, good and strong across the back, with long fingers. I am going to show you how to make the Debussy speak! You could be a fine pianist, little Judy."

"Thank you, Dr. Grico."

"It's Dr. Brico," she said, rolling the *r* and searching my face. "Can you be your best for me, little Judy?" I was being asked to behave as though I were responsible and adult, and I felt about four years old. I looked down at my brown oxfords, wondering how the polish had rubbed off in so many spots. I suddenly wished I could hide them—maybe by sticking them under the x-ray machine they had at the shoestore to show whether new shoes were too long for your toes.

"Will you do your best for your Tante Antonia?"

I looked at Dr. Brico, and didn't know if I could live up to her expectations. But I sensed, as young as I was, that she would drive me until I longed to live up to my own. I didn't know how different from hers they were to be.

Dr. Brico had studied piano in music schools at Berkeley and in New York and Germany with some of the greatest teachers in the world, and she was an accomplished pianist as well as conductor. She taught a solid basis in technique using scales, exercises, Czerny, Hanon, and Chopin etudes; but her forte was the approach to the piano used by such masters as Horowitz and Rachmaninoff—that is, she thought of the piano as not a percussion but a stringed instrument. She taught the connected, lyrical line and what she held to be the greatest prize, a personal interpretation that stamped the performance indelibly as belonging to only one pianist. Technique was only the platform that allowed the personality of the individual musician to make itself known.

I raced through a Chopin etude at one of our early lessons, sight-reading from the page, hurrying to show her how fast and how well I could play, bundling dozens of notes up and flinging them into the room at rip speed. She stopped me before I could finish the piece, gently laying her hands across the keys so that I could not go on. She sighed.

''Anyone can play notes,'' she said. ''I want you to sing, to lilt, on the piano.''

I learned as much from her about singing as I learned about playing the piano. Melody must flow, the piano must sound like the line of a cello, the line of a voice. It was a pure magic she knew, and inspired.

''You will learn everything by analysis, and you will never play anything through without memorizing, except pieces for technique.''

I shook my head, stared at the floor.

''When you begin a piece, take the first measure, and analyze it until you can play it without looking at the music. When you have it down, go on to the next, and then the next.'' Only when I had memorized the entire piece, at a slow, thinking tempo, would I know what the whole melody sounded like, and only later, after careful correction of my memorization, did she allow me to bring anything up to tempo. My early roughshod habit of speeding through pieces was over.

Dr. Brico always knew exactly what she wanted, as did some of the other strong, self-determined women I had known. Mrs. Munson, my piano teacher in Los Angeles, had supported herself through her teaching. My choir teacher in school, Violet McCarthy, was a woman whose determination to teach music and be self-supporting was not thought of as unusual. Though they were self-supporting professionals, I wouldn't have known to call these women feminists.

From the scrapbooks she showed me, I knew Dr. Brico had studied with the best musicians in the world and conducted many orchestras. She was a woman, whereas everyone else in the pictures in her scrapbook and in her studio was a man, except the female singers she had conducted, her friend Mrs. Page, and Juliana, the queen of the Netherlands. Sometimes a bitterness showed; she might speak of having had tough luck; she yearned for more contact with her friends, the people in the photographs. She went to Europe each summer on the *Queen Elizabeth* or the *France,* taking a piano student or two to listen to opera at Salzburg and Bayreuth; and though she went alone to see Albert Schweitzer in Lambarene, Africa, joining him at his little organ in the jungle to study Bach among the lepers, she always came home to Denver, home to me.

Something had happened to land her in Denver, like a big fish out of its depth. I had the feeling that someday I would know the real story of her life. Meanwhile, I saw her as the ultimate heroine, strapping her weapons to her back, the baton and the scores, roaming the forest like Diana the Huntress, the daughter of a god, the heiress to music and light.

For my twelfth birthday, in May, there was a surprise in the living room of our duplex house on Willow Street. The brown spinet both my father and I had played for years was gone, and in its place was a shining grand piano. Dr. Brico had told my parents I must have a fine instrument to practice on, and there it was. She was a wonder worker. I fell to it with a will, practicing with real pleasure.

But no matter how hard I did my exercises and learned pieces, according to Dr. Brico I never practiced enough. Our sessions together were soon tumultuous, filled with her praise, or tears, as she railed at me to practice more. She took me to rehearsals of her orchestra for inspiration so I could see what it meant to be committed. I sang in the choruses of her operatic productions: *Pagliacci* and *Eugene Onegin, The Marriage of Figaro* and *The Magic Flute.*

"*Andiam, andiam*!" I sang, dressed in a peasant costume for a performance at the Denver Auditorium. The clown in *Pagliacci* wept, the soprano laughed, and Dr. Brico's baton flashed. It was exciting and seductive. Sometimes I would sing so enthusiastically that my untrained voice would become hoarse.

Toscanini came to Denver to conduct the Denver Symphony and invited his old friend Antonia to join the rehearsals. He gave the board of directors hell for not letting her conduct the symphony as a guest, not letting her take over once in a while for the regular conductor, Saul Caston. She took me with her to the Toscanini rehearsals, and I followed her around, carrying her bags and her scores. We sat in the hall, listening to the rehearsal and watching the maestro, who was dressed in a black sweater and pants with his hair flying around his head, his baton flashing. He looked immense and conducted without a score, from memory. That impressed me terribly, and I wondered if he memorized by analysis.

After one rehearsal, Dr. Brico took me up to the podium and introduced me to the great man. He was hardly taller than I. His face beamed with a smile, his eyes lit up behind his glasses. "I am pleased to meet you. Dr. Brico says you are a very gifted pianist," Toscanini said to me. "Take care of your hands, little one. They are very beautiful and will make beautiful music."

It was not that I doubted my own talent. I was at ease with music, and overcoming the difficulties of perfecting the technique was a matter of time, of practice, of minutes and hours behind the piano. But I doubted my ability to do enough, go far enough, be perfect enough. It was as if I had a shameful secret that prevented me from ever doing or being anything that anyone wanted me to be.

• • •

"Oh, I wouldn't want to spoil you for your classical studies!" He [George Shearing, a blind pianist] was smiling, but very serious. George read Braille music and played concertos with orchestras, as well as doing his jazz, yet he wanted me to continue with my classical studies. My father, who made his living in pop music, also wanted me to be a classical pianist. It seemed strange that both of them wanted me to have what they had left behind.

I begged, and he declined again, but he finally gave in, and I studied his fingers as they formed around the chords to "Laura." I learned it note by note. I memorized it by analysis! Dr. Brico found out about it, of course.

"Little Judy, you'll ruin yourself with all that jazz!" she said to me.

My Debussy and Chopin scores had bite marks on all the corners, where my parakeet, who kept me company as I practiced, had taken little chunks out of them with his beak. Practicing scales was pure drudgery, and it always seemed to me that everyone in my family was having a good time while I plodded through my exercises. My only consolation was that sometimes I could prop up a favorite novel in front of my score and read while I practiced. So there were parakeet bites in *The Count of Monte Cristo* and *Madame Bovary* as well.

• • •

Soon after, I talked my father into renting me an old National guitar with a twangy sound and ancient strings. It came with seven free jazz lessons. I skipped the lessons and taught myself.

I was still working on the Rachmaninoff concerto, trying to get it ready for the concert with Dr. Brico's orchestra, but I had fallen in love with folk music. I was terrified to tell Dr. Brico that I didn't want to study the Rachmaninoff anymore. But I knew I had to.

On the day I finally summoned up the courage to tell her, I walked to the door of her studio like someone condemned, imagining the worst; and it was worse than I could have imagined. We had a terrible scene: she cried, she begged; I cried, I begged her to understand. Finally, she became furious.

"Can't you see you are throwing your career away?" I bowed my head. "Do you know how many pianists would give up everything just to be able to play as you can? You are ungrateful, you cannot see the thing that is right in front of your nose. I can't believe you are able to be this callous to what God has given you. You have the hands, you could go right to the top."

She didn't know I had a guitar, and when I told her it was the last straw. I was ruined, Dr. Brico said.

I walked out of her studio and onto the sidewalk without looking back. In my heart, I would look back for years, and perhaps even today a part of me still looks back. The call of folk music was stronger than even this strong and powerful woman. The wonderful Rachmaninoff Piano Concerto no. 2, which I had memorized, would go unplayed with her orchestra. She had said I was making a mistake and I had to struggle not to believe her. I didn't know then what the Buddhists say, that all decisions are right.

• • •

I arrive at the Mayflower Hotel in an elegant suit from Givenchy and high heels, my hair up under a cranberry red felt hat. My makeup is carefully done, I carry a new purse from an Italian shop on Madison Avenue. I am looking my best for this special occasion. I go into the lobby to pick up Dr. Brico for our annual lunch at the Russian Tea Room. She comes to New York once a year from Denver.

''You look wonderful. I am so glad you put your hair up, you look like a grown-up.''

I can't contain my pleasure that she noticed—quite a difference from that first meeting, so many years ago, when she saw a girl with pigtails, scruffy oxfords, dog-eared music.

At the Tea Room, we order borscht and lamb. The maitre d', Richard Baron, knows us both. He embraces us and shows us to our table.

''No onions, no celery, no pork,'' says Dr. Brico, shaking her head vehemently at Richard, who is smiling.

''You know there is never any pork or celery or onions in our borscht,'' he says.

''Here,'' she says to him before he can go off to get our order, ''take our picture, will you?'' She thrusts a camera into Richard's hands. ''Just push that button.'' Richard clicks the camera. Antonia and I are immortalized together at the Tea Room, smiling into the bright flash.

After our lunch, I take Antonia to a rehearsal of the National Dance Institute's event that is coming up in a few months. I have a part in it, singing some of the songs I wrote and serving as our mistress of ceremonies. She was thrilled to see the children dancing, and afterward she said to me, ''You know how I never could forgive you for giving up and not becoming a great pianist?''

I'll say I remember. How can I forget? For many years I would invite Dr. Brico to hear me sing, in Denver, or in New York, at Carnegie, with symphonies. I always introduced her from the stage as my beloved teacher, and she would come backstage afterward, take my hands in hers, and look at me with a deep sigh.

''You really could have gone places, little Judy,'' she would say. I could never get a response to what I was doing rather than to what she thought I should be doing.

"Well, I finally got over that," she says to me today. I cannot believe my ears.

And she talks about the songs I have just done for this rehearsal at the Felt Forum.

I still don't believe I've heard her correctly.

"Oh, they were just some little songs," I say. "No," she says. "You are marvelous."

I walk as if in a dream, as if under water. For thirty years I have longed for these words. But I never thought it possible. I'm exuberant. A circle is completed; my friend, my mentor, my nemesis, my imperfect and perfectly beloved teacher, Antonia.

STUDENT: IVAN DOIG

(1939–)

Journalist and author.

TEACHER: FRANCES CARSON TIDYMAN

Too many times each schoolday, I would look up and meet a set of cool gray eyes which could have outdrilled even Grandma's. The face around them was dark-browed, unadorned, and somehow both musing and ominous. Frances Carson Tidyman, who through a full generation had been scanning the students in her English classes as if they were muddy pebbles in a sluice box, had me under her steadiest focus.

What I already had begun to know about Mrs. Tidyman was as unsettling as her stare. She was the least likely presence to be found in a small farmtown school: a mysteriously spiced waft of booklore and speculative notions and astonishing languages and . . . oddnesses. It was circulated that she cared almost nothing for money—that she habitually turned down the salary raises due her to forestall a day when the school could not afford her, and that she paid in stores by asking what amount was needed, scrawling the sum into whatever counter checkbook the clerk happened to hand her, and forgetting the matter forever. In Valier, this quick blink of a system worked well enough. But in the county's main shopping town of Conrad, it left a patter of misbanked checks bouncing behind her, and her husband had at last to fund a bank account there solely to cover her offhand signatures.

As with finance, she seemed to declare, so with time and costume. They meant no more to her than that she eventually had to appear somewhere, with something on. This brought about her fame for occasionally gardening with her nightgown on, dark hair maned free and spilling to the waist—and, of course, her flowers and vegetables encouraged to ally into whatever clumps and jumbles they would.

At school, she would arrive in dark plain dresses so alike that it could hardly be traced when she changed one for another; bunned her hair into a great black burl at the back of her neck; clopped from class to class in the severest of shoes. She was buxom, much like Grandma with a half more plumped on all around her mounding in front and behind was very nearly more than the lackadaisical dresses wanted to contain. Leaning forward from the waist as she hurried about, she flew among us like a schooner's lusty figurehead prowing over a lazy sea.

The mind of Mrs. Tidyman was somewhat like that jostling garden of hers—sprigged here with the Greek and Roman myths she knew so entirely that she recited them to her children for bedtime stories, sprouting somewhere else with blood-red bouquets from Shakespeare, twining now into a tale such as having seen the cowboy artist Charlie Russell when she attended the university in Missoula: *In the midst of a sorority tea someone deposited him with us—dozens of fluffy girls, you understand, and he had been drinking for the ordeal—and then the utmost indignity, they took his hat from him and he had nothing to do with his hands, and sat helpless, imprisoned . . .*

The foliage of her learning laced everywhere through the school. She taught all the English courses, first- and second-year Latin, occasionally a course in Spanish, directed the plays, advised for the yearbook and newspaper, and oversaw the library. It could not be imagined where she might exist except in the midst of all this. She had taken leave for enough years to have four sons, and afterward decided the absence had been a mistake. Chinese peasant women did it properly, she reasoned, giving birth to their babies in the fields and going right on with their toil.

That earliest watching I felt from this unprecedented woman, it turned out, was to see whether I was a thief. A few times a year, a school-wide set of vocabulary tests was given, every student then ranked against national statistics. The first test-time fell in the second week after I enrolled at Valier, and I attacked with joy. If there was one knack in me, it was to hold in mind any word I had ever seen, much the way Dad could identify any sheep from all others. When this first of the set of tests was scored, no one among the seniors, juniors or sophomores achieved better than a respectable 50. One of my classmates soared to a 60, well up in the national percentiles. My paper lofted off to an unscorable 75.

Before I had time to get the grin off my face, Mrs. Tidyman had asked me into the library, locked the door, and with as much tact as she could muster—somewhere close to none—wondered abruptly whether I had come across the answer sheet before the national test. Whatever denial I stammered to her—what nightmare was this, did I have to prove myself stupid before I would be trusted here?—she had a better one in the making. *All right. There are three more tests in the next three days, and I have the answer sheets secure. We'll just see how you score on them.*

Three times more I gapped everyone else in the school and shot out the top of all percentiles. I didn't know whether to be triumphant or apprehensive, but before I had much time for either, Mrs. Tidyman again was hauling me into the library, clicking the lock, eyeing me relentlessly. *You know, you really ought to take my Latin class next year. Latin will be an advantage for you in the use of English. And you should write for the school paper, there's good practice. And I want to know what you read. I have a houseful of books if you can't find enough here . . .*

I gulped the relief of being out from under Mrs. Tidyman's suspicion, and sat back to see what the gale of her approval would bring. In the classroom, each hour with her began like a conjuring, or a parody of one. She would clomp in and back herself onto a high stool behind a thin-legged lectern. At last secure in midair she would revolve toward the class, the entire billow of her far up over us, with the lectern-top before her as if commanded to hover there. Then her hand deep into her dress front, and out of that vault of bosom would come eyeglasses, tethered on a neck chain which still did not entirely stop her from losing them a few times each day; a balled handkerchief; a fountain pen, likely leaking; perhaps a fat ring of keys, or a shredding blizzard of notes to herself. Up would come her head from an unperturbed inventory of this rummage. A mild glare or a stern look of fondness—her shadings of expression could be baffling—fastened onto the last of the class to go quiet. With it might fall the entire total of her irony, the query *Do you mind if I begin now?*

At last supplied and delivered, she set at us. The day's assigned reading might be thumped open and launched into sheerly for the entrancement of hearing herself aloud: *'It was the best of times, it was the worst of times, it was the age of wisdom, it was the age of foolishness'—oh, people, can you hear those phrases ring against one another?* . . . If there was agony and tragedy, so much the richer fancy: *'As flies to wanton boys, are we to the gods; they kill us for their sport.' When I read the headline of an airplane crash, people, first I wish that no one I know was killed. Then that no one from Montana was killed. Then that no one from this country. Then that no one at all would have been killed—oh, people, the casual lightning bolts which come down on us* . . . She would escort Richard Cory and Miniver Cheevy to their poetic dooms one instant, bring Ivanhoe galloping in to the bleats of chivalry's trumpets the next. Now Lady Macbeth in gore, now Portia pleading against blood. In Latin class, Mrs. Tidyman never could have us read in Caesar's *Commentaries* without declaiming on Caesar the man; could not declaim on Caesar without sketching Roman society; could not sketch the Romans without embracing all the Mediterranean, on and on in a widening spiral of lore and enthusiasm, glasses flying in her hand and bosom wheeling above the lectern like turrets searching for new fields of gunnery.

But it was the grammar of English that exalted her most. Day after day we would troop to the blackboard to take apart sentences for her, phrases chalked to one another like scaffolding, being shown how a clause dovetailed here, an infinitive did the splicing there, the whole of it planed and beamed together as her pointer whapped through a reading of the revealed sentence. For her the language held holy force, and she shuddered at any squander of it. In what must have been her fullest spate of forgiveness, she once apologized about one of the townswomen: *Once you get used to her split infinitives, you'll find she's a very nice person.* And so Mrs. Tidyman hovered at me from her heights of language, declaiming, rhapsodizing, unabashedly giving favor to any of us who seemed rapt. I was more than rapt, held by her whirligig of language and learning as if I were a ball swung on a tether. *I bet she thinks she glommed onto some-*

thing when you came to that school, Grandma assessed after one of my reports about Mrs. Tidyman. *Maybe,* I said, as if I hadn't had the answer drilled into me by gray eyes.

• • •

As if arguing against myself, in the spring of 1961 I finished up my intended four years at Northwestern by being awarded a scholarship for a year of graduate study. I bargained a military deferment out of my draft board, and set to work again at the school of journalism. A pair of messages marked my completion of that year. When the last pages of my thesis were handed back from their final reading by one of my research advisors, a note was clipped atop: *Around 1836 and 1837, people used to stand on the dock in New York and wait for the latest installment of the Pickwick Papers. With something of the same anticipation, I've waited for and read the chapters of your thesis.* The other arrived from Grandma: *Dearest Ivan. Well dear one I have sad news for you. Mrs Tidaman that you liked so much at Valier died a couple days ago. I'll send you the clipping out of the Gt Falls [Montana] paper when I get my hands on it. Gertie says in her letter that Mrs. Tidaman fell at school and broke her hip and died somehow of that. I'm sorry dear I know she was a wonderfull person to you . . .*

STUDENT: ANGELA DAVIS

(1944–)

Author, professor and political activist.

TEACHER: HERBERT MARCUSE

During my second year at Brandeis, I had picked up *Eros and Civilization* by Herbert Marcuse and had struggled with it from beginning to end. That year he was teaching at the Sorbonne. When I arrived in Paris the following year, he was already back at Brandeis, but people were still raving about his fantastic courses. When I returned to Brandeis, the first semester of my senior year was so crowded with required French courses that I could not officially enroll in Marcuse's lecture series on European political thought since the French Revolution. Nevertheless, I attended each session, rushing in to capture a seat in the front of the hall. Arranged around the room on progressively higher levels, the desks were in the style of the UN General Assembly room. When Marcuse walked onto the platform, situated at the lowest level of the hall, his presence dominated everything. There was something imposing about him which evoked total silence and attention when he appeared, without his having to pronounce a single word. The students had a rare respect for him. Their concentration was not only total during the entire hour as he paced back and forth while he lectured, but if at the sound of the bell Marcuse had not finished, the rattling of papers would not begin until he had formally closed the lecture.

One day, shortly after the semester began, I mustered up enough courage to put in a request for an interview with Marcuse. I had decided to ask him to help me draw up a bibliography on basic works in philosophy. Having assumed I would have to wait for weeks to see him, I was surprised when I was told he would be free that very afternoon.

From afar, Marcuse seemed unapproachable. I imagine the combination of his stature, his white hair, the heavy accent, his extraordinary air of confidence, and his wealth of knowledge made him seem ageless and the epitome of a philosopher. Up close, he was a man with inquisitive sparkling eyes and a fresh, very down-to-earth smile.

Trying to explain my reasons for the appointment, I told him that I intended to study philosophy in graduate school, perhaps at the university in Frankfurt, but that my independent reading in philosophy had been unsystematic—without regard for any national or historical relations. What I wanted from him—if it was not too much of an imposition—was a list of works in the sequence in which I ought to read them. And if he gave me permission, I wanted to enroll in his graduate seminar on Kant's *Critique of Pure Reason*.

''Do you really want to study philosophy?'' Professor Marcuse asked, slowly and placing emphasis on each word. He made it sound so serious and so profound—like an initiation into some secret society which, once you join, you can never leave. I was afraid that a mere ''yes'' would ring hollow and inane.

''At least, I want to see if I am able,'' was about the only thing I could think of to answer.

''Then you should begin with the Pre-Socratics, then Plato and Aristotle. Come back again next week and we will discuss the Pre-Socratics.''

I had no idea that my little request would develop into stimulating weekly discussions on the philosophers he suggested, discussions which gave me a far more exciting and vivid picture of the history of philosophy than would have emerged from a dry introduction-to-philosophy course.

• • •

During the last year at Brandeis, I made up my mind to apply for a scholarship to study philosophy at the university in Frankfurt. Marcuse confirmed my conviction that this was the best place to study, given my interest in Kant, Hegel and Marx. The remaining months of the school year were consumed by intensive preparation in philosophy, German language and the final requirements for my B.A.

degree, including a year-long honors project on the Phenomenological Attitude, which I thought I had discovered in the works of the contemporary French novelist Robbe-Grillet. The most challenging and fulfilling course was the graduate seminar that Marcuse conducted on the *Critique of Pure Reason*. Poring over a seemingly incomprehensible passage for hours, then suddenly, grasping its meaning gave me a sense of satisfaction I had never experienced before.

STUDENT: JOHN C. BOARD

(1936–)

Common citizen.

TEACHER: MISS LUCILE SIZELOVE

Miss Lucile Sizelove was her name; public school teaching was her occupation. History and government were her loves, but citizenship, with its rights and its responsibilities, was her passion. For five years she was my teacher, and I grew to love her. Now, some 37 years since I left her classroom, I know beyond all doubt that, except for my parents, no other person did more to craft, shape, and mold my life. So dominant, in fact, has been her influence that there have been times I almost resented it. The standards of citizenship she expounded and demanded were so rigorous and yet so compelling that they became the criteria by which I measured my own conduct as well as that of my fellow citizens and our political leaders.

I was aware of Miss Sizelove before, as a seventh-grader at Alexander J. Kent High School in Kentland, Indiana, I first saw her. Kentland was a small Hoosier town and anonymity was a rare achievement. With only six grades in the public grade school and six grades in the public high school, Kentland's teachers were especially visible and subject to the constant scrutiny of its citizens. By the time I arrived as a student, Miss Lenore Winters, the first grade and the longest tenured teacher in town; Miss Mary E. Kitzmiller, teacher of Latin, English, and high school librarian; and Miss Lucile Sizelove were teaching the children of the children who had been their first charges.

When the school year began in 1948, 28 of us entered Alexander J. Kent High School as seventh-graders. At that time, the faculty included eleven full-time teachers, the school principal (who also taught some classes), and the superintendent.

Of the teachers I encountered on my first day at A. J. Kent, I remember only Miss Sizelove. As is commonly the case with seventh-graders, we were apprehensive, excited, confused, high-strung, rambunctious. We were a band of barbarians, each a bundle of unbridled energy. We raced from one classroom to another. We charged into Miss Sizelove's room.

Silence!

Her eyes stripped each of us naked to our souls.

Absolute silence!

Her eyes pierced, probed, and punctuated. Not a word was spoken.

Absolute, absolute silence!

Some squirmed in their seats.

Some cleared their throats.

No one spoke.

Absolute and deadly silence!

She stood before us and glared at us.

Her right hand rested on her desk, her left hand on her hip, and her eyes searched each of us out individually and encompassed all of us collectively.

Silence!

Finally, she spoke.

She spoke slowly, de-lib-er-ate-ly, softly.

"I would appreciate it," she said, "when you enter this classroom the next time that you do so in an orderly and civilized manner."

"I do not appreciate my furniture being rearranged," she said.

"I do not want the desks moved out of place one inch. In fact, I do not want anything moved at all."

"Do you understand?" she asked.

"If you do not understand," she stated, "I have ways to make you understand because I know how to box ears."

Box ears!

I had never heard the term; I couldn't visualize ears being boxed, but I never doubted that it was a horrible form of punishment. I didn't move; I was frozen. But I wasn't afraid, just puzzled.

"I know how to box ears." I didn't doubt her word and neither did anyone else. In the six years during which we knew her, Miss

Sizelove never laid a hand on any student. She never had to. Her most effective forms of discipline were her eyes with their penetrating stare, and her voice with its quiet strength.

In truth, Miss Sizelove was a gentle person, a caring teacher, and a complete individual. She lacked any trace of pretension, was forthright in her actions and manners, and thoughtful in her deliberations. She believed deeply and sincerely, but she only took the speaker's stump when we behaved in any way that failed to meet her ideal of how young Americans should act.

"You have the duty . . .

"You of all people in the world have the responsibility . . .

"Democracy will not survive if you behave in your adult lives as you have just behaved.

"The United States of America cannot persevere if every one of you does not exhibit greater dedication to your tasks.

"It is your responsibility, it is your duty, it is your moral obligation as citizens to . . . "

For Miss Sizelove, it mattered not what a person's occupation was. She was not influenced by lineage, fortune, or social status in the community. In her eyes, all were equal. Every pupil received equal treatment, equal opportunity, equal sternness, equal compassion. And no one—no student, no parent, no member of the community—ever questioned her fairness. There was no reason to do so. I have never known a person who demonstrated such judiciousness in every aspect of her or his life.

By the time I became Miss Sizelove's student, she had taught 33 years. And her entire teaching career, with the exception of her first year in Newtown, Ohio, and her second year in Morocco, Indiana, had been in Kentland. She taught five classes, each requiring a separate preparation. Her schedule included seventh-grade social studies, eighth-grade United States history, tenth-grade world history, eleventh-grade United States history, and twelfth-grade civics.

We never had a substitute teacher for Miss Sizelove's classes except in the eighth grade when she was briefly hospitalized and, later, in high school, when she travelled to Germany. She returned from Germany not by herself, but with Anna and Karen, a German woman and her daughter, whom she sponsored for United States citizenship. This was a bold step: In Kentland, the trauma of World War II had not been forgotten. One of Miss Sizelove's colleagues thought it a terrible deed. "We have enough people in this country to take care of without importing displaced persons,'' she said. ''We should take care of our own people first.'' In my mind, I sided with Miss Sizelove because I hadn't seen much evidence of our doing or even caring about doing what the other teacher said we should do. Besides, through Miss Sizelove, I had come to know Anna and Karen and liked them. They were from another country, and they added a new dimension to my life that made me realize there was a world beyond the confines of Kentland.

With the responsibility for teaching five different classes, Miss Sizelove—as all of my teachers—had a heavy teaching load. I did not realize this at the time, but I came to understand her situation when I began my own teaching career. How she planned and carried out many of the things she incorporated into her teaching still amazes me.

It began in the seventh-grade and lasted throughout my total years with her as a student. Miss Sizelove introduced and sustained my awareness of what was happening in the world. She accomplished this through discussion on current events. Every Friday, it seems, we were engaged in a review of noteworthy and newsworthy events through panel discussions and debates. No issue was too small and none was too advanced for us to tackle and discuss, but we were to be prepared on the subject. Sometimes, however, she surprised us with impromptu subjects.

''In Kentland,'' she said, ''there is an unwritten rule that no Negro may sleep over night. None has ever been allowed to do so. Is this, in the context of our government, right?''

We offered our opinions, which were not enough.

''Where in the Constitution does it state that a person, regardless of color or creed, has the right to sleep wherever he or she wishes?''

We countered with the ideological tenets of the Bill of Rights and whatever other constitutional knowledge we could muster. We probed the morality of the issue as well as the legality. We drew upon what historical knowledge we had to make the case that any American citizen should be able to sleep and live and work in any community. Still, Miss Sizelove was not satisfied.

''If what you say is true,'' she said, ''then what are you going to do about it? It is not enough to say that the cat should be belled.''

Miss Sizelove wed theory to action with a virtuosity I have seldom witnessed. She made us see that abstract theory remains sterile until translated into concrete action. She introduced us to the meaning of commitment and, in the process, to the meaning of democracy.

I marveled then as I marvel now how Miss Sizelove led us through Indiana, United States, and European history without ever once relying on lecture notes. She knew her subject matter thoroughly. This should not imply that her facts and opinions were cut and dried, because she also showed us how historical issues could be widely interpreted; there was room for economic, social, geographical, or political interpretations of the same historical issue. And there were rare times when she brought to our class people who had personally witnessed an historical event.

I shall never forget, for example, the day when Dr. Van Kirk came to speak to our class. He had served as a physician in World War I. He covered, of course, many aspects of the war, but when he spoke about the war's ending at the eleventh hour of the eleventh day of the eleventh month of 1918, his whole manner and demeanor were uncomfortably mesmerizing.

''Of course, we knew for weeks that the War was ending. Finally, in its last hours after the armistice had been signed in a railway car in Compiègne, France,'' he said, ''we knew the exact hour when the fighting was to stop, but the fighting continued. In those hours, in those last six hours, all I could think about was how many fine, young American boys were being needlessly and senselessly killed.'' Then he broke down and wept unashamedly before our eyes.

Miss Sizelove also taught us that civility is the heart of civic virtue. As I have mentioned, one of her loves was Indiana history. Through her we learned about the Northwest Territory; came to appreciate the uniqueness of Indiana's first constitution in 1816 that recognized that equal opportunities should be extended to all; and came to appreciate, too, how an educational system equally open to all and ranging from the elementary grades to a tuition-free state university was incorporated into a new constitution in 1850. We also learned about the cultural contributions of Theodore Dreiser; Paul Dresser; Lew Wallace; and, of course, George Ade, Hoosier humorist, playwright and Kentland native. We were aware, too, of Warren T. McCray, Indiana's 30th governor whose home was just one block from our high school.

Prudence on Miss Sizelove's part came with the manner in which she spoke about former Governor McCray who, at the time, was the only governor in any of the states whose career had ended with conviction for fraud and imprisonment. Governor McCray had been dead for years, but one of his daughters, Marian, (who was my Sunday school teacher) and his only son, George, were still living in the McCray home and were Miss Sizelove's immediate neighbors.

It was not that Miss Sizelove side-stepped the facts about Governor McCray's shortcomings. But she held tight to an unwritten code that we would not embarrass either Marian or George by questioning them about any aspect of their lives as the children of one of Indiana's governors.

It was in my senior year that two events occurred in Miss Sizelove's class that I shall always remember, events that demonstrate her skills as a teacher. For one six-week period, our class became a "senate." We formed parties, elected officers, studied (and learned) parliamentary procedure. The entire legislative process became our subject matter. So well did we do in class that Miss Sizelove prevailed upon our superintendent to have us demonstrate our skills at a parents' open house. That we did, and for our performance we suffered the ire of our teacher. What we had done, in fact, was to "show off." I did not think we were that bad; I could not detect the affliction of "senioritis" of which we were accused the next day. Where we had fallen short was not in argumentation or preparation or forensic skill. No, our crime had been that we had not projected ourselves as good and responsible elected officials. We had given the impression that we held in low regard the high calling of public service. In short, we had not demonstrated the good citizenship the public deserved of elected officeholders.

The other event was a mock trial. The case was a personal injury suit in which one member of the class sued another for $50,000 as the result of injuries sustained from an automobile accident. Every member of the class participated. Terry Shirk served as judge; Jim Beatty and Jim Walker served as attorneys for the defendant; Ruth Portteus and Marilyn Beekman as attorneys for the plaintiff; John Spencer was the clerk of the court; Darwin Clark and Patty Bedinger were bailiffs; Sally Newland and Janice Edwards were court recorders; Leonard Lovell the sheriff; Betty Zell and I were doctors; Margaret Weldon and Ralph Hays were jury commissioners; and the remaining class members served as witnesses at the trial. Each of us prepared for our duties by working with our counterparts in the community. I studied the brain, the skull, and x-rays with a local physician, Dr. Wilbur Mathews. Our studies culminated with a day-long trial. The jury was selected from the senior classes from the other four high schools in Newton County.

Through such events, through visits to the legislature in Indianapolis, through witnessing a murder trial venued to Newton County from Lake County, through class visits by people such as Dr. Van Kirk, and through Miss Sizelove's conduct of her classes and the reading she required of us—the essays, book reports, written examinations—we learned. We learned the subject matter, yes. But we learned more: The greatest lesson was to be good citizens.

"If ever you are asked," she said, "to run for public office, you must do so. If ever you are asked to serve on the school board, you must. If ever you are asked to serve on a county committee, you must. You must do these things because our system of government will not and cannot survive if its citizens do not participate. It is not enough just to vote. You must exercise every right for which our forefathers fought, died, and sacrificed. This is your duty; this is your responsibility. You must exercise the freedom of speech and speak out when your government is acting irresponsibly. You must exercise the freedom to assemble peaceably when public policy victimizes the people. Just because these rights are written in our documents does not mean they will last. They will not last if you do not exercise them."

I graduated from high school in May 1954. I received a state scholarship to Ball State Teachers College in Muncie, but the greatest boost I received was moral support and encouragement from Miss Sizelove. Not every teacher believed in me as did Miss Sizelove. Our school's coach told my father not to be too disappointed when I flunked out of college; I just didn't have what it would take to be scholastically successful. In truth, I doubted it myself, but Miss Sizelove did not and I knew it.

Throughout college and my early years of teaching, I always visited Miss Sizelove whenever I returned to Kentland. She was especially helpful to me then as we discussed, among other things, teaching. I felt grown up when, on one visit, I learned that she smoked. It came as a shock to me, but together we sat in her living room, lit up our methol Kool cigarettes, puffed away, and talked for hours about world events, our latest adventures in reading, politics, historical figures, and whatever came to our minds.

I also owe to Miss Sizelove my love for reading. When I was in the fifth grade, our class used to make regular visits to the public library where Miss Virginia Rinard captivated us by the stories that she read to us. I always took a bundle of books home with me, but then never opened them. Years later the librarian would remind me that I had announced to her, "Miss Rinard, I don't like to read and I'm not checking any more books out of the library." It was in the summer between my junior and senior years in high school that I learned to appreciate reading. Before school was out, I asked Miss Sizelove for help. "Would you," I asked, "make up a list of books for me to read during the summer? I must learn to make it a habit to read."

I can't remember all 12 of the books on her list, but I do remember struggling through Louisa May Alcott's *Little Men* and *Little Women* and J. M. Barrie's *The Little Minister.* But this I know: I finished reading every book Miss Sizelove assigned me. And a lifelong habit took hold.

Miss Sizelove died in 1969. It is hard for me to remember when it was that I last saw her, because she has been so much a part of my life. Her early death spared her three historical events that, I believe, would have shaken the foundations of her passion for good citizenship. One was the prolongation of the Vietnam War. Another was the forced resignation of Richard Nixon as President of the United States. The third was the vast corruption in the Reagan Administration. These acts would have enraged her.

When Richard Nixon resigned on August 9, 1974, I was attending a summer leadership program for local officers of the Montana Education Association. Our evening dinner was delayed by the televised speech in which the President announced his resignation. Everyone, it seemed, cheered the news, but I remember standing in back of the crowd with tears running from my eyes. It was not that I did not believe Richard Nixon should not have resigned his office. No, it was because he had broken the fiduciary faith that Miss Sizelove had instilled in us about our government and its leaders. Over the years, I have come to appreciate many of the accomplishments of the Nixon Administration. But, try as I have, I have not yet reached the point of being able to forgive Mr. Nixon for acts that denigrated the Office of the President of the United States. I have not been able to forgive his violation of the code of honor Miss Sizelove cherished—and taught her students to cherish.

Miss Sizelove knew I wanted to be a history teacher. I suspect that she also knew that her influence explained this aspiration.

I began teaching in 1958 and was certified to teach my major, social studies, as well as my minor, English. For nine years, though, I taught English. Finally, after having earned a master's degree in United States History from the University of Wyoming in 1965 and having had a year's study beyond my master's degree at the University of Montana in 1968, I was able, in 1969, to transfer from an English position at Charles M. Russell High School in Great Falls, Montana, to a history position. I recall that on Monday, September 8, as I was erasing the blackboard at the end of the day in my classroom, I thought of Miss Sizelove. I wanted to write her and tell her that, finally, after ten years since I had entered the profession she ennobled, I was now teaching the subject that was my first love—and had completed my first full day with my students. I also wanted to tell her that it was my hope to teach the subject as well as she had taught me.

I left school and arrived at home where, by habit, I looked through my mail and opened a letter from my mother. In it she told me that Miss Sizelove had died. I phoned the McMullan Funeral Home in Kentland where, I learned, her family and friends had just returned from burying my teacher, Miss Lucile Sizelove.

EPILOGUE

Experience has taught me that it is the exception when any one person can claim exclusivity to an accomplished fact. Certainly, in the compilation of this anthology, I have been assisted by many helpful people. Their aid has come in many forms and it would be an impossible task to single out each and every person who has contributed to this volume of recollections of teachers. Be this as it may, I have relied on certain individuals whom I cannot help but acknowledge.

My wife, Mait, has stood by me for over 25 years and—more than any other person—has freed me to be my own person and supported me as I have pursued quixotic adventures. A daughter of Swedish immigrants, she has realized the dream of pursuing an education that so many harbored when they left the shores of their native lands and sailed for America. She has not disappointed those dreamers. Mait is a superior student, a loving wife and mother, and a person whose laughter pleases the gods and those around her.

From the beginning of my research for this volume, Margaret R. Knispel, a 27-year veteran English teacher in the Hillsboro and Beaverton, Oregon Public Schools and a retired National Education Association professional staff employee, fueled my energy and spirit. Margaret is but one example of the dedication that teachers devote to their positions. For the first 26 years that Margaret taught, she never missed a day of teaching except for those taken for professional purposes. She even delayed a medical operation and scheduled it to take place during one Christmas break so that she would not miss school. Her last year of teaching was marked by a tragedy and, only then, was her perfect record broken.

Dr. Arthur E. Wise, formerly Director of the Center For The Study of The Teaching Profession of The Rand Corporation and currently President of the National Council for Accreditation of Teacher Education, endorsed my idea for this anthology and freely offered his sage advice and counsel throughout its creation. A lot of things Art Wise is but, most importantly, he is a scholar, gentleman, and, thankfully, a visionary.

Thomas P. Mondani, the Executive Director of the Connecticut Education Association (CEA) and my immediate supervisor, gave me his support and overlooked my grumpiness because he knew I was trying, not only to do my job for CEA, but also to get this anthology put together. I could write much about Tom, but his encouragement of diversity in thinking and his demonstration of patience are top among his virtues. I have learned from working with him.

Two outstanding teachers, teacher leaders and personal friends—Mary Hatwood Futrell, past President of the National Education Association, and Mark D. Waxenberg, President of the Connecticut Education Association—perpetually renew my belief in the goodness of my fellow human beings who chose teaching as their careers. As long as our public schools, teachers and students have such advocates as colleagues, children, democracy and freedom shall be safeguarded.

Three associates—Michael Lydick, James "Jimmy" O'Brien, and Roger Gay—have been especially helpful by their presence and their willingness to share their individual expertise with me.

I stand in reverential awe of real writers, those people who—from the warp and woof of their minds and souls—create and masterfully arrange words and ideas and produce the magic of novels. Gloria Naylor is one of these people and I thank her for her words of encouragement that always came at the right times as I labored on this production.

Just as I am in awe of writers, I marvel at those who assist writers by their editing skills. Carl Luty is such a person, a true lapidarian with words.

Dr. Gene M. Gressley, my mentor at the University of Wyoming, is an intellectual dynamo who has provided me with his moral support for many of my varied ventures. Over the past 28 years, he has never lost his faith in me even when most of my ventures failed. Gene is a tenacious optimist and believer. I thank him for these qualities.

Because their interest, moral support and encouragement have meant much to me, I give my thanks to Bob Chase, Helene Gerstein, Jim Ewing and Nancy Rearick.

To Bill Henderson, the publisher of this volume, I owe a special debt of gratitude. He is the one who, at 4:34 P.M. on December 7, 1989, said, "yes", and caused a new world to open its doors to me and this anthology to become a reality.

Finally, I owe profound gratitude to Roger K. White, M.D. Without his counsel and intervention at a crucial period in my life, I would not have lived to experience all that I have herein described and more.

While I have singled out Miss Lucile Sizelove as being the one teacher who had the greatest influence on my life, I have felt the presence of the spirits of certain other teachers as I have worked on pulling this anthology together. These teachers are Mrs. Grace O'Neill (Liberty Loan Grade School in Illinois); Mrs. Eleanor Messman Monjon, Mrs. Gertrude Peek Smith and Mr. Leslie C. Gordon (Raub Grade School in Indiana); Mrs. Frances Winters Schuh and Mrs. Mabel Schanlaub (Kentland Grade School); Mr. R. D. Lutz, Mrs. Kathleen O'Connor Funk and Miss Mary Elizabeth Kitsmiller (Alexander J. Kent High School); Dr. Phyllis Nelson Yuhas, Dr. Lucile Clifton, Dr. Floy Ruth Painter and Dr. Louis E. Inglehart (Ball State Teachers College); Dr. Gene M. Gressley (University of Wyoming); Dr. H. Duane Hampton and Dr. William B. Evans (University of Montana); and Mrs. Mary Bates and Ms. Ione Pierron (University of Oregon).

Without the vast resources of the libraries used in putting together this anthology and the expertise, knowledge and help provided me by their librarians, this book would not be. I am grateful, therefore, not only for the resources, but also the librarians of the following public and private libraries in Connecticut: the Portland Public Library, Russell Library in Middletown, Hartford Public Library, Yale University Libraries, Homer Babbidge Library at the University of Connecticut, Elihu Burritt Library at Central Connecticut State University, and the Olin Memorial Library at Wesleyan University in Middletown.

For assistance in helping me locate or obtain photographs of the teachers included in this anthology, I am indebted to the following gracious people: Denny L. Stufflebeam, Webster City Community

Schools in Webster City, Iowa, (Grace Bidlack); Hollee Haswell, Columbia University, and Andrea La Sala, American Museum of Natural History, (Franz Boas); George D. Brightbill, Temple University, Richard M. Buck, Performing Arts Research Center, and Berdeen E. Pigorsh, Reprographic Services, The New York Public Library, (Giuseppe Boghetti); William C. Parson, Library of Congress, (Naida Boulanger); Vickie Makings, *The Denver Post,* (Antonia Brico); Elizabeth Keul, Robin McElheny, Louise Ambler and Elizabeth Gombosi, Harvard University, (Edward Tyrell Channing); David J. Stanhope, Jimmy Carter Library, and Pat Thrower, the *Columbus Ledger-Enquirer,* (Julia Coleman); Cynthia Pulis, Office of Dan Rather, CBS News, and Hugh Cunningham, (Hugh Cunningham); Dirk Van Tuerenhout and Alma D. Williams, Tulane University, (Peter Davis); Earle E. Coleman, Princeton University, (Samuel Davies and Woodrow Wilson); Patrick M. Quinn, Northwestern University and Steven Mandeville-Gamble and Margaret J. Kimball, Stanford University, (Bernard De Voto); Sandra E. Fitzgerald, *The Indianapolis Star/News,* and Lisa Lussier, Indiana Historical Society Library, (Laura Donnan); Elaine Owens, Mississippi Department of Archives and History, (Lorena Duling); Alaine L. Will and Lois G. Hendrickson, University of Minnesota, (Oscar W. Firkins); Barbara Soper, Buffalo and Erie County Public Library, and Sally Schlaerth, *The Buffalo News,* (Frank S. Fosdick); Elizabeth Keul and Robin McElheny, Harvard University, (Felix Frankfurter); Douglas Brown, Groton School in Groton, Massachusetts, (Amory Gardner); Daria D'Arienzo, Amherst College, (Charles E. Garman); Sally Schlaerth, *The Buffalo News,* and Margery N. Sly, Smith College, (Marion Gemmel); Betty Smith, Susquehanna County Historical Society and Free Public Library, and Doris Deakin, The Monday Club, Susquehanna, Pennsylvania, (Mary Graves); Robin McElheny, Harvard University, Marie-Hélène Gold, Radcliffe College, and Richard Hocking, (Agnes Boyle O'Reilly Hocking); Robin McElheny, Harvard University, and Lynne K. Fonteneau, Williams College, (Mark Hopkins); the Superintendent of Schools in Centerville, Indiana, Inezetta Eliason Stiver, great great niece of Samuel K. Hoshour, Centerville, Indiana, and Gisela S. Terrell, Butler University, (Samuel K. Hoshour); Stanley T. Seki, Principal of McKinley High School in Honolulu, Hawaii, (Ruth King); Butler T. Henderson, New York City, and Minnie M. Johnson, South Carolina State College, (Nelson C. Nix); Dr. John M. Christianson, Superintendent of Mitchell

School District No. 17–2 in Mitchell, South Dakota, (Robert Pearson); Bev Whitlock, Minneapolis *Star/Tribune,* (Anna Von Helmholtz Phelan); Michael M. Kaplan and Mary Wyly, The Newberry Library, (Santee Sioux); Barbara M. Smith, Rutgers College, and Earl Reed Silvers, Jr., (Earl Reed Silvers); William H. Brower, Perkins School For The Blind in Watertown, Massachusetts, (Anne Mansfield Sullivan); Catherine Davidson, Columbia University School of Law, (Thaddeus C. Terry); Gail Stoltz, Democratic National Committee, Rachel Van Gordon, Valier, Montana, and John and Thomas C. Tidyman, (Frances Carson Tidyman); Gretchen Viehmann, Museum of The City of New York; Richard M. Buck, Performing Arts Research Center, and Berdeen E. Pigorsh, Reprographic Services, The New York Public Library, (Ella Toëdt); President Robert L. Hess, Brooklyn College of The City University of New York, (Louis Warsoff); and President John McCall, Professor Douglas Wilson and Carley R. Robinson, Knox College, (Philip Green Wright).

For their professional assistance in the process of my obtaining permissions to reprint the excerpts from the autobiographies contained in this anthology, my appreciation is extended to the following people: Shirley Chisholm; John Coolidge; Joan Daves; Ivan Doig; Patricia Felmar; Butler T. Henderson; Tim Kantor and Layne Shroder; Mrs. Earl Schenck Miers; Marian N. Nelson; Louis Nizer; Dr. Norman Vincent Peale; Vivian Perlis; Marian Reiner; Thomas Rockwell; Margaret Sandburg; Charles and Dorothy G. Van Doren; Michael Greaves (Alfred A. Knopf, Inc.); Pamala L. Korton (The American Institute of Architects); Roberta Goodman, (Angela Davis); Judy Beresford (Ayer Company, Publishers); Alice Baer (Bernard Geis Associates); Julie R. Rosner (Bill Adler Books, Inc.); Virginia A. Copelin and Walter T. Conn (Broadman Press—The Sunday School Board); David Lefkowitz (Curtis Brown Ltd.); Carol Christiansen (Doubleday); Harold J. Dies (The Dreiser Trust); Karen R. Griffey and Warren C. Fortson (Fortson and White, P.C.); Louise Bates (Grosset & Dunlap); Maureen Rafferty and Judi Kincaid (Harcourt Brace Jovanovich, Inc.); Marilyn Small and Carol Schreiber (Harper & Row); Beth Kiley (Harvard University Press); Jeanne L. Harmon and Ray Search (High Plains Historical Society); Julie Jackson and Kathy Pohl (Houghton Mifflin Company); Gordon Kato (International Creative Management, Inc.); Dr. James M. Gifford (The Jesse Stuart Foundation); Itzik Becher (Julian Bach Literary Agency,

Inc.); Eugene R. Lehr and James C. Roberts (Library of Congress, Reference and Bibliography Section); Jill F. O'Connell and Morgan Perkins (Little, Brown and Company); Edith Golub, Agnes Fisher and Judith Fernandez (Macmillan Publishing Company); Dave Tislow (McGraw-Hill, Inc.); Lillian Jackson (Morehouse College); Peter Mayer and Rebecca Mancini (Penguin USA); Joan Palatine (Princeton University Press); Jose G. Arroyo (The Putnam Publishing Group); Florence Sawyer (Rand McNally); Ann Sandhorst (Random House, Inc.); Todd Norton and Joy Harris (The Robert Lantz—Joy Harris Literary Agency); Carolyn Krupp (Russell & Volkening, Inc.); Alice Corring (Simon & Schuster, Inc.); Peter J. Wolverton (St. Martin's Press); Patricia Freeman-Lynde (The University of Georgia Press); Harriet P. Stockanes and Barbara G. Griswell (University of Illinois Press); Doris M. Ayres (Unwin Hyman Limited); William Finnegan (Vantage Press, Inc.); Mary E. Ryan (W. W. Norton & Company); Jeanne L. Crane (Warner Books, Inc.); and Jennifer Coe (William Morrow & Company, Inc.).